Reconstructing American Legal Realism &
Rethinking Private Law Theory

Reconstructing American Legal Realism & Rethinking Private Law Theory

Hanoch Dagan

OXFORD
UNIVERSITY PRESS

OXFORD
UNIVERSITY PRESS

Oxford University Press is a department of the University of Oxford. It furthers the University's
objective of excellence in research, scholarship, and education by publishing worldwide.

Oxford New York

Auckland Cape Town Dar es Salaam Hong Kong Karachi Kuala Lumpur Madrid
Melbourne Mexico City Nairobi New Delhi Shanghai Taipei Toronto

With offices in

Argentina Austria Brazil Chile Czech Republic France Greece Guatemala Hungary
Italy Japan Poland Portugal Singapore South Korea Switzerland Thailand
Turkey Ukraine Vietnam

Oxford is a registered trade mark of Oxford University Press in the
UK and certain other countries.

Published in the United States of America by
Oxford University Press
198 Madison Avenue, New York, NY 10016

© Oxford University Press 2013

Library of Congress Cataloging-in-Publication Data
Dagan, Hanoch.
  Reconstructing American legal realism & rethinking private law theory / Hanoch Dagan.
    pages cm
  Includes bibliographical references and index.
  ISBN 978-0-19-989069-9 ((hardback) : alk. paper)
1. Law—Philosophy. 2. Realism. 3. Law—United States—Philosophy.
I. Title. II. Title: Reconstructing American legal realism and rethinking private law theory.
  K341.D34 2013
  346'.001—dc23
                                                                    2013006144

9 8 7 6 5 4 3 2 1
Printed in the United States of America on acid-free paper

Note to Readers
This publication is designed to provide accurate and authoritative information in regard to
the subject matter covered. It is based upon sources believed to be accurate and reliable and is
intended to be current as of the time it was written. It is sold with the understanding that the
publisher is not engaged in rendering legal, accounting, or other professional services. If legal
advice or other expert assistance is required, the services of a competent professional person
should be sought. Also, to confirm that the information has not been affected or changed by
recent developments, traditional legal research techniques should be used, including checking
primary sources where appropriate.

(Based on the Declaration of Principles jointly adopted by a Committee of the
American Bar Association and a Committee of Publishers and Associations.)

For Tehyiah and Uri

TABLE OF CONTENTS

ACKNOWLEDGMENTS

The chapters of this book heavily draw on essays that have appeared previously, and I gratefully acknowledge permission to incorporate them in this volume: *The Realist Conception of Law*, 57 U. TORONTO L.J. 607 (2007); *Between Rationality and Benevolence: The Happy Ambivalence of Law and Legal Theory*, 62 ALABAMA L. REV. 191 (2010); *The Character of Legal Theory*, 96 CORNELL L. REV. 671 (2011); *The Limited Autonomy of Private Law*, 56 AM. J. COMP. L. 809 (2008); *Legal Realism and the Taxonomy of Private Law, in* STRUCTURE AND JUSTIFICATION IN THE PRIVATE LAW 147 (Charles Rickett & Ross Grantham eds., 2008); *Remedies, Rights, and Properties*, 4(1) J. TORT. L. art. 3 (2011); *Pluralism and Perfectionism in Private Law*, 112 COLUM. L. REV. 1409 (2012); *Private Law Pluralism and the Rule of Law, in* PRIVATE LAW AND THE RULE OF LAW (Lisa Austin & Dennis Klimchuk eds., forthcoming 2014). All of these essays are revised and updated, and they are all reprinted here with proper adaptations, aimed at minimizing repetitions and moving some footnotes to the text while combining, shortening, or eliminating quite a few others.

One of these essays ("The Character of Legal Theory") is coauthored with Roy Kreitner. I am grateful to Roy for this intellectually stimulating collaborative effort as well as for his invaluable comments on each of the other essays. Numerous other friends and colleagues have also generously commented on various chapters, many of them on more than one or two: Greg Alexander, Anne Alstott, Marc Amstutz, Jill Anderson, Ori Aronson, Lisa Austin, Shyam Balganesh, Aharon Barak, Jane Baron, Itzik Benbaji, Eyal Benvenisti, Yishai Blank, Armin von Bogdandy, Sam Bray, Richard Briffault, Rick Brooks, Alan Brudner, Arudra Bura, Mauro Bussani, David Carlson, Mindy Chen-Wishart, Eric Claeys, Hugh Collins, Nili Cohen, Margit Cohn, Anne Dailey, Nestor Davidson, Donald Davis, Avihay Dorfman, Shai Dotan, Neil Duxbury, David Dyzenhaus, David Enoch, Bill Eskridge, Chris Essert, Pasquale Femia, Stanley Fish, Tali Fisher, Daniel Fitzpatrick, Charles Fried, Heather Gerken, Guy Goldstein, Jim Gordley, Michael Graetz, David Grewal, Thomas Gutmann, Andrew Halpin, Philip Hamburger, Henry Hansmann, Alon Harel, Ron Harris, Michael Heller, Daniel Hemel, Martijn Hesselink, Rick Hills, Adam Hofri-Winogradow, Amy Kapczynski, Lorenz Kähler, Greg Keating, Stephanie Keene,

Hagi Kenaan, Duncan Kennedy, Alon Klement, Dennis Klimchuk, Russell Korobkin, Shelly Kreiczer-Levy, Sudhir Krishnaswamy, David Lametti, Shai Lavi, Amnon Lehavi, Daphna Lewinsohn-Zamir, Amir Licht, Shahar Lifshitz, Mark Lotman, Jon Macey, Daniel Markovits, Menny Mautner, Mark McKenna, Tom Merrill, Ralf Michaels, Paul Miller, Jennifer Mnookin, Trevor Morrison, Pierre Moyse, Stephen Munzer, Kali Murray, Jennifer Nedelsky, Neil Netanel, Sachin Pandya, Nick Parrillo, Jeremy Paul, James Penner, Eduardo Peñalver, Ronen Perry, Heikki Pihlajamaki, Ariel Porat, Iddo Porat, Robert Post, Dan Priel, Uriel Procaccia, Amit Pundik, Sharon Rabin-Margaliot, Jeff Rachlinski, Andrzej Rapaczynski, Joseph Raz, Alex Reinert, Doug Rendleman, Arthur Ripstein, Roberta Romano, Craig Rotherham, Florian Rödl, Jed Rubenfeld, Chaim Saiman, Irit Samet, Fred Schauer, Tony Sebok, Yoram Shachar, Scott Shapiro, Ken Simons, Joe Singer, Hillel Sommer, Henry Smith, Steve Smith, Stewart Sterk, Simon Stern, Rob Stevens, Madhavi Sunder, Gunther Teubner, Chantal Thomas, Chris Tomlins, Peter Turner, Laura Underkuffler, Mariana Valverde, Stephen Waddams, Rachael Walsh, Rivka Weill, Ernie Weinrib, Christiane Wendehorst, Dan Wielsch, Steven Wilf, Steve Wizner, Katrina Wyman, Assaf Yaakov, Elkow Yankah, Jonathan Zasloff, Noah Zatz, Ben Zipursky, Peer Zumbansen, and two anonymous referees of Oxford University Press, as well as participants in legal theory workshops at Amsterdam, Bar-Ilan, Cardozo, Columbia, Haifa, Hebrew, IDC, Ramat-Gan, Tel-Aviv, Toronto, UCLA, the University of Connecticut, Washington & Lee, and Yale law schools, and in the Alabama Law School 2010 Meador Lectures on Rationality, the Cornell-Tel Aviv Conference on The Future of Legal Theory, the Yale Law School Graduate Seminar, the University of Toronto Faculty of Law Critical Analysis of Law workshop, the "Beyond the State? Rethinking Private Law" confer-ence at the Max Planck Institute for Comparative and Private International Law, the USC Conference on Property, Tort and Private Law Theory, the King's College London Conference on Moral Values and Private Law, the Villa Vigoni at Lake of Como Conference on Private Law Theory, the Annual Israeli Private Law Association Conference, the Fordham Property Works in Progress con-ference, the McGill Law School and the Harvard Law School Conferences on Progressive Property, and the University of Toronto Workshop on Private Law and the Rule of Law. I am also grateful to Terra Hittson (Columbia Law '12) and Batya Stein for superb editorial assistance and to the Cegla Center for Interdisciplinary Research of the Law at Tel-Aviv University for research funding.

CHAPTER 1

⌀

Introduction

I. THE TASK

Since its heyday in the 1930s, legal realism has not ceased to attract the imagination of American (and other) legal minds.[1] Even though some, such as Ronald Dworkin, have tended to dismiss American legal realism as standing for an (admittedly implausible) nominalistic understanding of law,[2] many others share the conviction that legal realists have made a significant contribution and transformed American legal discourse.[3] Hence the cliché "we are all realists now."[4] Different theorists, however, give different reasons for this truism. Some associate legal realism with a crude revolt against formalism,[5] implying that realism's only (putative) contribution to law is to deconstruct it. Others believe that legal realists not only challenged formalist orthodoxy but also offered some, albeit preliminary and rudimentary, insights that were later taken up by more mature jurisprudential schools—notably law and economics

---

1. The term "realism" in this context should not be confused with its technical philosophical meaning in fields such as epistemology (the belief that objects of perception exist independently of the mind), ontology (the position that universals exist independently of particulars), or philosophy of science (the view that scientific theories are at least approximately true and that scientific terms have genuine referents). *See* MICHAEL MARTIN, LEGAL REALISM: AMERICAN AND SCANDINAVIAN 2–3 (1997). Instead, legal realism stands for the conception of law as a set of institutions typified by three constitutive tensions, namely: between power and reason, science and craft, and tradition and progress.

2. *See* RONALD DWORKIN, TAKING RIGHTS SERIOUSLY 15–16 (1978).

3. *See, e.g.,* Anthony T. Kronman, *Jurisprudential Responses to Legal Realism,* 73 CORNELL L. REV. 335 (1998).

4. *See* LAURA KALMAN, LEGAL REALISM AT YALE, 1927–1960, at 229 (1986).

5. *See* MORTON WHITE, SOCIAL THOUGHT IN AMERICA: THE REVOLT AGAINST FORMALISM 11 (1957).

and critical legal studies—which indeed either claim to be or are portrayed as true descendants of legal realism.[6]

Both foes and friends of American legal realism thus imply that, apart from the (surely important) goal of setting the historical record straight, the contemporary benefits of studying legal realism are rather marginal. Nominalists, who reduce phenomena to their singular manifestations, can hardly contribute to our understanding of law because they strip law of any distinctive characteristic. And if legal realism stands only for antiformalism, those of us who are already convinced that legal formalism (at least in the sense that realists presented it) is a nonstarter, have nothing further to explore. The same unflattering conclusion follows also from the view that legal realism is an eclectic and potentially incoherent set of rudimentary ideas about law, which inevitably come into sharp conflict once they are properly fleshed out (a task left to the realists' successors).[7] Finally, if any particular contemporary descendant of legal realism turns out to be its "true" heir, the project of reviving American legal realism—the task of this book—is again rather futile. If the realist vision of law is basically reducible to one or another more or less known jurisprudential school, be it empirical social science,[8] pragmatic instrumentalism,[9] critical legal studies,[10] old-fashioned nihilism,[11] or philosophical anarchism,[12] we might do better consulting scholars in these schools, who present richer and more sophisticated accounts of their own approaches than the ones that can be distilled from realist literature.

As the title of this book suggests, I beg to differ, and I will argue that legal realism offers important, unique, and by now mostly forgotten jurisprudential insights. This book presents a charitable reading and a contemporary rendition of the legacy of American legal realism. It thus provides an appealing alternative to the current prevailing perspectives on law. My reconstruction of this realist legacy is not intended as a piece of intellectual history. I am not concerned here with tracing the intellectual roots of realist ideas,[13] with

6. *See, e.g.*, Joseph W. Singer, *Legal Realism Now*, 67 CAL. L. REV. 467, 532 (1988).

7. *See, e.g.*, MORTON HORWITZ, THE TRANSFORMATION OF AMERICAN LAW, 1870–1960, at 169, 208–12 (1977); *see also, e.g.*, GARY MINDA, POSTMODERN LEGAL MOVEMENTS 26, 28–30 (1995).

8. *See* JOHN HENRY SCHLEGEL, AMERICAN LEGAL REALISM AND EMPIRICAL LEGAL SCIENCE (1995).

9. *See* ROBERT SAMUEL SUMMERS, INSTRUMENTALISM AND AMERICAN LEGAL THEORY (1982).

10. *See* HORWITZ, *supra* note 7, at 270–71.

11. *See* BRUCE A. ACKERMAN, RECONSTRUCTING AMERICAN LAW 6–22 (1984).

12. *See* Michael Steven Green, *Legal Realism as a Theory of Law*, 46 WM. & MARY L. REV. 1915 (2005).

13. *See, e.g.*, EDWARD A. PURCELL, JR., THE CRISIS OF DEMOCRATIC THEORY: SCIENTIFIC NATURALISM AND THE PROBLEM OF VALUE (1973); James E. Herget & Stephen Wallace, *The German Free Law Movement as the Source of American Legal Realism*, 73 VA. L. REV. 399 (1987).

evaluating legal realism as a historical movement,[14] or with assessing the scholarship of a particular realist scholar.[15] Instead, my purpose is to present a useful interpretation of legal realism, drawing from realist texts a vision of law that is currently relevant—indeed, valuable.[16] With this aim in mind, I ignore the many excesses (and some sheer follies) found in realist literature and read these texts in the best possible light.[17] The same approach informs my interpretation of the texts I use and guides me in their selection and in the emphases I ascribe to them. This charitable perspective on realism further explains why I focus on some authors, particularly Oliver Wendell Holmes, Benjamin Cardozo, Karl Llewellyn, and Felix Cohen,[18] and marginalize others, notably Jerome Frank and Thurman Arnold.

In my reconstructed realist account, law is conceived as a dynamic institution, or set of institutions, that embodies three constitutive tensions: between power and reason, between science and craft, and between tradition and progress. (I deliberately chose a softer term such as "tension" rather than stronger ones such as "contradiction." The relationships I discuss are not contradictory. Yet, although the terms in the pairs are not antonyms, they each refer to alternative allegiances, to competing states of mind and perspectives. The difficulty of accommodating them is thus similar to that of reconciling incommensurable goods or obligations.) In the realist conception, what is most distinctive about law is the difficult accommodation of these constitutive tensions. Law is neither brute power nor pure reason; it is neither only a science nor merely a craft; it is neither exhausted by reference to its past nor adequately grasped by an exclusively future-oriented perspective. Legal realists reject all these reductionist understandings of law (e.g., reducing law to brute power, or reducing law to only a science), which are in vogue in contemporary jurisprudence. For the realist, law is defined by these three tensions. A conception of law purporting to dissolve these tensions obscures at least one of the legal phenomenon's irreducible characteristics, and is thus hopelessly deficient.

One way of presenting the aim of this book, then, is as an exposure of the ambiguity in the cliché "we are all realists now" and of the problem it evokes. This cliché is correct in the sense that many contemporary legal theories continue the realist project by refining and elaborating one realist tenet, be it its

14. *See, e.g.*, WILLIAM TWINING, *Talk about Realism*, 60 *N.Y.U. L. REV.* 329 (1985).

15. In particular, this book is not an intervention in the fierce debate on the philosophy of Oliver Wendell Holmes.

16. As William Twining notes, "[d]ead jurists have their uses. They can be treated . . . as sources of ideas that have a potential significance that transcends the particular context in which they were introduced." *See* William Twining, *Other People's Power: The Bad Man and English Positivism, 1897–1997*, 63 BROOK. L. REV. 189, 189 (1997).

17. *Cf.* RONALD DWORKIN, LAW'S EMPIRE 52–53 (1986).

18. My list of legal realists is indeed inclusive and follows HORWITZ, *supra* note 7, at 169–92. *See also* ANDREW L. KAUFMAN, CARDOZO 203, 217, 314, 451 (1998); *but cf.* Thomas C. Grey, *Modern American Legal Thought*, 106 YALE L.J. 493, 497–502 (1996).

challenge to legal formalism or its account of one of the features that, according to legal realism, are constitutive of law. Yet the cliché is also misleading in the sense that, by focusing on one aspect of the realist "big picture" of law, the contemporary descendants of legal realism lose sight of its core insight and thus miss out on its greatest promise: keeping the constitutive tensions of law constantly before us. The point of reconstructing and reviving the realist understanding of law is precisely the possibility of restoring this promise and reinstating the realist agenda for future research and debate.

II. LEGAL REALISM

I begin this book with an effort to reconstruct the realist conception of law. Chapter 2 uses texts by legal realists (notably Holmes, Cardozo, Llewellyn, and Cohen) in order to demonstrate how major claims attributed to legal realism fit into a particular understanding of law.[19] My claim in the chapter, however, is not the discovery of legal realism's true essence. The reading of legal realist literature suggested here is unashamedly influenced by my own convictions about law, though I do not pretend to have invented the ideas I present. The conception of law outlined in Chapter 2 emerges as the underlying understanding of a sufficient number of realist texts to justify being called, as the chapter is entitled, "The Realist Conception of Law." The success of the chapter thus depends on both the cogency of my understanding of law as presented, and the measure of its fit to legal realist scholarship. Because Chapter 2 lays the foundations of the book as a whole, I summarize its main claims here in slightly greater detail.

* * *

The starting point of the realist account of law is its non-positivism. H.L.A. Hart's response to the realist claim of doctrinal indeterminacy is frequently presented as decisive, but is rather beside the point. Through his distinction between core and penumbra in any given norm, Hart effectively addressed the problem of rule indeterminacy,[20] but the realist claim that pure doctrinalism is a conceptual impossibility is not based on the indeterminacy of discrete rules. For legal realists, the profound and inescapable reason for doctrinal indeterminacy is the availability of multiple, potentially applicable doctrinal sources.

19. *Cf.* Brian Leiter, *Rethinking Legal Realism: Toward a Naturalized Jurisprudence*, 76 TEXAS L. REV. 267, 269 (1997). Leiter rejects the claim that talking about the core of realism apart from the views of individual writers is meaningless, and argues that this core can be found by searching for a common denominator of views endorsed by people commonly thought to be realists. Although I share this methodological premise, I disagree with Leiter's substantive claim that the core claim of legal realism is that "in deciding cases, judges respond primarily to the stimulus of the facts." *Id.*
20. H.L.A. HART, THE CONCEPT OF LAW 123, 141–42, 144 (1961).

More precisely, the irreducible choice among rules competing to control the case (all of which can be expanded or contracted), together with the many potential ways of interpreting or elaborating any legal concept, means that legal doctrine is always open to multiple readings, and the judicial task is not one of static application.

The realist claim, concerning an inevitable gap between doctrinal materials and judicial outcomes, evokes two major concerns. First, what can explain past judicial behavior and predict its future course? Second, and even more significant, how can law constrain judgments made by unelected judges? How, in other words, can the distinction between law and politics be maintained despite the collapse of law's autonomy in its positivist rendition? The legitimacy prong of the realist challenge is particularly formidable because, as legal realists show, it is bolstered by the insidious tendency of legal doctrinalism to obscure contestable value judgments made by judges and to entrench lawyers' claim to an impenetrable professionalism, improperly shielded from critique by nonlawyers.

Legal realists answer this challenge by insisting on a view of law as a going institution (or set of institutions) distinguished by the difficult accommodation of the three constitutive yet irresolvable tensions mentioned above: between power and reason, science and craft, and tradition and progress.

* * *

Although the realist conception of law finds room for both power and reason, it appreciates the difficulties of their coexistence. The realists' preoccupation with power is justified not only by the obvious fact that, unlike other judgments, those prescribed by law's carriers (mainly judges) can recruit the state's monopolized power to back up their enforcement. It is also premised on the institutional and discursive means that tend to downplay some dimensions of law's power. These built-in features of law—notably the institutional division of labor between "interpretation specialists" and the actual executors of their judgments, together with our tendency to "thingify" legal constructs (i.e., treat them as a non-modifiable part of our natural or ethical environment) and accord them an aura of obviousness and acceptability—render the danger of obscuring law's coerciveness particularly troubling. They explain the realists' wariness of the trap entailed by the romantization of law.

Although realists are preoccupied with power, they reject as equally reductive the image of law as *sheer* power (or interest, or politics). They insist that law is also a forum of reason, and that reason imposes real—albeit elusive— constraints on the choices of legal decision makers, and thus on the subsequent implementation of state power. Law is never *only* about interest or power politics; it is also an exercise in reason giving. Furthermore, because so much is at stake when reasoning about law, legal reasoning becomes particularly urgent and rich, attentive, careful, and serious. Reasons can justify law's coercion only if properly grounded in human values. Realists are thus impatient with attempts to equate reason giving with parochial interests or arbitrary power. They also find such exercises morally irresponsible because they undermine both the possibility of criticizing state power and the option of marshaling the law for morally required social change.

And yet, realists are also wary of the idea that reason can displace interest, or that law can exclude all force except that of the better argument. Because reasoning about law is reasoning about power and interest, the reasons given by law's carriers should always be treated with suspicion. This caution accounts for the realists' endorsement of value pluralism, as well as for their understanding of law's quest for justification as a perennial process that constantly invites criticism of law's means, ends, and other (particularly distributive) consequences.

Legal realists do not pretend they have solved the mystery of reason, or demonstrated how reason can survive in law's coercive environment. Their recognition that coerciveness and reason are doomed to coexist in any credible account of the law is nonetheless significant. Making this tension an inherent characteristic of law means that reductionist theories employing a too cynical or overly romantic conception of law must be rejected because both theories reduce law to either sheer power or pure reason. This approach also steers us toward a continuous critical awareness of the complex interaction between reason and power. It thereby seeks to accentuate the distinct responsibility incumbent on the reasoning of and about power, minimizing the corrupting potential of the self-interested pursuit of power and the perpetuation of what could end up as merely group preferences and interests.

* * *

I turn now to the type of reasons realists invite into the legal discourse and thus introduce law's second constitutive tension.

Realists argue that the forward-looking aspect of legal reasoning relies on both science and craft. Realists recognize the profound differences between, on the one hand, lawyers as social engineers who dispassionately combine empirical knowledge with normative insights, and, on the other, lawyers as practical reasoners who employ contextual judgment as part of a process of dialogic adjudication. They nonetheless insist on preserving the difficulty of accommodating science and craft as yet another tension constitutive of law.

Realists emphasize the importance of empirical inquiries, such as investigating the hidden regularities of legal doctrine in order to restore law's predictability, or studying the practical consequences of law in order to better direct the evolution of law and further its legitimacy. But my prototype realists reject any pretense that knowledge of these important social facts can be a substitute for political morality. They realize that value judgments are indispensable, not only when evaluating empirical research but also when simply choosing the facts to be investigated. Moreover, they are always careful not to accept existing normative preferences uncritically. Legal realists insist that neither science nor an ethics that ignores the data of science offers a valid test of law's merits. Legal analysis needs both empirical data and normative judgments.

Because law affects people's lives dramatically, these social facts and human values must always inform the direction of legal evolution. But while legal reasoning necessarily shares this feature with other forms of practical reasoning, the realist conception of law also highlights that legal reasoning is, to some extent, a distinct mode of argumentation and analysis. Hence, realists pay attention to the distinctive institutional characteristics of law and study their potential virtues, while still aware of their possible abuse. The legal realists, like many other legal theorists, focused their attention in this respect on adjudication. They argue that the procedural characteristics of the adversary process, as well as the professional norms that bind judicial opinions—notably the requirement of a universalizable justification—provide a unique social setting. These features establish the accountability of law's carriers to law's subjects, and encourage judges to develop what Cohen terms "a many-perspectived view of the world" or a "synoptic vision" that "can relieve us of the endless anarchy of one-eyed vision."[21] Moreover, because the judicial drama is always situated in a specific human context, lawyers have constant and unmediated access to human situations and to actual problems of contemporary life. This contextuality of legal judgments ensures lawyers a unique skill in capturing the subtleties of various types of cases and in adjusting the legal treatment to the distinct characteristics of each category.

* * *

The extended realist treatment of science and craft derives from the conviction that law is profoundly dynamic, hence my third constitutive tension. Law's inherent dynamism implies that the legal positivist attempt to understand law statically by sheer reference to verifiable facts—such as the authoritative commands of a political superior or the rules identified by a rule of recognition—is hopeless. In the realist conception, law is "a going institution" or, in John Dewey's words, "a social process, not something that can be done or happen at a certain date." As a going institution, law is structured to be an "endless process of testing and retesting"; thus understood, law is a great human laboratory continuously seeking improvement.[22]

This quest "for justice and adjustment" in the legal discourse is typically constrained by legal tradition. Law's past serves as the starting point for

---

21. Felix S. Cohen, *Field Theory and Judicial Logic,* in THE LEGAL CONSCIENCE: SELECTED PAPERS OF FELIX S. COHEN 121, 125–26 (Lucy Kramer Cohen ed., 1960).
22. John Dewey, *My Philosophy of Law,* in MY PHILOSOPHY OF LAW 73, 77 (1941).

contemporary analysis, and not only because it is an anchor of intelligibility and predictability. Legal realists begin with the existing doctrinal landscape because it may (and often does) incorporate valuable—although implicit and sometimes imperfectly executed—normative choices. This conservative inclination particularly typifies adjudication because the adjudicatory process (at its best) combines scientific and normative insights within a legal professionalism premised on institutional constraints and practical wisdom, so that its past yield of accumulated experience and judgment deserves respect. Although legal realists do not accord every existing rule overwhelming normative authority, they often begin with Llewellyn's idea that the case law system generates "a demand for moderate consistency, for reasonable regularity, [and] for on-going conscientious effort at integration." Realists celebrate common law's Grand Style, described by Llewellyn as "a functioning harmonization of vision with tradition, of continuity with growth, of machinery with purpose, of measure with need," mediating between "the seeming commands of the authorities and the felt demands of justice."[23]

Integrating power into their conception of law pushes realists, however, to be wary of implying that the pace of legal change should always be restrained or that legal normativity is exhausted by the subset of moral principles that are embedded in past legal, political, and particularly adjudicative practices. Therefore, realists are also cautious not to overemphasize adjudication at the expense of other legal institutions in which law is made, applied, interpreted, and developed.

* * *

Insofar as most descendants of legal realism are concerned, then, the statement that "we are all realists now" is seriously misleading because they, rather than carrying the realist legacy forward, have torn it apart by focusing on one aspect of the law (such as science or power), thus ignoring the central insight of legal realism: the three constitutive tensions. The disintegration of legal theory has robbed the realist conception of law of its most promising lessons. Contemporary accounts of law do enhance our understanding of law's characteristics, but the current debates between law-as-power and law-as-reason, law-as-science and law-as-craft, or law-as-tradition and law-as-progress are futile and harmful. From the perspective of legal realism, all these one-dimensional accounts of law are hopelessly deficient. Law can properly be understood only if we regain the realist appreciation of law's most distinctive feature: the

23. KARL L. LLEWELLYN, THE COMMON LAW TRADITION: DECIDING APPEALS 36, 38, 190–91, 217, 222–23 (1960); KARL L. LLEWELLYN, THE CASE LAW SYSTEM IN AMERICA 25, 77 (Paul Gewirtz ed., Michael Alsandi trans., 1933, 1989); KARL L. LLEWELLYN, *Law and the Social Sciences, in* JURISPRUDENCE: REALISM IN THEORY AND IN PRACTICE 357, 361–62 (1962); K.N. Llewellyn, *The Normative, the Legal, and the Law-Jobs: The Problem of Juristic Method*, 49 YALE L.J. 1355, 1385 (1940).

uneasy but inevitable accommodation of power and reason, science and craft, and tradition and progress.

III. OVERVIEW

Like all theories of law, the realist conception of law should partly be assessed by demonstrating how well it performs across a range of more specific questions. Chapters 3–9 were written as individual essays, addressing particular jurisprudential questions as well as several theoretical issues concerning private law, a focus of concern for most legal realists. These chapters tackle specific topics rather than necessarily follow the corpus of Llewellyn et al., but all of them still build, explicitly or implicitly, on the realist conception of law as a whole or on a specific realist claim or claims. Furthermore, I believe that the mutual support deriving from my reconstruction of the realist conception of law and discussion of these jurisprudential and legal topics helps expand, enhance, and refine the more abstract discussion of Chapter 2. My hope is that these contemporary mediations, which are all indebted to legal realists, will contribute to the cause undertaken by this book—the revival of American legal realism.

Chapter 3, "Between Rationality and Benevolence: The Happy Ambivalence of Law and Legal Theory," demonstrates the pervasiveness of the first constitutive tension of the realist conception of law—between power and reason—in both law and legal theory. More precisely, this chapter examines a somewhat related dualism: that between rationality and benevolence. It looks at the two central actors of the legal drama—the subjects of law and the carriers of law (that is, the ordinary people who are affected by private law and the judges who are the focus of legal theory). With respect to both, Chapter 3 explores the ambivalence of law and of legal theory that wavers between rationality, narrowly defined as the maximization of an agent's self-interest, and benevolence, broadly understood as behavior that moderates the pursuit of one's self-interest by taking into account the interests of other individuals or of the community as a whole. As Chapter 3 shows, law expects its subjects to be rational, but it also seeks to help them move beyond their rationality. It further demonstrates how legal theory presents an opposite images of judges: although the ideal judges would transcend their self- and group-interest, legal theory acknowledges this ideal neither will nor can be met, thus suspecting that judges are often rational actors themselves. These tensions may, at first glance, seem troubling. In line with the realist insistence on sustaining the tension between power and reason, however, Chapter 3 seeks to explain and ultimately celebrate these ambivalences and traces the complex ways whereby law and legal theory confront the challenge of sustaining them.

Chapter 4, "The Character of Legal Theory," uses the realist conception of law as the infrastructure for understanding the nature of legal theory. For nearly a century, legal scholars have vacillated between two strategies for dealing with the post-realist collapse of legal science (doctrinalism) as an autonomous discipline. There are two typical responses. The first response is to abandon legal theory for theories or methodologies from other fields of study, notably from the social sciences or the humanities. The second response is to disregard legal theory, replacing it with the celebration of law as a craft. Chapter 4 argues, however, that legal theory is a potent enterprise, which justifies separate naming. Legal theory, as best captured by legal realism, examines the coercive normative institutions of society and studies the traditions of these institutions and the typical crafts of their members. At the same time, legal theory continuously challenges these institutions and tests the desirability of their products. Of course, in doing so, legal theory will necessarily take lessons from other disciplines. Yet, Chapter 4 will demonstrate that legal theory promises a unique contribution to our analysis and thinking of law because of its constant attention to the unique and persistent tensions constitutive of law. Before elaborating on these features, Chapter 4 provides an outline of the three other post-realist important discourses about law: law and policy, sociohistorical analysis of law, and law as craft. Explaining these three discourses is key for analyzing how legal theory is significantly distinct, and important, both for its focus on law's constitutive tensions and for its effort to synthesize lessons of import from these three genres of legal scholarship.

Chapters 5–9 focus on private law. Chapter 5, "The Limited Autonomy of Private Law," studies the relationship between social values and private law adjudication. This chapter challenges the conventional, and diametrically opposed accounts of the relationship between these two, offered by private law autonomists and private law instrumentalists. Private law autonomists reject the significance of social values in private law while instrumentalists view private law as one of many forms of state regulation. I claim that neither theory provides a satisfactory account of private law. Autonomist theory is implausible because private law rests on a perfectionist view of society and, therefore, cannot claim to be indifferent to social values. But unlimited instrumentalism is also misguided because, as autonomists insist, the bipolar structure of private law litigation does indeed entail certain normative constraints. These two propositions yield the main conclusion of this chapter. In the spirit of legal realism, I claim that private law doctrines should be responsive to the social values appropriate to the pertinent category of human interaction they cover as well as to the normative constraints entailed by the bipolar structure of private law litigation. This chapter further explores the implications of this conclusion for three specific doctrinal issues: marital property, monetary remedies for breach of entitlements, and the right of entry (into property).

The title of Chapter 6—"Legal Realism and the Taxonomy of Private Law"—may seem surprising because legal taxonomy is frequently portrayed as a necessarily formalist (or doctrinalist) endeavor, and thus, antithetical to realism. I argue, however, that dismissing taxonomy as a tool is both mistaken and unfortunate. To be sure, realists should reject the idea that the purpose of taxonomy is only to organize legal rules, as they appreciate that taxonomy necessarily shapes and influences the law. And so realists can substantially contribute to the valuable enterprise of legal taxonomy. They can do so by reconstructing the role of taxonomy—incorporating their insights on its inherent dynamism and on the significance of contextual normative analysis to the evolution of legal categories. This reconstruction changes the goals of legal categorization to consolidating expectations and expressing law's ideals regarding distinct types of human interaction. Thus instead of attempting to describe or refine "eternal truths," legal taxonomy would be recast as a constantly reinvented rendition. Also, rather than dismissing context, realist taxonomies are sensitive to context and seek to create relatively narrow legal categories that properly reflect the complexity of our social life. And finally, rather than aspiring to produce legal categories that do not overlap, a realist legal taxonomy recognizes and accommodates some overlaps between the various legal categories.

Chapter 7, "Remedies and Rights," studies the relationship between rights and remedies and celebrates the multiplicity of our private law rights. Remedies obviously serve as instruments of rights enforcement but, as realists have repeatedly insisted, they also participate in the constitution of the rights they help enforce. Although institutional reasons bring about certain gaps between the content of rights and the judicial response to their infringement, the constitutive role of remedies introduces significant subtlety into the domain of rights. Thus, the choice of different remedies, as well as the possibility of incorporating qualifications, limitations, and even obligations, allows private law to accommodate qualitative (and normatively attractive) distinctions between different types of rights. This chapter highlights the multiplicity of our private law rights. It further contends that this variety as well as the contingent facts on which it partly relies should not be embarrassing. Quite the contrary, a truly liberal law must resist uniformity and celebrate multiplicity for enhancing both freedom and individuality. Thus by appreciating the multiplicity of private law and the normative value of the choices on which it relies (as well as their potential critical bite), private law theory can better understand the order embedded in this complex legal mosaic and, perhaps, even contribute to its improvement.

Chapter 8, "Pluralism and Perfectionism in Private Law," offers a more elaborate defense of this typical realist celebration of the common law preference for narrow legal categories. Against the contemporary trend toward monistic theories, which suggests that one regulative principle (one value or one particular balance of values) guides an entire legal field, this chapter calls for a pluralistic turn in private law theory. Private law theory, I argue, should seriously consider the existing structural pluralism of private law and celebrate, rather than suppress or marginalize, the multiple forms typical of private law. I maintain that a structurally pluralistic and moderately perfectionistic understanding of private law is not only descriptively but also normatively superior. As Chapter 8 claims, structural pluralism is an essential entailment of the liberal commitment to autonomy, understood as people's ability to be the authors of their lives, choosing among worthwhile life plans and being able to pursue their choices. This understanding of autonomy requires an adequate range of significantly divergent options, leaving enough room for individual choice. Indeed, given the diversity of acceptable human goods from which autonomous individuals should be able to choose and their distinct constitutive values, the state must recognize a sufficiently diverse set of robust frameworks enabling people to organize their lives. And because many of these plural values cannot be realistically actualized without the active support of viable legal institutions, law should facilitate (within limits) the coexistence of various social spheres embodying different modes of valuation. Despite the appeal of monism's global coherence, it is thus reasonable and even desirable for law to adopt more than one set of principles and, therefore, more than one set of coherent doctrines. The pluralism of private law should not, however, be confused with value neutrality. Although careful not to impose a specific conception of the good life on the citizenry and happy to introduce and facilitate diverse forms of human interaction and human flourishing, private law is far from being value-neutral. Each of its categories targets, in its own way and with respect to some intended realm of application, a set of human values that can be promoted by its constitutive rules. Although many of these rules function as defaults, the number of social interaction and cooperation frameworks that private law facilitates is limited and their content relatively standardized. These features allow private law not only to consolidate people's expectations regarding these core types of human relationships but also to express law's normative ideals for these types of human interaction.

Finally, Chapter 9, "Private Law Pluralism and the Rule of Law," considers whether this pluralist account of private law can, notwithstanding its multiplicity, its dynamism, and its disavowal of neutrality, comply with the rule of law. There are, or at least so I argue, two aspects to the rule of law: the requirement that law be capable of guiding its subjects' behavior, and the prescription that law not confer on officials the right to exercise unconstrained power. At first glance, a pluralist and perfectionist understanding of private law is vulnerable on both the guidance and constraint fronts, but this impression is fortunately incorrect. Private law pluralism does not support using case-by-case adjudication (which would indeed thwart guidance). In fact, it endorses (and requires) the use of stable, coherent, and properly narrow doctrinal categories. People are able to predict the consequences of their actions and to plan for the future because each private law institution is governed by precise rules and informative standards that derive from the regulative principles of these institutions. Both legislation and adjudication shape these institutions because, at least insofar as private law is concerned, courts are equally participatory and accountable as the legislature. By the same token, although the plurality of values presents a challenge, there is no basis to assume that judicial power is not constrained by the requirement of normative contextual inquiry epitomizing common law adjudication.

IV. CONCLUDING REMARKS

Legal realism has transformed American legal discourse, but now is treated mainly as either a confused amalgam of half-baked ideas or as a milestone that may be of interest to legal historians. Instead, I suggest taking American legal realism seriously. I thus present this book as an exercise in reconstruction, an attempt to recapture the lost legacy of legal realism in the service of contemporary legal scholarship. Only the realist conception of law as an ongoing institution accommodating three constitutive and irresolvable tensions—between power and reason, science and craft, and tradition and progress—captures law's irreducible complexity. This achievement is crucial to the reinvigoration of legal theory as a distinct scholarly subject matter, and is also inspiring for a host of other, more specific theoretical questions. I hope that the accounts offered in this book of topics as the rule of law, the autonomy and taxonomy of private law, the relationships between rights and remedies, and the pluralism and perfectionism that typify private law, demonstrate my debt to legal realism and contribute to the long-overdue renewal of American legal realism.

CHAPTER 2

✧

The Realist Conception of Law

OPENING REMARKS

For many readers, the idea of a realist conception of law—the title of this chapter—may seem an oxymoron, as they may think that the realist conception of law is false or nonexistent. Those who view the infamous predictive theory of law as synonymous with the legal realist conception of law would point to its well-known deficiencies. Others, who focus on the realists' suspicion of conceptual analysis, are likely to hold that legal realism fails to offer any interesting insights into the concept of law. And even these readers who tend to applaud the realists for their pioneering contributions to numerous contemporary schools of thought would probably find the idea of reconstructing a realist conception of law deeply perplexing: the fierce rivalry among these schools reflects, after all, significant disagreements about the nature of law, suggesting that rather than one singular realist conception of law there are many.

My task in this chapter is to challenge these convictions. I argue that legal realism is unique and important for its jurisprudential insights. Legal realism also stands for a specific conception of law irreducible to any other.[1] I seek to revive the legal realists' rich account of law as an ongoing institution (or set

---

1. As the text implies, legal realists are likely to view most jurisprudential debates as arguments—notably normative arguments—between competing conceptions of law rather than as claims about the one and only possible concept of law. This position has been proposed by some contemporary legal theorists as well. *See* David Dyzenhaus, *The Genealogy of Legal Positivism*, 24 Ox. J. Legal Stud. 39, 56 (2004); Liam Murphy, *The Political Question and the Concept of Law*, in Hart's Postscript 371, 381–84 (Jules Coleman ed., 2001); Stephen R. Perry, *Interpretation and Methodology in Legal Theory*, in Law and Interpretation 97, 112–13 (Andrei Marmor ed., 1995); Frederick Schauer, *The Social Construction of the Concept of Law*, 25 Ox. J. Legal Stud. 493 (2005). On the distinction between concept and conception, see B. Gallie, *Essentially Contested Concepts*, 56 Proc. Arist. Soc. (N.S.) 167 (1956).

of institutions) accommodating three sets of constitutive tensions—between power and reason, science and craft, and tradition and progress—and to show how the major claims attributed to legal realism fit into this conception of law. I claim that the contemporary heirs of legal realism have each focused on one element of a single constitutive tension rather than refining, as conventional wisdom might hold, a confused collection of rudimentary claims. Although contemporary accounts of law enhance our understanding of its characteristics, only the realist conception captures law's most distinctive feature: the uncomfortable, but inevitable, accommodation of these constitutive tensions.

Law can neither be brute power nor pure reason; it cannot be only a science or merely a craft; and it is neither concluded by reference to the past nor fully understood by a future-oriented perspective. Legal realists reject all these reductionist conceptions of law, which are in vogue in contemporary jurisprudence. For the realist, law is defined by these three tensions. A conception of law purporting to dissolve these tensions obscures at least one of the legal phenomenon's irreducible characteristics and is thus hopelessly deficient.

Part I of this chapter sets the stage by highlighting the depth of challenge legal realism poses to legal theory. Parts II, III, and IV then lay the foundations of the realist conception of law by addressing each of the three constitutive tensions: between power and reason, science and craft, and tradition and progress (respectively). I will show how legal realism, by accommodating these three constitutive and irresolvable tensions, captures law's irreducible complexity, thus emphasizing legal realism's enduring viability to legal theory.

I. From Critique to Reconstruction

The starting point of legal realism is its critique of formalism or doctrinalism. In this part I outline the formalist vision of law and demonstrate that the legal realists' critique of this vision remains relevant, despite some heroic attempts to domesticate it (in other words, to take the "bite" out of realism, or to dilute its radical implications). Realists claim that the multiplicity of legal sources renders the formalist pretense of doctrinal determinacy an insidious falsity. This claim entails devastating consequences for the legitimacy and authority of a formalist legal regime. Appreciation of this radical critique is thus necessary to set the ground for the presentation of the realist alternative, which takes to heart the ramifications of this critical lesson but is also deeply committed to rehabilitating law as a viable social institution that can be an instrument of justice.[2]

---

2. *See* Christopher L. Tomlins, *Framing the Field of Law's Disciplinary Encounters: A Historical Narrative*, 34 L. & Soc'y Rev. 911, 944 (2000).

A. Legal Formalism

Classical formalism—culturally personified in the figure of Christopher Columbus Langdell of Harvard Law School—stands for the understanding of law as an autonomous, comprehensive, and rigorously structured doctrinal science.[3] To be sure, over the years, the term "formalism" has been used for other claims as well,[4] but they are irrelevant for this chapter.[5] Furthermore, for the purpose of reconstructing the realist conception of law, it is sufficient that the by-now canonical account of classical formalism summarized here is the view against which legal realists revolt, even if it is—as some claim—a mere caricature.[6] This historical debate is particularly irrelevant here given both the revival of American legal formalism among some judges and scholars[7] and the European attempts to rehabilitate doctrinalism, understood as a "quest" for "systematic coherence" through "the development of general concepts and structures and the perception of these as internal to and operative within the legal system."[8] Furthermore, doctrinalism seems alive and kicking in American legal culture given "the ubiquitous practice, especially in the United States, of accusing judges who have reached substantively disagreeable results in appellate cases of having committed technical legal errors or 'mistakes,' rather than of simply having the wrong substantive views."[9]

In formalism, law is governed by a set of fundamental and logically demonstrable principles.[10] Two interrelated features of the formalist conception of

---

3. *See* Anthony T. Kronman, *Jurisprudential Responses to Legal Realism*, 73 CORNELL L. REV. 335 (1988).

4. *See* Duncan Kennedy, *Legal Formalism*, *in* 13 INTERNATIONAL ENCYCLOPEDIA OF THE SOCIAL AND BEHAVIORAL SCIENCES 8634 (2001).

5. Frederick Schauer argues that formalism stands for "decisionmaking according to rule," that is, by "screening off from a decisionmaker factors that a sensitive decisionmaker would otherwise take into account." Frederick Schauer, *Formalism*, 97 YALE L.J. 509, 510 (1988). Insofar as this understanding of formalism refers to *conventional* rules—namely, insofar as it relies on the social practice of law at a given time and place—my reconstruction of legal realism complies with it. *See infra* Chapter 9.

6. *See* ANTHONY J. SEBOK, LEGAL POSITIVISM IN AMERICAN JURISPRUDENCE 83–104 (1998); BRIAN Z. TAMANAHA, BEYOND THE FORMALIST–REALIST DIVIDE: THE ROLE OF POLITICS IN JUDGING 13–108 (2010); Noga Morag-Levine, *Formalism, Facts, and the Brandeis Brief: The Making of a Myth*, 2013 U. ILL. L. REV. 59.

7. *See* ANTONIN SCALIA, A MATTER OF INTERPRETATION 25 (1997); *see also, e.g., Symposium: Formalism Revisited*, 66 U. CHI. L. REV. 527 (1999).

8. Armin von Bogdandy, *The Past and Promise of Doctrinal Constructivism: A Strategy for Responding to the Challenge Facing Constitutional Scholarship in Europe*, 7 INT'L J. CONST. L. 364, 376, 379 (2009); *see also* Armin von Bogdandy, *Founding Principles*, *in* PRINCIPLES OF EUROPEAN CONSTITUTIONAL LAW 11, 14–18, 26 (Armin von Bogdandy & Jürgen Bast eds., rev. 2d ed., 2009).

9. Frederick Schauer, Legal Realism Untamed 10, *available at* http://ssrn.com/abstract=2064837.

10. *See* NEIL DUXBURY, PATTERNS OF AMERICAN JURISPRUDENCE 10 (1995); Paul D. Carrington, *Hail! Langdell!*, 20 L. & SOC. INQ. 691, 709–10 (1995).

law bear emphasis: the purported autonomy and closure of the legal world, and the predominance of formal logic within this autonomous universe.[11] Law, on this view, is "an internally valid, autonomous, and self-justifying science" in which right answers are "derived from the autonomous, logical working out of the system."[12] Law is composed of concepts and rules. With respect to legal concepts, formalism endorses "a Platonic or Aristotelian theory," according to which "a concept delineates the essence of a species or natural kind."[13] Legal rules, in turn, embedded either in statutes or in case law, are also capable of determining logically necessary legal answers: induction can reduce the amalgam of statutes and case law to a limited number of principles, and lawyers using syllogistic reasoning—classifying the new case into one of these fundamental pigeonholes and deducing correct outcomes—can provide right answers to every case that may arise.[14]

Because legal reasoning is characterized by these logical terms, internal to it and independent of concrete subject matter,[15] formalism perceives legal reasoners as technicians whose task and expertise is mechanical: to find the law, declare what it says, and apply its preexisting prescriptions. Because these doctrinal means generate determinate and *internally* valid right answers, lawyers need not—indeed, should not—address social goals or human values.[16]

B. *The Critique of Formalism*

The realist project begins with a critique of this formalist conception of law. Realists claim that the doctrinalism celebrated by the formalist enterprise does not, in fact, describe adjudication. Conceptually, they maintain

11. *See* Thomas C. Grey, The New Formalism 5–6 (Stanford Law School, Pub. Law and Legal Theory Working Paper Series, Working Paper No. 4, 1999), *available at* http://ssrn.com/abstract=200732.

12. Richard H. Pildes, *Forms of Formalism*, 66 U. CHI. L. REV. 607, 608–09 (1999); *see also, e.g.*, Carrington, *supra* note 10, at 708–09.

13. Grey, *supra* note 11, at 11.

14. *See* DUXBURY, *supra* note 10, at 15; MORTON HORWITZ, THE TRANSFORMATION OF AMERICAN LAW, 1870–1960, at 16, 18 (1977); John Dewey, *Logical Method and Law, in* AMERICAN LEGAL REALISM 185, 188–89 (William W. Fisher III et al. eds., 1993); William W. Fisher III, *The Development of American Legal Theory and the Judicial Interpretation of the Bill of Rights, in* A CULTURE OF RIGHTS 266, 269 (Michael J. Lacey & Knud Haakonssen eds., 1993).

15. Scholars who offer reasons for adopting a formalist analysis for some specific set of legal questions fall outside the purview of formalism as a conception of law, because their call for formalism is viable, by its own terms, only insofar as, and to the extent of, its justification in realist terms. Roy Kreitner aptly terms this approach "local instrumental formalism." *See* Roy Kreitner, *Fear of Contract*, 2004 WISC. L. REV. 429, 437–38.

16. *See* HORWITZ, *supra* note 14, at 9–10, 15, 198–99; Carrington, *supra* note 10, at 707–08; Menachem Mautner, *Beyond Toleration and Pluralism: The Law School as a Multicultural Institution*, 9 INT'L J. LEGAL PROF. 55, 56 (2002).

that the indeterminacy and manipulability of the formalist techniques for divining the one essential meaning of legal concepts and deducing outcomes from legal rules render pure doctrinalism a conceptual impossibility. These descriptive and conceptual claims give rise to the realist normative criticism of legal formalism for masking normative choices and fabricating professional authority.

1. Doctrinal Indeterminacy

a. Hart's Challenge Beginning a charitable reconstruction of legal realism with a discussion of its claim of doctrinal indeterminacy may seem awkward. After all, H.L.A. Hart's famous conclusion that this claim is a "great exaggeration"[17] is usually taken as a truism.[18] But it is not. To be sure, Hart effectively addresses the narrower problem of rule indeterminacy, showing that the indeterminacy of discrete doctrinal sources is limited. However, realism views legal doctrine as hopelessly indeterminate not (or, at least, not primarily) because of the indeterminacy of discrete doctrinal sources but mainly because of their multiplicity. The indeterminacy of legal doctrine derives first and foremost from the available leeway in choosing the applicable rule rather than from the ambiguity of that rule once chosen.

Hart recognizes that doctrinal analysis affords some judicial latitude because of the vagueness of language and the multiplicity of human contingencies. But he insists that the gap between language and reality does not mean that there are no easy cases for the application of a given legal rule. He uses the example of a bylaw that forbids vehicles to enter a local park. Hart admits that "there is a limit, inherent in the nature of language, to the guidance which general language can provide," so that it may be disputable whether "vehicle" as used here includes bicycles, airplanes, and roller skates. But although these hard cases are the inevitable result of the open texture of language, there are also "plain cases constantly recurring in similar contexts to which general expressions are clearly applicable": if anything is a vehicle, a motorcar is one. This distinction between core and penumbra in any given norm is the premise of Hart's conclusion that, notwithstanding the realist critique, rules "are determinate enough at the centre to supply standards of correct judicial decisions."[19]

17. H.L.A. HART, THE CONCEPT OF LAW 144 (1961).

18. *See* Leslie Green, *The Concept of Law Revisited*, 94 MICH. L. REV. 1687, 1694 (1996); *see also, e.g.*, SCOTT J. SHAPIRO, LEGALITY 260 (2011).

19. HART, *supra* note 17, at 123, 141–42, 144. For an early incarnation of this argument, see John Dickinson, *Legal Rules: Their Function in the Process of Decision*, 79 U. PA. L. REV. 833, 846–47 (1996).

Hart's analysis can domesticate some realist claims regarding the inde-terminacy of discrete doctrinal (typically statutory) rules. Thus, it effectively addresses claims by John Dewey and Max Radin that no one can "signify rules so rigid that they can be stated once for all and then be literally and mechani-cally adhered to."[20] Indeed, insofar as the indeterminacy critique of doctrinal-ism relies on the inevitable ambiguity of the language of legal rules[21] and "the intrinsic impossibility of foreseeing all possible circumstances,"[22] it is limited to doctrinally hard cases. The indeterminacy of discrete doctrinal sources is not a serious threat to the formalist project.[23]

But Radin, who focuses on the indeterminacy of discrete statutory norms, anticipates Hart's point and concedes that the existence of a statutory rule "imposes certain limitations in the application."[24] In turn, Dewey's critique does not focus only on the indeterminacy of discrete doctrinal sources. Immediately after referring to the difficulty posed by the inherent gap between language and reality, Dewey adds that "questions of degree of this factor or that have the chief way in determining which general rule will be employed to judge the situation in question."[25]

b. Doctrinal Multiplicity While Dewey tackles the problem of doctrinal multi-plicity only implicitly, most realists present this element more explicitly and in far greater detail. Fully appreciating the magnitude and depth of doctri-nal indeterminacy, they claim, requires that we not look merely at one given rule. Rather, the main source of doctrinal indeterminacy is the multiplicity of doctrinal materials potentially applicable at each juncture in any given

20. Dewey, *supra* note 14, at 192.

21. *See* Max Radin, *Statutory Interpretation*, 43 HARV. L. REV. 863, 868–69 (1929). Radin extends his critique to other conventional methods of statutory interpretation, such as legislative intent. *Id.* at 870. For a Hart-like domestication of this claim, *see* ANDREI MARMOR, INTERPRETATION AND LEGAL THEORY ch. 8 (1992). For a critique, see Jeremy Waldron, *Legislators' Intentions and Unintentional Legislation, in* LAW AND INTERPRETATION 329 (Andrei Marmor ed., 1995).

22. Dewey, *supra* note 14, at 193.

23. Furthermore, even a more charitable reading of the realist critique of the deter-minacy of discrete rules does not fully capture the radicalism of the realist critique of doctrinalism. Thus, in highlighting the realist distinction between "a paper rule— the plain meaning of the language of a legal rule as set forth in a statute, regulation, or case—[and] the real rule as actually applied," Frederick Schauer seeks to "untame" legal realism, showing that it "challenges the very idea that the written down law is the source of legal determinacy." But as he correctly argues, the significance of *this* chal-lenge is contingent upon empirical questions. This realist claim "will have effects on our understanding of law that are in no way limited to the domain of cases that turn out to be worth fighting over in court" if but only if "even clear paper rules are [in fact] less outcome-determinative than many commentators, then and now, have supposed." Schauer, *supra* note 9, at 20, 28, 32–34.

24. Radin, *supra* note 21, 878–79.

25. Dewey, *supra* note 14, at 192.

case.[26] As legal norms are "in the habit of hunting in pairs"[27]—because legal doctrine always offers at least "two buttons" between which choice must be made—none of the doctrine's answers to problems is preordained, precise, or inevitable.[28]

Doctrinal multiplicity is endemic to law, mainly because of the fact—emphasized by Hans Kelsen (who was, of course, a prominent legal positivist)[29]—that no legal rule exists in solitude, and legal rules are always part of the legal system in which they are embedded. When assessing the claim of doctrinal indeterminacy, therefore, we must look at the legal doctrine as a whole, as lawyers always do. This broader perspective immediately highlights an element of choice that is obscured in any discussion focusing on the indeterminacy of discrete rules, including Hart's: because "the authoritative tradition speaks with a forked tongue,"[30] there is always some latitude in picking up the rule to be applied to the case at hand. For legal realism, the choice among doctrinal rules competing to control the case is the major (and inescapable) source of doctrinal indeterminacy or, more precisely, of doctrinal under-determinacy.[31] (Realists do not deny of course that legal doctrine rules out many—indeed, most—options, but they insist that there will always remain more than one option that can doctrinally apply.)

Thus, Karl Llewellyn claims that "*all* legal systems" are patchworks of contradictory premises covered by "ill-disguised inconsistency," because in all of them we find that "a variety of strands, only partly consistent with one another, exist side by side."[32] Any given legal doctrine, including the one guiding the lawyers' interpretative activity (the canons of interpretation),[33] suggests "at least two

26. The problem of doctrinal multiplicity goes beyond the multiplication of rule indeterminacy, as would be the case were the relevant legal norms approached sequentially.

27. Walter Wheeler Cook, *Book Review*, 38 YALE L. J. 405, 406 (1929) (reviewing BENJAMIN N. CARDOZO, THE PARADOXES OF LEGAL SCIENCE (1928)) .

28. FRED RODELL, WOE UNTO YOU, LAWYERS! 154, 160 (1940); *see also, e.g.,* JEROME FRANK, LAW AND THE MODERN MIND 138 (1949).

29. *See* HANS KELSEN, GENERAL THEORY OF LAW AND STATE 3, 110–23 (Anders Wedberg trans., 1946) (claiming that legal rules gain their validity—at times even their meaning—from being part of an effective legal system).

30. KARL N. LLEWELLYN, *Some Realism about Realism, in* JURISPRUDENCE: REALISM IN THEORY AND IN PRACTICE 42, 70 (1962).

31. *See id.* at 58; FELIX S. COHEN, *The Problems of Functional Jurisprudence, in* THE LEGAL CONSCIENCE: SELECTED PAPERS OF FELIX S. COHEN 77, 83 (Lucy Kramer Cohen ed., 1960); *see also, e.g.,* EDWARD A. PURCELL, JR., THE CRISIS OF DEMOCRATIC THEORY: SCIENTIFIC NATURALISM AND THE PROBLEM OF VALUE 90 (1973); Andrew Altman, *Legal Realism, Critical Legal Studies, and Dworkin*, 15 PHIL. & PUB. AFF. 205 (1986).

32. KARL N. LLEWELLYN, THE CASE LAW SYSTEM IN AMERICA 45 (Paul Gewirtz ed., Michael Alsandi trans., 1989) (1933). This critique was picked up by Roberto Unger. *See* ROBERTO M. UNGER, THE CRITICAL LEGAL STUDIES MOVEMENT 15–22 (1983).

33. *See* Karl N. Llewellyn, *Remarks on the Theory of Appellate Decision and the Rules or Canons about How Statutes Are to Be Construed*, 3 VAND. L. REV. 395 (1950).

opposite tendencies" at every point. For (almost) every case, then, lawyers find opposite doctrinal sources that need to be accommodated: a rule and an (frequently vague) exception, or a seemingly precise rule and a vague standard (such as good faith or reasonableness) that is also potentially applicable. The availability of such a multiplicity of sources on any given legal question, all of which can be either expanded or contracted, results in profound and irreducible doctrinal indeterminacy.[34]

Moreover, doctrinal multiplicity manifests itself even when we are dealing with one legal source, especially where that source is a case, rather than a statutory rule. (In fact, even statutory rules often include more than one norm at a time, thus generating a problem of multiplicity.) As Llewellyn explains, in distinguishing between *ratio decidendi* and *obiter dictum*, judges can rely either on the rule stated by the previous court or on the legally relevant facts (or on both). Furthermore, even if we focus on only one method, significant indeterminacy still remains. Thus, insofar as articulated rules are concerned, accumulative or alternative reasons generate "an intermediate type of authority," where each leg "is much more subject to challenge than it would be if the decision stood on it alone." Furthermore, even with regard to each reason given by the court for its decision, some ambiguity remains, both because judges tend to repeat their reasons and the rules they state—even though "the repetition seldom is exact"—and because opinions are always read "with primary reference to the particular dispute," so that some arguments must be confined to the case at hand and others enjoy a much more general applicability. Similar indeterminacy faces the method of figuring out the holding of a case by focusing on its legally relevant facts. Obviously, not each and every fact stated by the court is legally significant: some are discarded "as of no interest whatsoever . . . others as dramatic but as legal nothings." Moreover, the relevant facts are not treated as such, but are rather classified in categories that are deemed significant. But neither the selection of the pertinent facts nor their classification into categories is a self-evident or logically necessary undertaking. In all these ways, judges have significant discretion as to the question of how wide, or how narrow, the *ratio decidendi* of the case should be—that is, what should its scope be vis-à-vis other rules.[35]

---

34. *See* LLEWELLYN, *supra* note 32, at 51. For one example, see Hanoch Dagan, *Codification, Coherence, and Priority Conflicts, in* THE DRAFT CIVIL CODE FOR ISRAEL IN COMPARATIVE PERSPECTIVE 149, 151–52, 167–68 (Kurt Siehr & Reinhard Zimmermann eds., 2008). To be sure, none of this implies that the social practice of law at a given time and place would not provide insiders determinate answers to these doctrinal quandaries, as some critics of Llewellyn's claims regarding the canons of interpretations demonstrate. *See, e.g.,* Michael Sinclair, *"Only a Sith Thinks Like That": Llewellyn's "Dueling Canons," One to Seven,* 50 N.Y.L. SCH. L. REV. 919 (2005–2006).

35. *See* KARL N. LLEWELLYN, THE BRAMBLE BUSH 40–48 (1930); LLEWELLYN, *supra* note 32, at 25; KARL N. LLEWELLYN, THE COMMON LAW TRADITION: DECIDING APPEALS 77–91 (1960). To be sure, at any given time and place, the practice of precedent is

Similarly, legal realists maintain that the idea of inevitable entailments from legal concepts is false. Instead, they assert that the elaboration of any legal concept can choose from a broad menu of possible alternatives.[36] The heterogeneity of contemporary understandings of any given legal concept (such as property or contract) within and outside any given jurisdiction, as well as the wealth of additional alternatives that legal history offers, defies the formalist quest for conceptual essentialism.[37]

In sum, the main reason for the realist claim that judges are never fully constrained by legal doctrine is not the indeterminacy of any given rule, an indeterminacy that Hart domesticated. Rather, it is the question of whether the rule will contain a doubtful case. The multiplicity of doctrinal sources is the main reason for Justice Holmes's famous dictum, "[y]ou can give any conclusion a logical form."[38] In dealing with legal rules and legal concepts, the judicial task is never one of static application. At any given moment, legal doctrine contains competing trends that can apply to the particular case at issue.[39] Judges always need to choose "and perhaps also to re-formulate the victorious trend."[40]

2. Cloaking Choices, Fabricating Authority

The legal formalist project of focusing on "the niceties of [law's] internal structure [and] the beauty of its logical processes" is thus untenable.[41] It is also disturbing and harmful. By falsely presenting (often intuitive) value judgments made by judges as inevitable entailments of predetermined rules and concepts, formalism obscures these choices, shielding them from empirical and normative scrutiny and securing the unjustified claim of lawyers to an impenetrable professionalism.

robust enough so that different lawyers employ similar techniques for distinguishing between *ratio decidendi* and *obiter dictum. See* Kent Greenawalt, *Reflections on Holding and Dictum*, 39 J. LEGAL EDUC. 431, 433–34 (1989). But this only vindicates the realist claim that the real work of settling the content of the legal doctrine is done by these background understandings rather than by the doctrine strictly speaking.

36. Felix S. Cohen, *Transcendental Nonsense and the Functional Approach*, 35 COLUM. L. REV. 809, 820–21, 827–29 (1935); *see also* HORWITZ, *supra* note 14, at 202.

37. *See, e.g.*, HANOCH DAGAN, THE LAW AND ETHICS OF RESTITUTION 221–24, 315–16 (2004); HANOCH DAGAN, PROPERTY: VALUES AND INSTITUTIONS 3–84 (2011).

38. OLIVER W. HOLMES, *The Path of the Law*, *in* COLLECTED LEGAL PAPERS 167, 181 (1920); *cf.* RICHARD POSNER, LAW, PRAGMATISM, AND DEMOCRACY 81–82 (2003).

39. *See* Paul Gewirtz, *Editor's Introduction*, *in* LLEWELLYN, *supra* note 32, at xvi.

40. LLEWELLYN, *supra* note 32, at 92 n.1. For an attempt to domesticate this challenge, see LARRY ALEXANDER & EMILY SHERWIN, DEMYSTIFYING LEGAL REASONING 22–23 (2008).

41. Roscoe Pound, *Mechanical Jurisprudence*, 8 COLUM. L. REV. 605, 605 (1908).

a. Formalism as Cover-Up The formalist fallacy, claims Holmes, serves as a cover-up for "considerations of social advantage" that are "the very ground and foundation of judgments" and must not be left unconscious.[42] Felix Cohen elaborates on the theme of cloaking normative choices in his famous critique of the formalist use of legal concepts. Although using legal concepts is unavoidable, Cohen maintains this innocuous practice is risky because lawyers tend to "thingify" legal concepts. Lawyers' "language of transcendental nonsense" treats such concepts not as legal artifacts but as a non-modifiable part of our natural or ethical environment. And, thus, it misleadingly presents existing understandings of legal concepts as explanations and justifications for subsequent legal results. But "the magic 'solving words' of traditional jurisprudence," Cohen claims, neither explain nor justify court decisions. Worse still, when "the vivid fictions and metaphors of traditional jurisprudence are thought of as reasons for decisions," then "the author, as well as the reader, of the opinion or argument . . . is apt to forget the social forces which mold the law and the social ideals by which the law is to be judged."[43] (Hohfeld's reconstruction of rights discourse, discussed in Chapter 7, is part of the same move of exposing the choice behind seemingly natural legal constructs.[44]) Formalism is objectionable because, by pretending to find determinate doctrinal answers to legal questions, it bars the way to an open inquiry of the normative desirability of alternative judicial decisions, thus unduly essentializing contingent doctrinal choices.[45]

42. HOLMES, *supra* note 38, at 184.

43. Cohen, *supra* note 36, at 811–12, 820; *see also* Joseph Bingham, *What Is the Law?*, 11 MICH. L. REV. 1, 12 (1912). The astute reader will notice the deliberately limited use I am making of Cohen's argument. I do not dispute Jeremy Waldron's claim that legal concepts help "represent[] a nexus of connections" that "may be something of substantial importance for anyone proposing to change or repeal any one or more items in the array, or even for anyone proposing simply to apply one of the rules in the array to a particular set of events in a particular case." Jeremy Waldron, *"Transcendental Nonsense" and System in the Law*, 100 COLUM. L. REV. 16, 25 (2000). Nothing in the text is aimed at undermining, or in fact undermines, the role of the conceptual terminology of law in "keep[ing] track of the significance of legal changes in a complex patchwork of doctrine," thus facilitating "law's ability to flourish in an environment of complexity, diversity, and disagreement." *Id.* at 52–53. Indeed, while insisting that not "every non-empirical connection is discreditable and unimportant," Waldron himself is careful enough to add that "Cohen might be right in his distaste for conceptual arguments that trapeze around in cycles and epicycles without ever coming to rest on the floor of verifiable fact." *Id.* at 51.

44. *See* Wesley Newcomb Hohfeld, *Some Fundamental Legal Conceptions as Applied in Judicial Reasoning*, 23 YALE L.J. 16 (1913); *see also* Walter Wheeler Cook, *Privileges of Labor Unions in the Struggle for Life*, 27 YALE L.J. 779 (1918).

45. *See* OLIVER W. HOLMES, *Law in Science and Science in Law*, in COLLECTED LEGAL PAPERS, *supra* note 38, at 210, 230, 232, 238–39.

Dewey criticizes syllogistic reasoning along similar lines. He presents doctrinal exposition as the professional hazard of judges. The purpose of such an exposition "is to set forth grounds for the decision reached so that it will not appear as an arbitrary dictum." Doctrinal exposition, therefore, tends not to reveal all the problems and doubts a legal reasoner faces along the way, hence the appeal of syllogism, with its attendant misrepresentation. "Those forms of speech which are rigorous in appearance...give an illusion of certitude" and of a judicial opinion that is "impersonal, objective, rational." Moreover, when "the doctrine of undoubtable and necessary antecedent rules comes in," the old is sanctified. This, in Dewey's view, is "the great practical evil" of the syllogistic method. Privileging—indeed, perpetuating—the status quo in such a way breeds "irritation, disrespect for law, together with virtual alliance between the judiciary and entrenched interests that correspond most nearly to the conditions under which the rules of law were previously laid down."[46]

b. Formalism and Lawyers' Authority Unmasking the manipulability of legal doctrine raises severe concerns as to the authority of legal reasoners. Thus, Fred Rodell laments lawyers' success in making themselves "masters of their fellow men." Lawyers capture excessive social power by preventing any "brand competition or product competition." They are able to gain this unjustified privileged position by creating and preserving (at times self-deceptively) a distinct language with a scientific appearance: the discourse of legal formalism. Rodell vividly presents this language as "a maze of confusing gestures and formalities"—a hodgepodge of "long words and sonorous phrases" with "ambiguous or empty meanings" frequently "contradictory of each other." He further explains that lawyers are able to conceal the "emptiness" of doctrinal reasoning by their "sober pretense" that the doctrinal language—which is for nonlawyers "a foreign tongue"—"is, in the main, an exact science." Legal formalism is thus responsible for the unjustified privileged status of lawyers.[47]

---

46. *See* Dewey, *supra* note 14, at 191, 193.

47. RODELL, *supra* note 28, at 3–4, 6–7, 153, 157–58, 186, 189, 196, 198. Rodell's "cure" to these faults—to "get rid of the lawyers and throw the Law out of our system of laws" (*id.* at 249)—has been justifiably criticized. *See, e.g.*, Neil Duxbury, *In the Twilight of Legal Realism: Fred Rodell and the Limits of Legal Critique*, 11 OX. J. LEGAL STUD. 354, 370–72 (1991). But the claim that the nature of legal discourse affects the status of the legal profession and that the preservation of law's autonomy generates for lawyers far-reaching advantages is by now an almost mainstream position among sociologists of law. *See* Pierre Bourdieu, *The Force of Law: Towards a Sociology of the Juridical Field*, 38 HASTINGS L.J. 805, 819–21, 841–43 (1987); *see also* RONEN SHAMIR, MANAGING LEGAL UNCERTAINTY: ELITE LAWYERS IN THE NEW DEAL 5, 166 (1995).

C. *The Puzzle of Reconstruction*

1. Beyond Frankified Subjectivism

The realist attack on the formalist conception of law is too often misinterpreted to mean that judges exercise unfettered discretion to reach results based on their personal predilections, which they then rationalize with appropriate legal rules and reasons. Brian Leiter describes this view as the "Frankification" of legal realism and correctly charges its subscribers with the fallacy of viewing Jerome Frank—an extreme proponent of the "idiosyncrasy wing" of legal realism—as its typical representative. But Frank, as Leiter notes further on, is a minority voice.[48]

Mainstream legal realists reject Frank's subjectivism.[49] Thus, Cohen maintains that because law is a social institution, legal results are "large-scale social facts" that "cannot be explained in terms of the atomic idiosyncrasies of personal prejudices of individuals."[50] The "hunch theory of law" magnifies "the personal and accidental factors in judicial behavior" and ignores our daily experience of "predictable uniformity in the behavior of courts." Indeed, law, Cohen claims, "is not a map of unrelated decisions nor a product of judicial bellyaches. Judges are human, but they are a peculiar breed of humans, selected to a type and held to service under a potent system of governmental controls." Decisions genuinely peculiar are therefore bound to erode and be washed away in a system that provides for appeals, rehearings, impeachments, and legislation.[51] Although legal realists do not deny that the personalities of individual judges may affect outcomes in particular cases,[52] most believe that "[t]he eccentricities of judges balance one another,"[53] and the bulk of legal material falls into essentially predictable patterns.[54]

48. Brian Leiter, *Rethinking Legal Realism: Toward a Naturalized Jurisprudence*, 76 TEXAS L. REV. 267, 268–69, 283–84 (1997); *see also* Michael Ansaldi, *The German Llewellyn*, 58 BROOKLYN L. REV. 705, 775–77 (1992). For one invocation of the Frankified caricature of legal realism, see RONALD DWORKIN, JUSTICE IN ROBES (2006).

49. Frank himself never renounced his irrationalist view, encapsulated by the reference to "the judicial hunch." He merely believed that this hunch could become more benevolent. *See* ROBERT JEROME GLENNON, THE ICONOCLAST AS REFORMER 49–50 (1985); Bruce A. Ackerman, *Book Review*, 103 DEDALUS 119, 122 (1974) (reviewing JEROME FRANK, LAW AND THE MODERN MIND (1930)).

50. COHEN, *Field Theory and Judicial Logic, in* THE LEGAL CONSCIENCE, *supra* note 31, at 121.

51. Cohen, *supra* note 36, at 70.

52. For a poignant example—an exception that proves the rule—see Republic of Bolivia v. Philip Morris, 39 F. Supp. 2d 1008 (S.D. Tex. 1999).

53. BENJAMIN N. CARDOZO, THE NATURE OF THE JUDICIAL PROCESS 176 (1921); *see also* ANDREW L. KAUFMAN, CARDOZO 457–58 (1998).

54. *See* Karl N. Llewellyn, *My Philosophy of Law, in* MY PHILOSOPHY OF LAW: CREDOS OF SIXTEEN AMERICAN SCHOLARS 183, 196 (1941, 1987); Leiter, *supra* note 48, at 283–84; *see also, e.g.,* KENT GREENAWALT, LAW AND OBJECTIVITY 34, 68 (1992).

None of this undermines the realist claim that a gap will always exist between doctrinal materials and judicial outcomes. Law cannot be understood as a set of concepts and rules, able to transcend the legal tradition in which it is situated and independent of any extra-doctrinal understandings of the legal community.[55] Unlike its Frankified caricature, however, legal realism neither maintains that the gap between doctrine and law is filled with subjectivity nor denies the existence of legal reality. Mainstream realists agree with Benjamin Cardozo's critique of "the jurists who seem to hold that in reality there is no law except the decisions of the courts." This position, Cardozo argues, is fallacious because it denies the "present" of law: "Law never *is*, but is always about to be. It is realized only when embodied in a judgment, and in being realized, expires." This denial of an existing legal reality is rejected because our daily experience disproves it: "Law and obedience to law are facts confirmed every day to us all in our experience of life. If the result of a definition is to make them seem to be illusions, so much the worse for the definition."[56]

Indeed, unlike their image in some caricatures of legal realism, realists do not challenge the felt predictability of the doctrine at a given time and place. While persuasively insisting that legal doctrine qua doctrine cannot constrain decision makers, they recognize that the convergence of lawyers' background understandings at a given time and place generates a significant measure of stability.[57] Hence, rather than threatening the rule of law, legal realism merely insists that law's stability and predictability do not inhere in the doctrine as such and rests instead on the broader social practice of law.[58] (I return to the realist understanding of the rule of law in Chapter 9.)

2. Refining the Realist Challenge

Realists claim that the formalist description of law's present (or legal reality) as synonymous with an autonomous system of concepts entailing necessary meanings and logically interconnected rules is misguided. Therefore, they also reject positivist theories insofar as they portray the standard judicial function

---

55. *Cf.* Brian Bix, Law, Language, and Legal Determinacy 181–82 (1993).

56. Cardozo, *supra* note 53, at 126–27; *see also* Richard Polenberg, The World of Benjamin Cardozo 159, 162–63 (1997). To this phenomenological reason Cardozo adds another, namely that legal nihilism "denies the possibility of law [by denying] the possibility of rules of general operation." Cardozo, *supra* note 53, at 126. Insofar as it is supposed to be an independent argument, it is circular because it assumes a positivist conception of law, defeated by the realist critique of formalism.

57. *See* Larry Alexander & Emily Sherwin, The Rule of Rules 32–34 (2001).

58. *See* Frederick Schauer, *Editor's Introduction*, *in* Karl N. Llewellyn, The Theory of Rules 1, 5, 7–8, 18, 20–24 (Frederick Schauer ed., 2011).

as the application of black-letter law,[59] and thus conceptualize law as if it were a self-regulating system of concepts and rules, a machine that, in run-of-the-mill cases, necessarily runs itself.[60] For legal realists, a credible conception of law must allow the people who make it to occupy center stage. Legal realists, in short, repudiate the equation of law with doctrine, insisting instead that law must be understood as an ongoing institution rather than a disembodied entity.[61]

This claim does not deny the existence of rules or quarrel with the present of law.[62] Realists emphatically recognize that law is a reasonably determinate terrain—that most lawyers will converge at any given moment on the "felt" law of a case.[63] But this raises a puzzle. Realists surely do not argue that law's determinacy—the fact that there are indeed easy cases in law—derives from the determinacy of legal doctrine as such.[64] So they must claim that law's determinacy derives from something else, something that goes to the most fundamental characteristics of law. But what can this "something else" be?

This question sums up the challenge of legal realism. The slippage between doctrine and outcomes, Anthony Kronman claims, raises two problems: intelligibility and legitimacy.[65] First, identifying the sources of the "felt law"—once sheer doctrine is no longer a viable candidate—is crucial to explain past judicial behavior (i.e., to render it intelligible) and predict its future course. Second, and even more significantly, if law is to rehabilitate its legitimacy, these sources should have redeeming qualities. Once the formalist myth of law as a set of agent-independent concepts and rules has been effectively discredited, these alternative sources must be capable of constraining judgments made by unelected judges and justifying their authority (i.e., to render it legitimate).

---

59. *Cf.* H.L.A. HART, *American Jurisprudence through English Eyes: The Nightmare and the Noble Dream*, 11 GA. L. REV. 969, 971 (1977).

60. *See* ROGER COTTERRELL, THE POLITICS OF JURISPRUDENCE 99, 110–12 (1989).

61. *See* Llewellyn, *supra* note 54, 183–84; *see also, e.g.*, SHAPIRO, *supra* note 18, at 32, 34; Michael C. Dorf, *Legal Indeterminacy and Institutional Design*, 78 N.Y.U. L. REV. 875, 878–79 (2003).

62. *Contra* THEODORE BENDITT, LAW AS RULE AND PRINCIPLE 25 (1978). Similarly, nothing in the realist legacy supports judicial hyperactivity vis-à-vis legislatures or prior courts, or denies the virtue of translating broad statutory mandates into a set of specified judge-made rules. *Contra* Frederick Schauer, *The Limited Domain of Law*, 90 VA. L. REV. 1909, 1939–41 (2004).

63. *See* LLEWELLYN, BRAMBLE BUSH, *supra* note 35, at 48; *see also, e.g.*, MICHAEL MARTIN, LEGAL REALISM: AMERICAN AND SCANDINAVIAN 39–40, 76 (1997); Brian Leiter, *Legal Indeterminacy*, 1 LEGAL THEORY 481 (1995).

64. In Leiter's terminology, realists claim that legal doctrine is always rationally indeterminate. For his distinction between causal and rational indeterminacy, see Leiter, *supra* note 63.

65. *See* Kronman, *supra* note 3, at 335–36; *see also, e.g.*, GLENNON, *supra* note 49, at 52; LAURA KALMAN, THE STRANGE CAREER OF LEGAL LIBERALISM 5 (1996); PURCELL, *supra* note 31, at 94.

The remainder of this chapter reconstructs the realist response to these challenges while developing its unique conception of law. The realist understanding of law presents an ideal, but it is decidedly not utopian. It emphasizes the human factor, with its inevitable frailties, and highlights the tensions inherent in law. It also suggests certain institutional, procedural, and discursive features that can alleviate—though by no means solve—these constitutive tensions of law. Although perhaps less glamorous, law is far more intelligible and considerably more legitimate in this account than in its (purported but mythical) formalist counterpart.

In the realist conception, law is a going institution—or rather a set of institutions[66]—that embodies three sets of constitutive tensions: between power and reason, science and craft, and tradition and progress. Parts III–V are devoted to separate discussions of these sets of constitutive tensions, demonstrating their prominence in legal realist literature while using this literature to explain why our understanding of law is deficient without an appreciation of their significance. The realist presentation of law's perennial features is far from complete or flawless. It is impossible to address here, let alone resolve, the questions and difficulties left open in the realist discourse, which bring to the fore several classic philosophical debates. Fortunately, this formidable undertaking is unnecessary for my task: reinstating the legal realist insight of keeping law's constitutive tensions at the core of our conception of law.

II. On Power and Reason

I begin with power and its tortuous relationship with reason (the first constitutive tension) as two prominent, yet not easily coexistent, features of law. Our starting point must be the coerciveness of law, because it adds to the challenge that legal realists face when attempting to reconstruct law. Judgments issued by the carriers of law are qualitatively different from all others in their ability to recruit the state's monopolized power to back up their enforcement.[67] The fallacy of the formalist algorithm is that it is judges' choices, not the doctrines they apply, that trigger coercion and power. It is precisely in this sense that the collapse of the formalist premise concerning the predictability and legitimacy of law is particularly devastating and that the need for reconstruction is singularly acute.

---

66. *See* Roy Kreitner, *Biographing Legal Realism*, 35 L. & Soc. Inq. 765, 779–81 (2010).

67. *See, e.g.*, Robin West, *Adjudication Is Not Interpretation*, *in* Narrative, Authority, and Law 89, 93–96, 174–76 (1993). I use the words "power," "force," and "coerciveness" more or less as synonyms and, likewise, use "reason," "justification," and "normativity" almost interchangeably.

Although the coerciveness of law and the challenges it poses have been too frequently ignored or domesticated, the portrayal of law as sheer power (or interest, or politics) is, realists claim, equally reductive. Law is also a forum of reason, and reason imposes real—albeit elusive—constraints on the choices of legal decision makers and thus on the entailed application of state power. Legal realists have neither solved the mystery of reason nor conclusively demonstrated how reason can survive in law's coercive environment. But their insistence that, in any credible account of the law, coerciveness and reason are fated to coexist and their preliminary account of the difficult accommodation of power and reason are important, especially when compared to more contemporary approaches that are typically reductionist and predicated on an overly romantic or far too cynical view of law.

A. Law as Public Force

Oliver Wendell Holmes begins *The Path of the Law* by strongly emphasizing law's coercive power. The reason law is a profession, says Holmes, is that "in societies like ours the command of the public force is entrusted by judges in certain cases, and the whole power of the state will be put forth, if necessary, to carry out their judgments and decrees."[68] This gloomy emphasis on force is not just an introductory gimmick. The claim that law is a coercive mechanism backed by state-mandated power weaves into and helps explain some important themes in Holmes's seminal essay.[69]

1. Power as Key to *The Path of the Law*

Consider Holmes's notorious dictum that "[t]he prophecies of what the courts will do in fact, and nothing more pretentious, are what I mean by the law."[70] At face value, this so-called predictive theory of law is riddled with flaws. Law as prediction makes no sense for judges addressing legal questions—are they to predict their own behavior? If so, surely they can never be wrong.[71] Furthermore, even if we set aside this difficulty by acknowledging that judges

---

68. HOLMES, *supra* note 38, at 167.

69. On the significance of questions of power to realism generally, see Gregory S. Alexander, *Comparing the Two Legal Realisms—American and Scandinavian*, 50 AM. J. COMP. L. 131, 132 (2002).

70. HOLMES, *supra* note 54, at 173. Karl Llewellyn expands this claim to other law carriers as well: sheriffs, clerks, jailers, and lawyers. *See* LLEWELLYN, BRAMBLE BUSH, *supra* note 35, at 3.

71. *See, e.g.*, Felix S. Cohen, *The Problems of a Functional Jurisprudence*, 1 MOD. L. REV. 5, 17 (1937); David Luban, *The Bad Man and the Good Lawyer: A Centennial Essay on Holmes's The Path of the Law*, 72 N.Y.U. L. REV. 1547, 1577–78 (1997).

cannot see law in this way,[72] a predictive theory of law is seriously misleading. As Hart argues, legal norms are taken not only as predictions of judicial action but also as standards and guides for conduct and judgment, and as bases for claims, demands, admissions, criticism, and punishment. The predictive theory "obscures the fact that, where rules exist, deviations from them are not merely grounds for a prediction that hostile reactions will follow or that a court will apply sanctions to those who break them, but are also a reason or justification for such reaction and for applying the sanctions."[73] This failure to appreciate the normativity of law is significant because it ignores the "internal point of view" of people who accept the rules and voluntarily cooperate in maintaining them, usually the majority. From that point of view, "the violation of a rule is not merely a basis for the prediction that a hostile reaction will follow but a *reason* for hostility."[74] Needless to add, this second flaw undermines another important theme of *The Path of the Law*: Holmes's endorsement of the perspective of the bad man who "cares only for the material consequences" of his acts and discounts other reasons for action, "whether inside the law or outside of it, in the vaguer sanctions of conscience."[75]

Another contested Holmesian theme is his call for separating law from morality. Holmes acknowledges that "[t]he law is the witness and external deposit of our moral life" and that its "practice tends to make good citizens." Yet he complains that "law is full of phraseology drawn from morals," which confusingly "invites us to pass from one domain to the other without perceiving it." In order to avoid this trap, Holmes suggests banishing from the law "every word of moral significance" and adopting instead other words "which should convey legal ideas uncolored by anything outside the law."[76] At face value, these statements are embarrassingly shallow. Not only does the claim about law's moral function undermine the one about the impropriety of using words with moral content in legal discourse (or vice versa), but the latter claim, as David Luban notes, is a non sequitur. "The bare fact that legal words diverge from their extralegal counterpart doesn't mean that they are different words with different meanings." Replacing morally laden legal words with artificial terms is not really possible, because the moral and legal meanings are systematically related: "The moral baggage and nontechnical meanings of legal terms

---

72. See LLEWELLYN, *On Reading and Using the Newer Jurisprudence, in* JURISPRUDENCE, *supra* note 30, at 128, 142; *see also* MARTIN, *supra* note 63, at 16, 30, 32–37, 72–74; J.M. Balkin, *Understanding Legal Understanding: The Legal Subject and the Problem of Legal Coherence*, 103 YALE L.J. 105, 110–12, 128–29, 131–36, 139–43 (1993); Bingham, *supra* note 43, at 10.

73. HART, *supra* note 17, at 84.

74. *Id.* at 90; *see also, e.g.*, BENDITT, *supra* note 62, 39, 86–88; JOSEPH RAZ, *The Relevance of Coherence, in* ETHICS IN THE PUBLIC DOMAIN: ESSAYS IN THE MORALITY OF LAW AND POLITICS 261, 280–81 (1994); *infra* Part I.A of Chapter 3.

75. HOLMES, *supra* note 38, at 171; *see also id.* at 174.

76. *Id.* at 170–71, 179.

indeed co-exist with more specialized senses as the legal discourse develops them, but this is common respecting words that are used in multiple contexts (that is, respecting words, period)."[77] Moreover, as Cardozo claims, judges are duty-bound "to maintain a relation between law and morals"; the "contrasts between law and justice" should not obscure "their deeper harmonies."[78]

It is crude to think about law solely in terms of prediction, and it is awkward to advocate an impermeable separation of law from morality and celebrate the amoral perspective of the bad man. But these severe flaws become marginal, almost beside the point, if we interpret Holmes's claims more charitably, reading them as a means to bolster the assertion that coercion is a constitutive feature of law, that law is not just a "system of reason."[79] Recall that Holmes emphasizes prediction because people are afraid of the danger they may face when confronting the law, which is "so much stronger than themselves"; indeed, this is why the object of prediction is "the incidence of the public force through the instrumentality of the courts."[80] Likewise, Holmes's separation thesis, as well as his espousal of the bad man's prudential point of view rather than that of the socialized good citizen,[81] are best read as methodological devices for opening up some liberating distance for the addressees of law's coercive judgments and for depriving law of some of "the majesty got from ethical associations." Only after we wash the notion of duty with this "cynical acid," explains Holmes, will the realm of legal duties shrink and grow more precise.[82]

Along these lines, Llewellyn criticizes the "confused tradition [in which] if it is Legal, it is *therefore* Right enough." It is mistaken to assume any inherent convergence between law and justice. Law should be separated from morality in order to "hold the responsibility for working toward the Right and the Just within the hard legal frame... to *de*fuse and *de*confuse the merely authoritative... from the Just or the Right, and to get into the pillory so much of the Law as has no business to be Law."[83] Indeed, whereas the fusion of law and morality tends to present law only in terms of justice and truth, rather than as comprising acts of power, separating law from morality can help preserve

77. Luban, *supra* note 71, at 1567–69.

78. CARDOZO, *supra* note 53, at 133–34; *see also* SHAPIRO, *supra* note 18, at 114, 217.

79. HOLMES, *supra* note 38, at 172–73; *see also* COTTERRELL, *supra* note 60, at 57–74, 77–79.

80. HOLMES, *supra* note 38, at 167.

81. *See* Stephen R. Perry, *Holmes versus Hart: The Bad Man in Legal Theory*, in THE PATH OF THE LAW AND ITS INFLUENCE: THE LEGACY OF OLIVER WENDELL HOLMES, JR. 158, 165–66 (Steven J. Burton ed., 2000).

82. HOLMES, *supra* note 38, at 174, 179; *see also id.* at 171–72.

83. K.N. Llewellyn, *The Normative, the Legal, and the Law-Jobs: The Problem of Juristic Method*, 49 YALE L.J. 1355, 1372–73 (1940).

our capacity for morally responsible and morally informed legal criticism.[84] Similarly, we should think of the "bad man" metaphor as a caution against viewing law through "rose-tinted spectacles" that serve to "filter out the seamy side of law and those elements that deserve criticism." Taking the bad man's detached perspective, at least intermittently,[85] can help deprive law of its mythic significance and emphasize its coercive implications.[86]

2. The Elusiveness of Law's Power

Hardly anyone denies law's coercive power. Even Hart, who gives normativity center stage in legal theory, recognizes the feature distinguishing law from other normative systems that also impose obligations (such as rules of grammar or rules of etiquette): the seriousness of the social pressure behind legal rules.[87] Nevertheless, Holmes should not be criticized for rehashing a familiar point. The constitutive role of power and coercion in the practice of law is slippery and tends to be obscured.

To begin with, although law is rather forthright about monopolizing legitimized force in society,[88] its coercive effects extend to include other, more figurative, and thus less transparent, ways of wielding power. Law tends to essentialize (or at least privilege) its own contingent choices—which too often turn out to work for "entrenched interests"[89]—thus legitimizing them and delegitimizing other alternatives. This point, which surfaces in Cohen's discussion of legal concepts and Dewey's analysis of syllogistic reasoning, is elaborated by critical legal studies scholars. Thus, Robert Gordon explains that people tend to perceive legal prescriptions as "natural and necessary" or, at least, as "basically uncontroversial, neutral, acceptable." This makes law one of those "clusters of beliefs...which [is] profoundly paralysis-inducing because [it] make[s] it so hard for people...even to *imagine* that life could be different

84. *See* Robin West, *Three Positivisms*, 78 B.U. L. Rev. 791, 792–93, 795 (1998); *see also* Neil Maccormick, H.L.A. Hart 24–25, 158–60 (1981); Murphy, *supra* note 1, at 387–92, 398–99.

85. As with any case of membership, legal actors—including citizens—cannot simultaneously identify with the values of their group and critically assess the values' cogency. Nonetheless, reflective members can and should occasionally take a critical perspective of these values. *See* Andrew Mason, Community, Solidarity and Belonging: Levels of Community and Their Normative Significance 58–59 (2000).

86. *See* William Twining, *Other People's Power: The Bad Man and English Positivism, 1897–1997*, 63 Brook. L. Rev. 189, 205, 208–13, 218–20, 222–23 (1997); *see also* Shapiro, *supra* note 18, at 185–86.

87. *See* Hart, *supra* note 17, at 84; *see also infra* Part I.A of Chapter 3.

88. *See, e.g.*, Kelsen, *supra* note 29, at 21; Joseph Raz, The Concept of a Legal System 3 (2d ed. 1980).

89. *Cf.* Dewey, *supra* note 14, at 193.

and better." Though legal structures are built "with human intentions," people come to believe that they must be the way they are.[90]

There are further important features of law that tend to mask the exercise of power—both material and figurative—by law's carriers. The institutional division of labor between "interpretation specialists" (i.e., judges) and the executors of their judgments (i.e., police officers) facilitates law's coerciveness by encouraging the former to delegate violent activity to the latter while disconnecting judges from the violent outcomes that follow from their interpretive commitments.[91] Similarly, as we have seen, the formalist legal algorithm, in misleadingly offering an agent-independent methodology that can yield one right answer, downplays the legal actor's choices, enabling actors to dodge responsibility for the coercive measures inevitably ensuing from their legal activity. Even post-realist theories, such as Dworkin's, tend to obscure the dimensions of power and interest by suggesting, for example, that an ideal judge (Hercules) can totally transcend his or her self-interest and group affiliation.[92]

The risk of blurring the coerciveness of law is particularly high with respect to private law, which structures our daily interactions and tends to blend into our natural environment.[93] Not surprisingly, then, legal realists focus on exposing the contingency of the concepts and rules of property, contract, and tort law in an attempt to expose the hidden ways in which law applies its power. Cohen's critique about the "thingification" of property illustrates this well. Courts justify the protection of trade names on the grounds that if someone has created a thing of value, she is entitled to protection against deprivation because a thing of value is property. "The vicious circle inherent in this reasoning is plain," Cohen explains. "It purports to base legal protection upon economic value, when, as a matter of actual fact, the economic value of a device depends upon the extent to which it will be legally protected." This flawed reasoning obscures the coercive and distributive effects of law. What courts actually do in these cases is to establish "inequality in the commercial exploitation of language," thus creating and distributing "a new source of economic wealth or power." Traditional legal discourse shields these decisions from normative critique and is thus tantamount to "economic prejudice

90. Robert W. Gordon, *New Developments in Legal Theory, in* THE POLITICS OF LAW: A PROGRESSIVE CRITIQUE 413, 418–21 (David Kairys ed., 2d ed. 1990); *see also, e.g.,* MARK KELMAN, A GUIDE TO CRITICAL LEGAL STUDIES 290–95 (1987); Bourdieu, *supra* note 47, at 837–39.

91. *See* ROBERT COVER, *Violence and the Word, in* NARRATIVE, VIOLENCE, AND THE LAW 203 (Martha Minow et al. eds., 1993).

92. *See* RONALD DWORKIN, LAW'S EMPIRE 259–60 (1986); *see also* ERNEST J. WEINRIB, THE IDEA OF PRIVATE LAW 14–15 (1995) (referring to law as "an exhibition of intelligence" and emphasizing "the personal self-effacement" of its carriers).

93. *See, e.g.,* Robert W. Gordon, *Unfreezing Legal Reality: Critical Approaches to Law,* 15 FLA. ST. U. L. REV. 195, 212–14 (1987).

masquerading in the cloak of legal logic." Unchecked, law may serve "to per-petuate class prejudices and uncritical assumptions which could not survive the sunlight of free ethical controversy."[94]

Similarly, Louis Jaffe argues that legal permissions and delegations—us-ing custom or usage as a source of law, granting power to property-holders and promisees, as well as respecting internal decisions of various forms of association—allow specific segments of society to determine "the substance of economic and social arrangement." The fact that this power is covert—that it is obscured by the legal rhetoric of permissions or delegations—should not shield participation in lawmaking by private groups from an analysis of what it is: a form of lawmaking.[95] Indeed, the most important contribution of legal realism to private law discourse is *not* in criticizing laissez-faire economics.[96] Rather, the realist lesson here is the critique of the way doctrinalism tends to absolve private law from normative justification.[97]

B. *The Power of Reason and the Reason of Power*

When legal realists emphasize law's coerciveness (despite the institutional and discursive diffusion of law's power) and highlight the distributive and expres-sive implications of the choices of law's carriers, they introduce a formidable challenge. Situating power in the midst of jurisprudence is threatening to law because it is not clear how power and reason (or coerciveness and normativ-ity) can ever be accommodated. Although realists are aware of this difficulty, they resist the temptation of reductionism and argue that the uncomfortable cohabitation of power and reason is key to a proper understanding of law.

1. The Difficulty

At first glance, the challenge posed by the notion that power (or coercive-ness) is a constitutive feature of law seems easy to handle. We might imag-ine that law's coerciveness can just be added to its normativity, both being two distinct characteristics of law, separate but complementary strategies for securing compliance. But Meir Dan-Cohen, who attributes this view to Hart,[98] considers it simplistic because it ignores the potential tension (or downright

---

94. Cohen, *supra* note 36, at 814–18, 840.

95. Louis L. Jaffe, *Law Making by Private Groups*, 51 HARV. L. REV. 212 (1937).

96. *See* Heikki Pihlajamaki, *Against Metaphysics in Law: The Historical Background of American and Scandinavian Legal Realism Compared*, 52 AM. J. COMP. L. 469, 473–77 (2004).

97. *See generally* MORRIS R. COHEN, LAW AND THE SOCIAL ORDER: ESSAYS IN LEGAL PHILOSOPHY (1933).

98. This view could also have been attributed to Thomas Aquinas. *See* THOMAS AQUINAS, SUMMA THEOLOGICA Q. 95, a. 1.

contradiction, in Dan-Cohen's view) between coerciveness and normativity. Power cannot simply be appended to norms without affecting them, because backing imperatives with coercion detracts from the normative force that an authority's utterances might otherwise have had. Coercion is designed to bring about the commanded behavior independently of the agent's own values and desires. Thus, coercion undermines the legal norm's normative appeal, invalidating any possible reason for deference and voluntary obedience (be it gratitude, identification, or trust). Power, or the threat of inflicting power, does not append itself to normativity but, rather, displaces it.[99]

Writing more than 50 years before Dan-Cohen sharply articulated this difficulty, Llewellyn also appreciated the challenge of accommodating law's coerciveness and its claim for normativity. Law "reaches beyond the normation of oughtness into the imperative of mustness," and, at times, law "is neither right nor just." But, although law enforces its prescriptions, law "is not brute power exercised at odds with, or without reference to the going order." Law claims "observance, obedience, authority, effectiveness" because law "is the effective expression of the *recognized going order* of the Entirety concerned." As such, it is not enough for law to claim and effectively enforce its supremacy. Law needs an additional "element of recognition that what is done or commanded or set as imperative or as norm is part of the going order of the Entirety concerned." Although any given specific rule need not be approved, "[t]he content and substance of the norms and activities of the imperative System, as a whole, must be felt by the Entirety [and] concerned to serve that Entirety reasonably well." This requirement of normativity is not easy to comply with, however. Because law lends "a tremendous power" to judges, politicians, and police forces, it is naturally perceived by others as a mere "imperative" set by an "interferer."[100]

In other words, Llewellyn subscribes to Holmes's view whereby power must play a central role in any credible conception of law. He further acknowledges that, because the interests and preferences of legal reasoners are always (at least potentially) part of the legal drama, law's coerciveness threatens its normativity. But Llewellyn refuses to accept the reductive view that law is power. Although the coexistence of power and normativity is admittedly uncomfortable, Llewellyn claims struggles for power and normative discourse are

99. Meir Dan-Cohen, *In Defense of Defiance*, 23 Phil. & Pub. Aff. 24, 26–27, 29, 48–49 (1994). Dan-Cohen calls his claim about the relation between coerciveness and normativity disjunctive, and he distinguishes it from the reductive view in which the normativity of law is entirely a matter of law's coerciveness. *Id.* at 26. But by insisting that normativity and coercion are at odds with each other, the disjunctive approach undermines any claim of law as we know it—that is, law as public power—to carry any normative meaning.

100. Llewellyn, *supra* note 54, at 1364, 1367, 1370, 1381; *see also* Morris R. Cohen, *My Philosophy of Law, in* My Philosophy of Law, *supra* note 54, at 31, 41.

inextricably linked in law:[101] "Protagonists of divergent normations struggle to capture the backing of the *system* of imperatives; and that is a struggle
for power, and by way of power and strategy. The protagonists struggle also
to persuade relevant persons that such capture will serve the commonweal;
that is both a tactic for capture and a tactic for more effective operation after
capture."[102]

When rejecting the idea that law collapses into sheer power (or interest, or
politics), realists part ways with many contemporary students of the realist
critique of formalism. Unlike many lawyer economists, they do not see law
as a set of (explicit or implicit) transactions among factions, each trying to
maximize its share.[103] Unlike many critical scholars, realists deny that law
merely secures the existing structures of power by immunizing the prevailing ideology from political critique.[104] Llewellyn's contrary notion, stating that
struggles for power in law always involve persuasion about the common good,
is not aimed at dismissing, or even lessening, the concern about legal actors
using reason as a mere mask for power and interest (hence the realist commitment to constantly challenge existing law, to which I shortly turn). Rather,
insisting that justification plays a central role in law—that law is never *only*
about interest or power politics—is critical because of its indispensable role in
preserving the very possibility of criticizing existing law and of recruiting law
for morally required social change.[105] If reason is left out of our conception of
law, as reductionist theories of "law as power" suggest, there is no point in a
moral critique of law and (almost) no choice but to affirm its current application of power. Because the consequences of severing law from moral reasoning
are just as grave as those of conflating law with morality, every effort should
be made to avoid them also. Too much is at stake to renounce the realist project of reconciling law's coerciveness with its claim to normativity.

101. The discussion that follows may also apply to Holmes and may help explain why,
after emphasizing law's coerciveness, he still celebrates law as the voice of reason and
thus "one of the vastest products of the human mind." *See* HOLMES, *supra* note 38, at
194, 201–02; *cf.* Thomas C. Grey, *Plotting the Path of the Law*, 63 BROOK. L. REV. 19, 21,
25–26, 46, 51, 57 (1997).

102. Llewellyn, *supra* note 83, at 1382–83; *see also id.* at 1362–63 (discussing two
"urges": "to use available social machinery to serve personal, sub-group or other ends
[that] are at odds with interest of some other members of the Entirety" and "a contrast-
ing urge . . . to seek the welfare of the Entirety concerned"). *See also* Mathilde Cohen,
Reasons for Reasons, in APPROACHES TO LEGAL RATIONALITY 119 (Dov M. Gabbay et al.
eds., 2010); *cf.* DAGAN, PROPERTY, *supra* note 37, at ch.7 (discussing the intricate role
of reasons in the way interest groups compete for power).

103. *See* RICHARD A. POSNER, ECONOMIC ANALYSIS OF LAW 529, 535–37 (6th ed.
2003); Frank H. Easterbrook, *Foreword: The Court and the Economic System*, 98 HARV. L.
REV. 4, 15–17 (1984).

104. *See, e.g.,* Robert W. Gordon, *Law and Ideology*, TIKKUN 3(1) 14, 16, 85 (1988);
Austin Sarat & Thomas R. Kearns, *Making Peace with Violence*, in LAW, VIOLENCE, AND
THE POSSIBILITY OF JUSTICE 49, 50, 66, 69–71 (2001).

105. *See, e.g.,* STEVEN J. BURTON, JUDGING IN GOOD FAITH 19–21 (1992).

2. Reasoning about Power

The realist sketch of the way in which law accommodates both power and reason begins with the idea that law's power invites reason. Because law is a coercive mechanism backed by state-mandated power, legal discourse—our public conversation about state-mandated coercion—must be a justificatory discourse, an exercise in reason giving.[106] But reasoning about power has both important perils and unique advantages. Its perils require a suspicious and critical attitude toward legal reasoning. Its potential advantages revolve around the special burden of responsibility experienced by legal reasoners. This burden ensures that law's carriers (and other legal reasoners) are held accountable, thus counteracting some of the negative effects experienced by the coercive power of law.

a. A Jurisprudence of Ends Legal realists insist that legal reasoning, insofar as it addresses the evaluation of the law or is aimed at directing its development, should be oriented toward the human ends served by law.[107] Lawyers, they argue, must forthrightly justify legal prescriptions in terms of their promotion of human values. (Indeed, as I argue below, these values should play a crucial role in prescribing rules, rather than in deciding individual cases.) Legal institutions and legal doctrines must be evaluated in terms of their effectiveness in promoting their accepted values and the continued validity and desirability of these values.[108] Because legal prescriptions affect people at large rather than the litigating parties only, legal reasoning should not blind itself to these broader social ramifications.[109] (This injunction poses a significant difficulty to private law, given its bilateral structure. I take up this challenge in Chapter 5.)

---

106. *See, e.g.*, LLEWELLYN, *supra* note 30, at 70–71.

107. *See, e.g.*, CARDOZO, *supra* note 53, at 99–102; Pound, *supra* note 41, at 611–12.

108. For a powerful statement of the inevitability of applying moral judgments as part of legal discourse (even in its most descriptive aspects), see Roscoe Pound, *A Comparisons of Ideals in Law*, 47 HARV. L. REV. 1, 2–3 (1933); *see also, e.g.*, ROBERT SAMUEL SUMMERS, INSTRUMENTALISM AND AMERICAN LEGAL THEORY 20–21 (1982); Thomas W. Bechtler, *American Legal Realism Revaluated, in* LAW IN SOCIAL CONTEXT: LIBER AMICORUM HONOURING PROFESSOR LON L. FULLER (Thomas W. Bechtler ed., 1978) 3, 20–21; Thomas C. Grey, *Freestanding Legal Pragmatism*, 18 CARDOZO L. REV. 21, 26, 41–42 (1996). Pound was ambiguous as to the legal force of values that do not yet enjoy a sufficiently robust empirical pedigree. *See* Roscoe Pound, *The Ideal Element in American Judicial Decision*, 45 HARV. L. REV. 136, 136–37 (1931). This question forms one of the core debates between positivists and non-positivists. *Compare* Joseph Raz, *Legal Principles and the Limits of Law*, 81 YALE L.J. 823, 852–54 (1972), *with* RONALD DWORKIN, TAKING RIGHTS SERIOUSLY 46, 58–65, 68 (1978).

109. *See* Max Radin, *My Philosophy of Law, in* MY PHILOSOPHY OF LAW, *supra* note 54, at 285, 299.

Thus, Holmes claims that once the "duty of weighing" considerations of "social advantage" becomes "inevitable," legal reasoning must be concerned with providing reasons that refer to social ends. In turn, this new focus is bound to extract legal discourse from its disciplinary solitude: jurists will have to study, Holmes predicted, "the ends sought to be attained and the reasons for desiring them," and this inquiry will necessitate the introduction of insights and methods from other disciplines into legal discourse. Holmes explicitly mentions the beneficial use of criminology and, especially "the schools of political economy"—hence his dictum that "the black-letter man may be the man of the present, but the man of the future is the man of statistics and the master of economics."[110] Similarly, Roscoe Pound agonizes over the "separa-tion of jurisprudence from the other social sciences" and "the conviction of its self-sufficiency" because they generate "a narrow and partial view that was in large part to be charged with the backwardness in meeting social ends...and the gulf between legal thought and popular thought on matters of social reform." He further insists on *"the impossibility of a self-centered, self-sufficient science of law"* and calls for "unity of the social sciences."[111]

Following these pronouncements of the interdisciplinary approach to law, Chapter 4 attempts to distill a meaningful notion of legal theory that does not depend on using the methodology of another discipline. But at this stage it is enough to note that opening up legal discourse to insights from other disciplines—acknowledging the continuity between legal reasoning and other forms of practical reasoning—inevitably upsets lawyers' claim to spe-cialized knowledge and expertise.[112] As Holmes puts it, lawyers' language of proof or the assertion of absolute, "once and for all" rightness, must be aban-doned. "Law cannot be dealt with as if it contained only the axioms and cor-ollaries of a book of mathematics"; it cannot be treated as a matter of "doing the...sums right." Because law requires reference to social beliefs or policy concerns, it is "not capable of exact quantitative measurement, and there-fore not capable of founding exact logical conclusions." Legal discourse must become much more contingent, and jurists must become much more modest: they should "hesitate where now they are confident, and see that really they are taking sides upon debatable and often burning questions." Disagreement (among individuals, groups, and branches of government) turns out to be a constitutive feature of law.[113]

---

110. HOLMES, *supra* note 38, at 184, 187–89, 195.
111. Roscoe Pound, *The Scope and Purpose of Sociological Jurisprudence*, 25 HARV. L. REV. 489, 510–11 (1912).
112. *See* POSNER, *supra* note 103, at 73; *see also, e.g.,* HORWITZ, *supra* note 14, at 193.
113. HOLMES, *supra* note 38, at 180–82, 184.

b. Constant Criticism; Value Pluralism This understanding of law as a forum of reason must rely, at least to some extent, on an optimistic conviction of our ability to recognize and be influenced by good moral reasons.[114] And yet, because reasoning about law is reasoning about power and interest, the reasons given by legal actors should always be taken with a grain of salt. (In fact, if we could be absolutely sure that law's reasons invariably overlap with morality, it would be mistaken to even talk about law's power in any interesting way.) Law's normativity can be preserved only if it is treated with suspicion, only if lawyers are constantly reminded of the other, much less glorified, constitutive element of law—its coerciveness. Therefore law must constantly invite criticism of both its underlying reasons and its (particularly distributive) consequences. Thus, realists espouse Holmes's proposition that no part of the law is immune to reconsideration: "No concrete proposition is self-evident, no matter how ready we may be to accept it."[115]

Echoing Holmes's separation thesis, legal realists claim that the fact that law's endorsement of certain rules and values "reaches beyond the *normation* of oughtness into the *imperative* of mustness" and, moreover, tends to produce "a sense of rightness, a claim of right,"[116] must affect the tone of law's justificatory discourse. Appreciating the risks of habitual reaffirmation, realists typically approach their normative inquiries in a critical and pluralistic spirit. They conceptualize justice as a "perennial quest for improvement in law, functioning as symbol to represent the need of constant criticism and constant adaptation of law to the changing society that it articulates." Legal realists perceive human values as "pluralistic and multiple, dynamic and changing, hypothetical and not self-evident, problematic rather than determinative."[117] (American legal realists have hardly articulated—let alone defended—their pluralism, a task I take up at Chapter 8.)

c. Responsible Argumentation Legal realists claim that law's coerciveness is not only a challenge to law's legitimacy but also a source of certain worthy qualities in legal discourse. "[W]ith power organized behind the official-Legal," Llewellyn explains, "official imperatives become for anybody with a purpose, high or low, a force to [channel] to his aid." To put it differently, in

---

114. *See, e.g.*, Martha Nussbaum, *Why Practice Needs Ethical Theory: Particularism, Principle, and Bad Behavior, in* THE PATH OF THE LAW AND ITS INFLUENCE, *supra* note 81, at 50, 74, 76–77.

115. HOLMES, *supra* note 38, at 181; *see also, e.g.*, LLEWELLYN, *supra* note 30, at 55. For a modern articulation, see JEREMY WALDRON, LAW AND DISAGREEMENT 111–12, 176–87 (1999).

116. Llewellyn, *supra* note 83, at 1364, 1368.

117. Hessel E. Yntema, *Jurisprudence on Parade*, 39 MICH. L. REV. 1154, 1169 (1941); *see also, e.g.*, LLEWELLYN, *On the Good, the True, the Beautiful in Law, in* JURISPRUDENCE, *supra* note 30, at 167, 211–12; PURCELL, *supra* note 31, at 41–42. Not all legal realists

contemporary society, legal discourse becomes an arena of social deliberation precisely because it is the arena where power is divided and interests collide. What is at stake is not only material—as law produces and maintains "the groupness of the group"—but also expressive as law is an institution that can properly "speak for the Whole of Us." Law's material and expressive power is what brings to the legal discourse the protagonists of various ideals and conflicting views, making it "inescapably one place, in which [people] face group responsibility."[118] Thus, law's coerciveness always "stands under a requirement of accountability." Unlike other domains of force and power, the power of law is always held to account.[119]

Indeed, the ubiquity of coercive power in law—its indispensability—and the corresponding high stakes of legal reasoning implies that (as Joseph Raz recently put it) "it is essential to the law that it recognizes that its use of power is answerable to moral standards and claims to have reconciled power and morality."[120] Thus, facing the responsibility of affecting the direction of law's coerciveness requires every legal actor who participates in the evolution of law and affects its development to justify and persuade us that his or her way will better promote pertinent human goods and values. "Legalistic normation...has its own sophisticated claims to being just" by choosing between conflicting claims "in tune with the net requirements of the Entirety." Law is an arena with a "persistent urge to purport to speak for the Entirety, and, in some measure, to make the purport real."[121]

This sense of acute responsibility also helps explain why legal realists, who are by and large careful not to disregard radical alternatives, reject moral skepticism or relativism.[122] Because "the process of responsible decision...pervades the whole of law in life"—because lawyers' everyday business requires "choice, decision, and responsibility"—legal realists find the use of "moral insights"

subscribe to value pluralism. Cohen, for instance, was a utilitarian. *See, e.g.*, FELIX S. COHEN, ETHICAL SYSTEMS AND LEGAL IDEALS 17, 42, 145, 187–88, 220, 229 (1933); *cf.* SUMMERS, *supra* note 108, at 42–44.

118. Llewellyn, *supra* note 83, at 1365, 1382, 1387; LLEWELLYN, *Law and the Social Sciences*, *in* JURISPRUDENCE, *supra* note 30, at 357–58.

119. Anthony T. Kronman, Monotheism and Violence (unpublished).

120. JOSEPH RAZ, BETWEEN AUTHORITY AND INTERPRETATION: ON THE THEORY OF LAW AND PRACTICAL REASON 1 (2009). *See also* JOHN GARDNER, LAW AS A LEAP OF FAITH: ESSAYS ON LAW IN GENERAL 142–43, 169–72 (2012).

121. Llewellyn, *supra* note 83, at 1398–99.

122. *See, e.g.*, Guido Calabresi, *An Introduction to Legal Thought: Four Approaches to Law and the Allocation of Body Parts*, 55 STAN. L. REV. 2113, 2121 (2003). Some legal realists were indeed value skeptics, but they were clearly the minority. *See, e.g.*, SUMMERS, *supra* note 108, at 42. Even Frank—who "might have been a skeptic to the point of nihilism"—aimed at producing "activists," not "paralyzed doubters." Robert W. Gordon, *Professors and Policymakers: Yale Law School Faculty in the New Deal and After*, *in* HISTORY OF THE YALE LAW SCHOOL 75, 101 (Anthony T. Kronman ed., 2004).

indispensable to law.[123] Realists are impatient with some critical scholars' characterization of reason as "a means of discipline, a coercive technology for the social regulation of passion and emotion,"[124] and with the attendant equation of normative reasoning with parochial interests and arbitrary power.[125] Legal reasons refer to ideals of justice, and, as Hessel Yntema claims, not every ideal will do: "ideals of justice not related to human needs are not true ideals."[126] While always inviting challenges to law's most accepted commonplaces, realists bracket out skeptical doubts that undermine any possibility of both justification and criticism.[127] Accordingly, legal realists subscribe to philosophical pragmatism if (and only if) pragmatism stands for a commitment to the constant exposure of beliefs to experience and to arguments that might overturn them, while insisting that there are better (even best) objective answers to the questions we face.[128] Realists engage in a *constructive* reexamination of law's existing rules and of the values they promote.[129]

Thus, for example, the realist undertaking to remove the seemingly neutral and inevitable mask of private law concepts and rules is not aimed at subverting the possibility of a just legal order or even, necessarily, the desirability of the existing one. Although the risks of essentializing private law's contested choices and of concealing its distributive and expressive effects are endemic, private law may be redeemed. Along these lines, realist authors argue that private property is not only "dominion over things" but "also *imperium* over our fellow human beings," and that traditional legal discourse fails to justify "the extent of the power over the life of others which the legal order confers on those called owners." But exposing private law's distributive effects

---

123. Harry W. Jones, *Law and Morality in the Perspective of Legal Realism*, 61 COLUM. L. REV. 799, 801, 809 (1961).

124. Gary Peller, *Reason and the Mob: The Politics of Representation*, TIKKUN 2(3) 28, 92 (1987); *see also, e.g.*, Gary Peller, *The Metaphysics of American Law*, 73 CAL. L. REV. 1151, 1155 (1985).

125. *See, e.g.*, DUNCAN KENNEDY, A CRITIQUE OF ADJUDICATION 109–13, 147–48, 155 (1997). For Kennedy, post-realist legal rhetoric "is structured in matched pairs of contradictory argument-bites." It is "a system of contradictory buzzwords that are always available and therefore never persuasive in and of themselves." Thus, law is "manipulable at retail, as well as at wholesale, level," open to the introduction of ideology through the "Trojan horse of policy," which Kennedy characterizes as "a fudge-word." *See also, e.g.*, Peller, *supra* note 124, at 1152–53.

126. Hessel E. Yntema, *The Rational Basis of Legal Science*, 31 COLUM. L. REV. 925, 955 (1931); *see also, e.g.*, DON HERZOG, WITHOUT FOUNDATIONS: JUSTIFICATION IN POLITICAL THEORY 232, 237–38 (1985).

127. *See* ALAN BRUDNER, THE UNITY OF THE COMMON LAW: STUDIES IN HEGELIAN JURISPRUDENCE 269–77 (1995).

128. For an account of pragmatism along these lines, see CHERYL MISAK, TRUTH, POLITICS, MORALITY: PRAGMATISM AND DELIBERATION 49, 56–57, 74, 98 (2000).

129. *See* EDWIN W. PATTERSON, JURISPRUDENCE 552–53 (1953); *see also, e.g.*, WOUTER DE BEEN, REALISM REVISITED (2008); Howard Etlanger et al., *Foreword: Is It Time for a New Legal Realism?*, WIS. L. REV. 335, 345 (2005); *cf.* Green, *supra* note 18, at 1968–69

and counteracting its pretence of neutrality (or even obviousness) is never the end point of the analysis for legal realists; rather, it is the beginning.[130] It is a means of facilitating a constructive critical inquiry: recognizing that property is a form of government that allows, and even requires, "all those considerations of social ethics and enlightened public policy[,] which ought to be brought to the discussion of any just form of government," to apply to the law of property.[131]

Reason and power are destined to blend together within legal discourse. With reason in place, law should never be equated with sheer power. Legal realists, therefore, find it unduly defeatist—indeed, irresponsible—to postulate that power is bound to displace reason. And yet, because law's power is so susceptible to abuse by its carriers, realists are equally suspicious regarding the idea—which they see as dangerously naïve—that reason can displace interest or that law can exclude all force except that of the better argument. The realist conception of law is careful not to imply that interest and power can ever be superseded.

Rejecting both purist alternatives, the realist conception of law accepts the uncomfortable accommodation of reason and power as a constitutive feature of law while remaining acutely aware of the potentially devastating consequences of this unhappy union. It instructs us to observe, continually and critically, the complex interaction of reason and power, hoping to accentuate the distinct sense of responsibility involved in the reasoning of and about power[132] as well as to minimize the corrupting potential entailed in the self-interested pursuit of power. One important consequence of this instruction is the caution with which realists approach monistic theories of justice and their insistence on ongoing legal criticism. Another, and no less important, consequence is the rejection of cynicism as a response to law's justifications

(confusing the realist reformist agenda with anarchism because he does not appreciate the realist distinction between law and doctrine).

130. *See, e.g.*, Gordon, *supra* note 122, at 95. Notwithstanding their rhetoric to the contrary, many critical legal scholars share this constructive spirit. *See, e.g.*, Duncan Kennedy, *The Effect of the Warranty of Habitability on Low Income Housing: "Milking" and Class Violence*, 15 FLA. ST. L. REV. 485 (1987).

131. *See* Morris R. Cohen, *Property and Sovereignty*, 13 CORNELL L.Q. 8 (1927). The text also represents a charitable reading of Robert Hale's critique of private law. *See* Robert L. Hale, *Coercion and Distribution in a Supposedly Non-Coercive State*, 38 POL. SCI. Q. 470 (1923); *cf.* BARBARA H. FRIED, THE PROGRESSIVE ASSAULT ON LAISSEZ FAIRE: ROBERT HALE AND THE FIRST LAW AND ECONOMIC MOVEMENT 10, 13 (1998); KENNEDY, *supra* note 125, at 292–94. The other possible reading of Hale's article—claiming the proposition that all the inequalities in the distribution of income and power are the direct result of legal allocation of background rules and that there is no distinction either between threats and promises or between coercion and consent—relies on an indefensible "mechanistic image of human agency." Neil Duxbury, *Robert Hale and the Economy of Legal Force*, 53 MOD. L. REV. 421, 443 (1990).

132. *See* DON HERZOG, POISONING THE MINDS OF THE LOWER ORDERS 151, 159 (1998).

of its current practices. This justification impulse is a fruitful source of social and moral progress because it forces, at the very least, a respectable façade, an idealized picture of law that can often challenge conventional opinions and practices.[133]

III. On Science and Craft

My discussion of reason so far has been abstract, and my concern now is to put some substance into realist ideas about legal reasoning. Replacing the (untenable) formalist algorithm with a realist jurisprudence of ends provides some direction but also adds a note of urgency to the difficulties of intelligibility and legitimacy. If legal doctrine per se does not dictate outcomes, what indeed constrains law's carriers? Does not the continuity between legal reasoning and other forms of practical reasoning collapse the distinction between law and politics, thus undermining law's legitimacy?[134]

Part of the answer to these questions lies in my last observation in Part II regarding the significance of legal tradition. Before we can discuss (in Part IV)

133. *See also infra* Section II.B of Chapter 7; *cf.* LLEWELLYN, THEORY OF RULES, *supra* note 58, at 40.

134. The concern that the continuity between legal reasoning and other forms of practical reasoning would collapse the distinction between politics and law animates Weinrib's revival of a natural law kind of formalism. Weinrib's formalism is different in many respects from the formalism discussed in Part I.A; notably, it is non-positivist, it distances itself from claims about the essence of concepts, it renounces any reliance on deductive logic, and it acknowledges the indeterminacy of legal doctrine and the attendant necessity of judgment in its elaboration and application. *See* WEINRIB, *supra* note 92, at 13, 15, 25, 30–31, 223, 225–26, 228–29. Nonetheless, Weinrib still insists on a "distinctively legal mode of justification" that relies solely on law's "immanent moral rationality," to the exclusion of any recourse to "independently valid goals." In particular, Weinrib argues that, in rendering legal judgments, lawyers and judges should rely only on the elaboration of "a legal relationship's internal principle of organization"—on the question of whether a justification "coheres with the other considerations that support the other features of the relationship"—and refrain from directly assessing "the substantive merit" or addressing the desirability of any particular legal relationships, arrangements, or determinations. It is this "priority of the formal over the substantive"—the focus solely on the demand of justificatory coherence—that, for Weinrib, differentiates law from politics, and allows lawyers to acknowledge the "political antecedents and effects" of law while insisting on the "specifically juridical aspect" of their endeavor. *Id.* at 7, 25, 33–35, 45–46, 208–209, 219, 225, 230. This chapter can be read as a response to Weinrib in two senses: it shows that there are distinctly legal features that may, at least at times, adequately address the concern about collapsing law into politics, and it points out some potential pitfalls that the implementation of his solution to this challenge might bring about. *See also* Part III of Chapter 9. This response, however, does not amount to an account of the rather intricate law/politics distinction. For a discussion of this distinction that seems to fit

the place of tradition in the realist conception of law, however, we need to address the realist blueprint for the forward-looking aspects of adjudication. Realist literature suggests two types of devices for constraining the discretion of those who direct the evolution of law: science, or, more precisely, scientific insights, both empirical and normative; and craft, or, more precisely, certain conventional features of adjudication, notably its contextual focus and its dialogic character.[135]

It may seem natural to present these two devices as competing, if not conflicting, responses to the realist challenge of reconstruction; this, at least, is their unfortunate predicament in contemporary scholarship.[136] Some realists, indeed, share this sense of rift and place themselves on one side of the emerging divide. My representative realists, however, especially Cohen and Llewellyn, do not share this view. For them, and thus for my reconstructed realist conception of law, science and craft are complementary rather than incompatible. As usual, neither Cohen nor Llewellyn fully worked out the terms of this uneasy coexistence, and this chapter does not attempt to fill that gap. Yet, partial as they are, their accounts suffice to allow us to appreciate what we are losing as long as protagonists of science and champions of craft keep competing rather than engaging each other.

A. Recruiting the Sciences

Identifying legal realism with the recruitment of science into law's service is a reasonable association. As Neil Duxbury observes, while legal formalism "had been scientific only in name," legal realists aspire toward a "truly scientific study of law," a "systemized study, deliberately focused toward getting an adequate knowledge of the entire social structure as a functioning and changing but coherent mechanism."[137] It is therefore not surprising that contemporary schools with a strong scientific emphasis—notably empirical legal research and economic analysis of law—are frequently identified as the rightful heirs of legal realism.[138]

---

the realist conception of law, see Robert Post, *Theorizing Disagreement: Reconceiving the Relationship between Law and Politics*, 98 CAL. L. REV. 1319 (2010).

135. *See* Kronman, *supra* note 3, at 336–38.

136. *See id.* at 339.

137. DUXBURY, *supra* note 10, at 80; *see also, e.g.*, STEPHEN M. FELDMAN, AMERICAN LEGAL THOUGHT FROM PREMODERNISM TO POSTMODERNISM: AN INTELLECTUAL VOYAGE 110 (2000).

138. For empirical legal research, see, e.g., JOHN HENRY SCHLEGEL, AMERICAN LEGAL REALISM AND EMPIRICAL LEGAL SCIENCE (1995). For the economic analysis of law, see Judith W. DeCew, *Realities about Legal Realism*, 4 LAW & PHIL. 405, 421 (1985); Edmund W. Kitch, *The Intellectual Foundations of Law and Economics* (1983) 33 J. LEGAL EDUC. 184, 184 (1983); Alan Schwartz, *Karl Llewellyn and the Origins of Contract Theory, in*

I do not deny the debt of these schools to legal realism, or their contribution to the realist project. Both the realist view of law as an instrument for the promotion of social goods, as discussed above, and the realist focus on social facts and commitment to scientific inquiry, as discussed below, corroborate the association between legal realism and the mobilization of social sciences for the purposes of legal discourse. And yet, legal realism should not be identified with a social-scientific perspective of law. As other contemporary heirs of legal realism, social-science–oriented lawyers also tend to twist the realist legacy by focusing solely on this aspect of the realist conception of law and omitting references to other components of the rich conception of law in which it is situated. Indeed, focusing on science does not only omit part of the picture of law but may also harmfully distort it. Thus, for example, the omission of craft might deform the education of lawyers, and the omission of power might unjustifiably immunize the projects of legal scientists from a normative and distributive critique.

1. Three Empirical Pursuits

Realists put a premium on studying the social facts pertinent to various legal endeavors and recommend focusing on three empirical pursuits: investigating the hidden regularities of legal doctrine in order to restore law's intelligibility and predictability; studying the practical consequences of law in order to better direct the evolution of law and further its legitimacy; and responding to the prevailing social mores—conventional morality in order to further stabilize law's objectivity and legitimacy.[139] To be sure, for legal realists, as opposed perhaps to sociologists of law, the significance of omitting robust empirical inquiries depends on a judgment of these inquiries' expected benefit to the project at hand vis-à-vis their cost. This means that for legal realists empirical work is not always needed, and that at times they may conclude that the implicit impressionistic empirical observations on which lawyers tend to rely are good enough. But even in such cases legal realists are happy to invite a rebuttal of these conjectures or of their judgment of their sufficiency. Although some reliance on commonsensical observations about social reality is inevitable, legal realists concede that, in some contexts, reality may turn out to be different from what people think it is. If this can be shown, either by providing relevant

THE JURISPRUDENTIAL FOUNDATIONS OF CORPORATE AND COMMERCIAL LAW 18 (Jody S. Kraus & Steven D. Walt eds., 2000).

139. There is a fourth type of empirical inquiry that is attributed to realism: situating law in a broader set of social norms. Its main champion was Underhill Moore. *See, e.g.,* Underhill Moore & Gilbert Sussman, *The Lawyer's Law*, 41 YALE L.J. 566 (1932); *see also* SCHLEGEL, *supra* note 138, at 115–46. For a survey and critique of some contemporary analogues, see Austin Sarat & Thomas R. Kearns, *Beyond the Great Divide: Forms of Legal Scholarship in Everyday Life, in* LAW IN EVERYDAY LIFE 21, 42–47 (Austin Sarat & Thomas R. Kearns eds., 1993).

empirical data or through a competing commonsensical account, legal realists would be delighted to revisit their conclusions.[140]

a. Exposing the Law in Action By collecting, processing, and analyzing data regarding existing judicial decisions, legal realists show the frequent divergence between law in the books and law in action. They further uncover the hidden regularities of judicial decisions and demonstrate that these regularities can account for existing law better than any formalist explanation can. Unlike law in the books, a realist restatement of the true elements that explain law in action is also helpful to practicing lawyers because it provides a credible basis for predicting future decisions.[141] Past cases are thus used, in Joseph Bingham's words, as "experimental guides to prognostications of future decisions."[142]

b. Guiding Law Reform Another type of empirical study is relevant to legal actors seeking to improve, rather than predict, the law. This path follows Pound's prescription for looking at "the actual social effects of legal institutions and legal doctrines," both in law reform and in the application and interpretation of existing law.[143] This project is epitomized in the famous "Brandeis brief," where a vast array of information regarding actual conditions in the mill and the foundry was used in the preparation of a formal legal brief to the Supreme Court involving the review of regulations on maximum working hours for laundresses.[144] In this and numerous other cases, "detailed knowledge of social fact [provided and still provides] a necessary demystifying first step toward the goal of social reform."[145]

c. Reflecting Conventional Morality Although rarely presented in this context, Cardozo's reliance on conventional morality as a source of guidance to judicial discretion also belongs in this category. Cardozo faced the challenge of objectivity: the risk that a jurisprudence of ends might degenerate into "a jurisprudence of mere sentiment and feeling." His response was that judges should not impose "upon the community as a rule of life [their] own idiosyncrasies

140. *See* Hanoch Dagan, *Restitution's Realism, in* PHILOSOPHICAL FOUNDATIONS OF UNJUST ENRICHMENT 54, 77–80 (Robert Chambers et al. eds., 2009).

141. *See, e.g.,* DUXBURY, *supra* note 10, at 80, 96, 127; FELDMAN, *supra* note 137, at 113; Etlanger et al., *supra* note 129, at 339–40.

142. Bingham, *supra* note 43, at 17.

143. Pound, *supra* note 110, at 513.

144. *See* Fisher et al., *supra* note 14, at 237; N.E.H. HULL, ROSCOE POUND AND KARL LLEWELLYN: SEARCHING FOR AN AMERICAN JURISPRUDENCE 29 (1997).

145. HORWITZ, *supra* note 14, at 189; *see also* SCHLEGEL, *supra* note 138, at chs. 2 & 4; Phoebe Ellsworth & Julius Jentum, *Social Science in Legal Decision-Making, in* LAW

of conduct or belief." Rather, judges must rely on "the life of the community"; they are duty-bound to "conform to the accepted standards of the community, the *mores* of the time," namely, the actual normative persuasions of law's constituents.[146]

2. Facts and Values

Influenced by the intellectual distinctiveness of the 1920s and 1930s, some realists subscribed to the view that the only real knowledge about society is both empirical and experimental. The claim is that nonempirical concepts are meaningless and that scholars should develop and employ devices enabling us to identify and measure social phenomena verifiably, without value judgments. On this view, methodology replaces political morality and social progress can be judged only in terms of knowledge and scientific expertise.[147]

The conception of the science of society has since been criticized.[148] In fact, my typical legal realists never embraced it. Both Cohen and Llewellyn were skeptical about the project of pure empiricism in facilitating legal predictability, evaluating existing rules, or considering law reform. Cohen clarifies in his discussion the two major pitfalls of the pretense that a scientific analysis of facts is enough to do the work.[149]

The first problem, in Cohen's view, is that whereas science can "throw light upon the real meaning of legal rules by tracing their effect throughout the social order," appraising this effect is the task of ethics. Moral judgment will always be necessary "in order to render normative significance to brute facts."[150] But this is not the only difficulty. Even the collection of facts on the consequences of a given rule necessarily involves "some discriminating criterion of what consequences are *important*," and "a criterion of *importance* presupposes a criterion of values"; "the collection of social facts without a

AND THE SOCIAL SCIENCES 581 (Leon Lipson & Stanton Wheeler eds., 1986); Michael C. Dorf, *Foreword: The Limits of Socratic Deliberation*, 112 HARV. L. REV. 4 (1998).

146. CARDOZO, *supra* note 53, at 105–106, 108; *see also* John C.P. Goldberg, *Community and the Common Law Judge: Reconstructing Cardozo's Theoretical Writings*, 64 N.Y.U. L. REV. 1324, 1335, 1338, 1372 (1990). Cardozo did cast doubt on the possibility of pure subjectivism. CARDOZO, *id.*, at 110–11; *see also, e.g.*, MELVIN ARON EISENBERG, THE NATURE OF THE COMMON LAW 15–19 (1988).

147. *See* PURCELL, *supra* note 31, at 15, 19, 21–22, 24–27, 31–32; *see also, e.g.*, HORWITZ, *supra* note 14, at 209, 211. There are some late repercussions of this approach. *See, e.g.*, POSNER, *supra* note 103, at 76.

148. *See, e.g.*, PETER NOVICK, THAT NOBLE DREAM: THE "OBJECTIVITY QUESTION" AND THE AMERICAN HISTORICAL PROFESSION (1998).

149. On Llewellyn, see William Twining, *The Idea of Juristic Method: A Tribute to Karl Llewellyn*, 48 U. MIAMI L. REV. 119, 151–52 (1993).

150. Felix S. Cohen, *Modern Ethics and the Law*, 4 BROOK. L. REV. 33, 45 (1934); *see also, e.g.*, GLENNON, *supra* note 49, at 43. For a critique of the economic analysis of

selective criterion of human values produces a horrid wilderness of useless statistics."[151] (Consider also the potential errors of an empirical project aimed at devising tools for credible prediction if it is purely quantitative, counting cases with no regard for the perceived importance of different cases within the legal community.) For these reasons, Cohen concludes that "legal description is blind without the guiding light of a theory of values."[152]

Rejecting the program of brute empiricism, Llewellyn and Cohen promote an account that grants empiricism a more modest—and more reasonable— role in the legal universe.[153] In this approach, the empirical phase in the legal analysis creates merely a "temporary divorce of Is and Ought." As Llewellyn explains, "value judgments must always be appealed to in order to set objectives for [the empirical] inquiry," yet descriptions of "what Is" should "remain *as largely as possible* uncontaminated" by the observer's normative commitments.[154] In their further endeavors—legislation, advocacy, counseling, and judging—lawyers should use the information gathered on the law in action and its impact in society, as well as "technical data of fact and expert opinion," in order to supplement, rather than supplant, the normative aspect of their judgment.[155] The distinction between the *is* and the *ought* is aimed, then, not at "ignoring or dismissing the *ought*" but, rather, at "making a future *is* into an *ought* for its time."[156] As Cohen insists, "[n]either science alone [n]or an ethics that ignores the data of science can offer a valid test of the goodness or badness of law."[157] Legal analysis needs both empirical data and normative judgments.

Interestingly, Cardozo also subscribes to a similar position on the integration of social data and moral evaluation.[158] Exclusive reliance on the social facts of society's mores might have seemed an attractive solution to his problem of judicial objectivity.[159] Yet, anticipating the contemporary (justified) qualms

---

law along similar lines, see Arthur Leff, *Economic Analysis of Law: Some Realism about Nominalism*, 60 Va. L. Rev. 451, 454–59 (1974).

151. Cohen, *supra* note 36, at 75–76.

152. *Id.* at 76; *see also, e.g.,* Lon L. Fuller, *American Legal Realism*, 82 U. Pa. L. Rev. 429, 457–58 (1974).

153. *Contra* Horwitz, *supra* note 14, at 5, 181, 210 (portraying Llewellyn's conception of legal realism as one of brute empiricism).

154. Llewellyn, *supra* note 30, at 55.

155. Llewellyn, *supra* note 117, at 189.

156. Myres S. McDougal, *Fuller v. The American Legal Realists: An Intervention*, 50 Yale L.J. 827, 835 (1941).

157. Cohen, *supra* note 150, at 45.

158. *Cf.* Bernard Schwartz, Main Currents in American Legal Thought 479–80 (1993).

159. Even the reference to conventional morality is not a magic cure, because "[t]he spirit of the age, as it is revealed to each of us, is too often only the spirit of the group in which the accidents of birth or education or occupation or fellowship have given us a place." Cardozo, *supra* note 53, at 174–75.

regarding reliance on conventional morality[160]—recall that *Plessy v. Ferguson* is heavily predicated on "the established usages, customs and traditions of the people"[161]—Cardozo refrains from excluding the normative dimension. In some cases, says Cardozo, the judge should not yield to prevailing community standards, because "[d]espite their temporary hold, they do not stand comparison with accepted norms of morals." These cases "impose a duty to act in accordance with the highest standards which a man of the most delicate conscience... might impose upon himself."[162]

This nuanced empiricism of Cohen, Llewellyn, and Cardozo helps outline the way legal realists integrate economic insights into legal discourse. While realists appreciate the moral significance of people's existing preferences, they nonetheless reject the idea—popular among some contemporary practitioners of the economic analysis of the law[163]—that these preferences should be the sole guide of social welfare, at least if the preferences are fully rational and aptly informed. Because the value of these preferences must rely on the injunction to respect people's right to be authors of their lives, preference satisfaction should be understood as *instrumental* to autonomy, which is of course *intrinsically* valuable. This means that certain preferences, even if prevalent, must be rejected (especially given the realist recognition of the expressive and shaping functions of law). This also means that law should promote *everyone's* autonomy, which entails particular sensitivity to the potential regressive implications of maximizing people's willingness to pay given the marginal utility of income,[164] and accordingly requires a commitment to corrective measures in appropriate contexts. Furthermore, because legal realists subscribe to value pluralism, they would also tend to be cautious toward the prevalent commensurability presupposition of economic analyses of law,[165] and prefer to incorporate the efficiency analysis in a broader normative account.[166]

These are all important and valuable refinements, but they may still be insufficient to fully address the challenge of legitimacy. Legal realists, who are always cautious not to romanticize law and its carriers, recognize this difficulty. As Cohen explains, because law is *"par excellence,* the field of controversies," judges' "personal frame of reference" is likely to have a significant

---

160. *See, e.g.,* WEST, *supra* note 67, at 106–08.

161. 163 U.S. 537, 550 (1896).

162. CARDOZO, *supra* note 53, at 108–10.

163. For a poignant example, see LOUIS KAPLOW & STEVEN SHAVELL, FAIRNESS VERSUS WELFARE 18–28, 413–31 (2002).

164. *See* Anthony T. Kronman, *Wealth Maximization as a Normative Principle,* 9 J. LEGAL STUD. 227, 240 (1980).

165. Alon Harel & Ariel Porat, *Commensurability and Agency: Two Yet-to-Be-Met Challenges for Law and Economics,* 96 CORNELL L. REV. 749, 751–67 (2011).

166. For a prime example for such an attitude by one of the founders of law and economics, see GUIDO CALABRESI, THE COSTS OF ACCIDENTS: A LEGAL AND ECONOMIC ANALYSIS (1970).

impact on their judgments. Judicial idiosyncrasies, á *la* Frank, will most likely disappear, as noted. But judges' normative commitments may still be shaped by "the attitudes of their own economic class on social questions."[167] Thus, although facts and values are indeed crucial building blocks in the realist conception of law, they are still only part of the puzzle. The challenges that realists pose to law's intelligibility and legitimacy cannot be fully addressed without an account of the institutional characteristics of the law, notably of (common law) adjudication, as well as the shared norms and traits of the legal profession. These distinctly legal features are cardinal components of the promise of law. Admittedly, even after adding these indispensable features of law, realists still lack flawless answers to the challenges of law's intelligibility and legitimacy. A human discipline such as law offers no such magic cures. Moreover, part of the realist project is to break away from the binary option of cynicism about law or its romanticization, cultivating instead a cautious acceptance of the moral propriety of existing law combined with a healthy dose of suspicion able to trigger informed moral criticism and instill an acute sense of responsibility in the legal mind.[168] The realist celebration of the legal craft, to which I now turn, should be read in this state of mind.[169]

B. The Legal Craft

Talking about law as a craft could be misleading. It might suggest that realists adhere to—or, indeed, support—a purely conventional conception of law.[170] Llewellyn claims that lawyers' "ways of doing," "working knowhow," "craftconscience," "operating techniques," "ingrained ways of work," and "habits of mind" give practitioners of the legal craft "a feeling of naturalness, even of courseness" regarding certain legal results. The ethos of the legal profession in general, and of the judicial office in particular, Llewellyn argues, generates real constraints that produce some "reasonable regularity" and thus effectively dispel the fear of "free discretion."[171]

---

167. Cohen, *supra* note 50, at 123–24; Cohen, *supra* note 36, at 72.

168. *Contra* Charles Clark & David Trubek, *The Creative Role of the Judge: Restraint and Freedom in the Common Law Tradition*, 71 Yale L.J. 255, 256, 263–65, 268–73, 275–76 (1961) (arguing that by rejecting the notion of judicial freedom and subjectivity Llewellyn obscures the impact of the judge's personal values and shields judges from the responsibilities of their creative freedom).

169. The text should not imply a sharp division between science and craft. I do not deny that there could be a social science examination of craft. Nor do I argue against the position in which science involves an element of craft in its elaboration of imaginative theoretical tools.

170. *See* Dennis Patterson, *Law's Practice*, 90 Colum. L. Rev. 575, 597–600 (1990).

171. Llewellyn, *supra* note 32, at 77; Llewellyn, Common Law Tradition, *supra* note 35, at 49, 214, 216–17; Llewellyn, *supra* note 54, at 183–84; *see also, e.g.,* Cohen, *supra* note 36, at 72 ("[J]udges are craftsmen, with aesthetic ideals, concerned with

Out of their context (which is added below), these statements may seem to anticipate Stanley Fish's account of lawyers as extensions of the know-how of their practice. Lawyers, on this view, are "not only possessed *of* but possessed *by* a knowledge of the ropes," and the only—albeit significant—constraint they face is the acceptance of their discursive, or interpretive, community.[172] But the realist account of the legal craft represents a significant departure from this reductive theory.[173] Together with Fish, legal realists use the immersion of lawyers in their craft to defend the realist conception of law against the accusation of judicial subjectivity, to show that "the iconoclastic buggy of an utterly free judicial prerogative [is] a fantasy or myth."[174] Unlike Fish, however, they suggest that the nature of the legal craft justifies, to an extent, the authority of law. In the realist conception of law, the characteristics of the legal craft not only help rehabilitate law's predictability but are also part of the justification of its claim to legitimacy.

1. Institutional Virtues

Recall Cohen's (and Cardozo's) challenge of objectivity. Opening up the legal discourse to extra-doctrinal facts and value judgments is not tantamount to giving carte blanche to judicial subjectivity, but it does raise a concern about group distortions due to the specific (privileged) social positioning of lawyers and judges. When facing this concern, both Cohen and Llewellyn find some comfort in the institutional virtues of law, or at least of one of its core fora: adjudication.

"The ancient wisdom of our common law," Cohen explains, "recognizes that [people] are bound to differ in their views of fact and law, not because some are honest and others dishonest, but because each of us operates in a value-charged field which gives shape and color to whatever we see." Hence, only "a many-perspectived view of the world can relieve us of the endless anarchy of one-eyed vision." The institutional structure of (common law) adjudication is aimed at generating exactly such a "human and social view of truth and meaning." It invites disagreements respecting questions of facts, opinion, and law, thus creating a forum where judges' normative and empirical horizons

---

the aesthetic judgments that the bar and the law schools will pass upon their awkward or skillful, harmonious or unharmonious, anomalous or satisfying, actions and theories.").

172. *See* STANLEY FISH, DOING WHAT COMES NATURALLY: CHANGE, RHETORIC, AND THE PRACTICE OF THEORY IN LITERARY AND LEGAL STUDIES 127 (1989); *see also* Brett G. Scharffs, *Law as Craft*, 54 VAND. L. REV. 2245 (2001).

173. Another distinction is that, by rejecting moral skepticism and relativism, the realist conception of law also rejects Fish's "conservative vision of the potential of criticism." For a powerful critique of Fish on this front, see WEST, *supra* note 67, at 137–51.

174. ANTHONY T. KRONMAN, THE LOST LAWYER 224 (1993).

are constantly challenged by conflicting perspectives. In this way, law as an institution encourages judges to develop a "synoptic vision" that is "a distinguishing mark of liberal civilization."[175]

For Llewellyn as well, the judges' authority derives not from their unique characteristics as individuals but, rather, from "the office." Judges are situated in an institutional environment that "presses upon the office holder a demand to be selfless. Time, place, architecture and interior arrangements, supporting officials, garb, [and] ritual combine to drive these matters home." When adjudicating between litigants, judges are not only expected to be impartial, but also "open, truly open, to listen, to get informed, to be persuaded, [and] to respond to good reason." They are driven to make an effort "toward patience, toward understanding sympathetically, toward quest for wisdom in the result."[176] The two most important features of that environment are the adversarial process and the judicial opinion. The legal drama is structured as a competition in reason giving, in which advocates of each side function as officers of the court, marshalling the authorities "on each side in support of one persuasive view of sense in life, as well as one view technically tenable in law."[177] At the end of this process judges must render an opinion. That opinion is intended to "bring and hold the writer's brethren together . . . [and] persuade them that it is a sound opinion." It also aims to show "losing counsel . . . [that] they have been fairly heard," provide "wise and cleanly guidance to the future," and persuade "the interested public that outcome, underpinning, and workmanship are worthy."[178]

Taken together, these structural characteristics of the judicial office have a "majestic power" to lift out of judges the best they have to offer, channeling them into the "service of the whole." They make courts "the most appropriate body of unelected officials to review other governmental agencies (torn between politics, favoritism, enthusiasm, specialized expertness, woodenness, lopsidedness, ambition and vision)." Judges need to "account to the public, to the general law-consumer" on a regular basis and in detail. They

175. COHEN, *supra* note 50, at 125–26. For Cohen's legal pluralism, see DALIA TSUK MITCHELL, ARCHITECT OF JUSTICE: FELIX S. COHEN AND THE FOUNDING OF AMERICAN LEGAL PLURALISM (2007). Similarly, Cardozo claims that judges are never "wholly free . . . to innovate at pleasure . . . in pursuit of [their] own idea of beauty or of goodness." Cardozo further proclaims that judges' training, coupled with "the judicial temperament" can "emancipate [them] from the suggestive power of individual likes and dislikes and prepossessions," broadening "the group to which [their] subconscious loyalties are due." CARDOZO, *supra* note 53, at 141, 176. For a similar take on adjudication in feminist scholarship, see Katharine T. Bartlett, *Feminist Legal Methods*, 103 HARV. L. REV. 829, 880–87 (1990).

176. LLEWELLYN, COMMON LAW TRADITION, *supra* note 35, at 46–47; *see also infra* Part III of Chapter 3.

177. LLEWELLYN, *American Common Law Tradition and American Democracy*, *in* JURISPRUDENCE, *supra* note 30, at 282, 308–10.

178. LLEWELLYN, COMMON LAW TRADITION, *supra* note 35, at 132.

thus become "experts in that necessary but difficult task of forming judgment without single-phased expertness, but in terms of the Whole, *seen whole*."[179]

Owen Fiss provides a succinct modern articulation of these institutional virtues that facilitate judges' bounded objectivity:

> Judges must stand independent of the interests of the parties or even those of the body politic (the requirement of judicial independence); the judges must listen to grievances they might otherwise prefer not to hear (the concept of a non-discretionary jurisdiction) and must listen to all who will be directly affected by their decision (the rules respecting parties); the judge must respond and assume personal responsibility for the decision (the tradition of the signed opinion); and judges must justify their decision in terms that can be universalizable (the neutral principles requirement).[180]

But Fiss goes on to suggest that the procedures of adjudication are therefore analogous to John Rawls's original position,[181] thus implying that judges can transcend their self-interest and their group alliances. The realist account of law's institutional virtues views such claims with caution given its emphasis on interest and power as indispensable characteristics of the legal field. True, these virtues make adjudication a unique public forum with potential for inclusiveness, entrenching the realist rejection of cynicism about law. Yet Llewellyn's and Cohen's (and Fiss's) discussions about the institutional virtues of adjudication should be read not as real-life descriptions but as accounts of the institution's ideal, which should serve as a benchmark for evaluating its daily operation. They should not set aside concerns about self-serving (and at times self-deluding) judicial judgment. Deference toward Rawlsian impartial representatives must be out of place insofar as law's carriers are concerned, even if we set aside the mundane—but often significant—problems of heavy caseloads and limited resources.[182] Rather than complacency, an appreciation of law's potential institutional virtues requires legal actors to constantly challenge smug legal truisms, including the portrayal of adjudication as a purely public-regarding institutional service.[183]

---

179. *Id.* at 48; LLEWELLYN, *supra* note 177, at 309–10.

180. OWEN FISS, THE LAW AS IT COULD BE 163 (2003); *see also id.* at 11–12, 14, 54–55, 68; JOHN RAWLS, POLITICAL LIBERALISM 235–36 (1993).

181. *See* FISS, *supra* note 180, at 163.

182. *Cf.* Paul Brest, *Interpretation and Interest*, 34 STAN. L. REV. 765, 770–71 (1982).

183. Along these lines, a charitable reading of Llewellyn's frequent reference to "the Whole" need not interpret his conception of society as a necessarily stable, coherent, and singular community.

2. Situation Sense

The judicial drama is not simply a dialogue about principles of abstract justice. Accordingly, the legal craft is not exhausted by the institutional features discussed above. A legal normative discourse is typically situated in a specific human context. It invokes, strengthens, and relies on the unique skill of lawyers to capture the factual subtleties of different types of cases and to adjust the legal treatment to the specific characteristics of each of these categories.[184] Legal realists claim that, because the contextuality of legal discourse is not only part of the legal ideal but also a typical element of legal know-how, it is both a reason for law's legitimacy and a source of its predictability.

a. Narrow Categories; Not Individual Cases The realist prescription for contextual inquiry is at times mistaken for an advocacy of ad hoc judgments. Indeed, a small minority among realists does endorse this dubious nominalistic approach.[185] Most realists, however, take a very different position.[186] They realize that law's use of categories, concepts, and rules is unavoidable—even desirable—and that, in most cases, many legal reasoners should simply follow rules,[187] which is why realists take pains to improve rules, relying on empirical data, normative commitments, and situation sense. In other words, as I argue in Chapter 9, a "rule-oriented realism" is not a contradiction in terms as long as we remember that the (limited) stability of rules at any given moment relies on—and is thus contingent upon—a convergence of lawyers' background understandings (discussed in this and the next part) and not upon the determinacy of the doctrine as such.

The realist, radical, doctrinal-indeterminacy claim implies a wide breadth of *potential* judicial choice, but it does not mean—indeed, it should not mean— that judges use, should use, or even consider using, such potential choice in every case—quite the contrary. Because legal realists are both aware of the amenability of the carriers of law to abuse of power and committed to the use of law for the furtherance of human values (as noted earlier), they must

184. *But see* FISS, *supra* note 180, at 24–26, 30–31, 52–53, 100–02 (noting the social function of courts is to give meaning to our public values rather than to resolve disputes).

185. *See, e.g.*, RODELL, *supra* note 28, at 169–74, 201–202.

186. *See, e.g.*, Andrew Altman, *The Legacy of Legal Realism*, 10 LEGAL STUD. FORUM 167, 171–72 (1986); Todd D. Rakoff, *The Implied Terms of Contract: Of "Default Rules" and "Situation Sense,"* in GOOD FAITH AND FAULT IN CONTRACT LAW 191, 216 (Jack Beatson & Daniel Friedmann eds., 1995).

187. Rules authoritatively settle disputes, thus securing the moral benefits of coordination, expertise, and efficiency. *See* ALEXANDER & SHERWIN, *supra* note 57, at 12–15; *see also, e.g.*, FREDERICK SCHAUER, *The Generality of Law*, in PROFILES, PROBABILITIES, AND STEREOTYPES 251 (2003); Frederick Schauer, *The Generality of Law*, 107 W. VA. L. REV. 217, 224–34 (2004).

respect and further the two respective faces of the rule of law: as a requirement that law be capable of guiding its subjects' behavior and as a prescription
that law not confer on officials the right to exercise unconstrained power.[188]
Therefore, they can, and indeed should, distance themselves from the dubious
nominalist approach of open-ended discretionary decision making. Legal realism neither endorses nor should it imply focusing on the equities of the particular case or the particular parties. Furthermore, realists need not subscribe to
the problematic strategy of rule-sensitive particularism, which allows judges
to depart from rules whenever the outcome of the particular case at hand so
requires while taking into account both substantive values and the value of
preserving the rule's integrity.[189] Rather, legal realism requires that because
the values underlying our legal doctrines are the normative infrastructure of
law, *some* legal actors—notably, legislators and judges of appellate courts—
should *occasionally* use new social developments and new cases (respectively)
as triggers for an ongoing refinement of the law and as opportunities for both
revisiting the normative viability of existing doctrines qua doctrines and reexamining the adequacy of the legal categorization that organizes these doctrines. My focus here is on this last claim: that, in order to benefit from the
unique situation sense of lawyers (as discussed below), legal categorization
should be examined critically, and legal categories should be relatively narrow.[190] (I return to legal taxonomy in more detail in Chapter 6.)

Thus, Llewellyn invites us to rethink law's received categories because,
although legal classification cannot be eliminated, "to classify is to disturb"
and hence "obscure some of the data under observation and give fictitious
value to others." For this reason, our classifications "can be excused only in
so far as [they are] necessary to the accomplishing of a purpose." And because
our purposes may change, we should periodically reexamine "the available
tradition of categories."[191] (Rethinking legal categorization is important for a
further reason, which is that it may help expose otherwise hidden, and sometimes unjustified, legal choices of inclusion and exclusion.)

Llewellyn finds wholesale legal categories (think of contracts or property)
"too big to handle," as they encompass too "many heterogeneous items." He
thus recommends "[t]he making of smaller categories—which may either be
sub-groupings inside the received categories, or may cut across them."[192] By

188. *See infra* Chapter 9.

189. *Contra* Emily Sherwin, *Rule-Oriented Realism*, 103 MICH. L. REV. 1578, 1591–94
(2005).

190. *See* Fisher, *supra* note 14, at 272–73, 275.

191. LLEWELLYN, *A Realistic Jurisprudence: The Next Step*, in JURISPRUDENCE, *supra*
note 30, at 3, 27; *see also, e.g.*, Walter Wheeler Cook, *Scientific Method and the Law*, in
AMERICAN LEGAL REALISM, *supra* note 14, at 242, 246.

192. LLEWELLYN, *Realistic Jurisprudence*, *supra* note 191, at 27–28, 32; LLEWELLYN,
supra note 30, at 59–60; *see also, e.g.*, Fisher, *supra* note 14, at 275.

employing these narrow categories, lawyers can develop the law while "testing it against life-wisdom." Again, the claim is *not* that "the equities or sense of the particular case or the particular parties" should be determinative; rather, it is that decision making should benefit from "the sense and reason of some significantly seen *type* of life-situation."[193]

b. Supplementing—Not Supplanting—Normative Analysis   Brian Leiter equates the realist prescription of "fact-guided decision making"[194] with "a natural-ized jurisprudence predicated on a pragmatic outlook," which he presents as the core claim of legal realism. For Leiter, realism stands for the view that, in deciding cases, judges generally respond to the stimulus of the facts of the case rather than to legal rules or reasons.[195] Leiter's conceptualization of the realist legacy has some support in the writings of legal realists.[196] The idea that a normative solution is inherent in the facts themselves, however, is fraught with difficulties.

A prescription for sensitivity to situations and facts is vacuous without gen-eral normative commitments. These commitments are indispensable if we are to resolve—as law always needs to do—conflicts between the very demands and interests that case sensitivity exposes. Although normative consensus within the affected group may emerge in some limited contexts,[197] in modern heterogeneous societies law cannot assume a robust, stable, and shared tra-dition that can guide lawyers in resolving these conflicts.[198] Moreover, even where such a convergence does exist, it should not conclusively define our aspirations concerning legal norms; law should always beware of perpetuating unjust social norms.[199]

---

193. LLEWELLYN, *The Current Recapture of the Grand Tradition, in* JURISPRUDENCE, *supra* note 30, at 215, 217, 219–20.

194. LLEWELLYN, *supra* note 32, at 77.

195. Leiter, *supra* note 48, at 267, 275, 277, 283; *see also, e.g.,* Brian Leiter, *Legal Realism, in* A COMPANION TO PHILOSOPHY OF LAW AND LEGAL THEORY 261, 269–71 (Dennis Patterson ed., 1996); Brian Leiter, *Legal Realism, in* BLACKWELL GUIDE TO THE PHILOSOPHY OF LAW AND LEGAL THEORY 50, 52–53 (Martin Golding ed., 2004). Leiter appeared to have somewhat modified his views on this front. *See* BRIAN LEITER, NATURALIZING JURISPRUDENCE: ESSAYS ON AMERICAN LEGAL REALISM AND NATURALISM IN LEGAL PHILOSOPHY 22 n.33 (2007).

196. For a particularly extreme version, see Joseph C. Hutcheson, Jr., *The Judgment Intuitive: The Function of the "Hunch" in Judicial Decision,* 14 CORNELL L.Q. 274 (1929). Even Llewellyn and Oliphant can sometimes be interpreted along these lines. *See* LLEWELLYN, COMMON LAW TRADITION, *supra* note 35, at 329; Herman Oliphant, *Facts, Opinions, and Value-Judgments,* 10 TEX. L. REV. 127, 138 (1932).

197. *But cf.* WILLIAM TWINING, KARL LLEWELLYN AND THE REALIST MOVEMENT 226–27 (1973).

198. *See, e.g.,* Robert Post, *Law and Cultural Conflict,* 78 CHI.-KENT L. REV. 485, 491–92 (2003).

199. *See* WILL KYMLICKA, CONTEMPORARY POLITICAL PHILOSOPHY 267–69 (1990); FISS, *supra* note 180, at 215–20; SUMMERS, *supra* note 108, at 58; Gewirtz, *supra* note 39, at xx–xxi.

For these reasons, I discard the idea that a situation sense can substitute for value judgments and, in line with my task of a charitable reconstruction, suggest a different reading of the realist contextualizing theme. In this view, attention to the "situation-type" exemplified by the case at hand supplements rather than supplants law's normative engagement.

c. *The Significance of Context* In this realist approach, attention to context is important for two reasons. The first reason emerges from Herman Oliphant's celebration of the traditional common law strategy of employing narrow legal categories, each covering relatively few human situations. This strategy "divide[s] and minutely subdivide[s] the transactions of life for legal treatment," with the desirable result of a significant "particularity and minuteness in the [legal] classification of human transactions." Such narrow categories help to produce "the discrimination necessary for intimacy of treatment," holding lawyers and judges close to "the actual transactions before them" and thus encouraging them to shape law "close and contemporary" to the human problems they deal with. In these ways, the traditional common law contextualist strategy facilitates one distinct comparative advantage of lawyers (notably judges) in producing legal norms: their daily and unmediated access to actual human situations and problems in contemporary life. When law's categories are in tune with those of life so that an "alert sense of actuality checks our reveries in theory," lawyers uniquely enjoy "the illumination which only immediacy affords and the judiciousness which reality alone can induce."[200] (A charitable reading of these claims of firsthand experience must have in mind the virtues of law as a competition of reason-giving discussed above: characterizing judges' encounters with life experiences as "many-perspectived," to use Cohen's term, is necessary in order to partly ameliorate the risk that the judges' experience of reality merely perpetuates the status quo even when unjust.)

Indeed, our lives are divided into economically and socially differentiated segments,[201] and each such "transaction of life" has some features that are of sufficient normative importance, which gain significance from the perspective of some general principle or policy that justifies a distinct legal treatment.[202]

200. Herman Oliphant, *A Return to Stare Decisis*, 14 A.B.A.J. 71, 73–74, 159 (1928). Raz's analysis of the phenomenon of distinguishing cases brings home a similar point. *See* JOSEPH RAZ, THE AUTHORITY OF LAW 183–97 (1979).

201. *See* PETER BERGER ET AL., THE HOMELESS MIND: MODERNIZATION AND CONSCIOUSNESS 63–82 (1973).

202. *See, e.g.*, MICHAEL WALZER, SPHERES OF JUSTICE: A DEFENSE OF PLURALISM AND EQUALITY (1993); ELIZABETH ANDERSON, VALUE IN ETHICS AND ECONOMICS (1993); Elizabeth Anderson, *Pragmatism, Science, and Moral Inquiry, in* THE FACE OF FACTS 10, 17 (Richard Wightman Fox & Robert B. Westbrook eds., 1998).

If law is to serve life, it should tailor its categories narrowly, and in accordance with these patterns of human conduct and interaction, so that it can gradually capture and respond to the characteristics of each type of case.[203]

Furthermore, instilling attentiveness to context into legal discourse helps to nourish some of the legal profession's most significant qualities. In interpreting Llewellyn's jurisprudence, Kronman conceptualizes these qualities in terms of sympathy and detachment: the uneasy combination between, on the one hand, the compassion that enables lawyers to imagine themselves in their clients' positions (or, for judges, in that of the litigants) so as to understand their experience from within and, on the other hand, the independence, coolness, and reserve that are prerequisites for the ability to pass judgment on the situation's merits.[204] This combination of sympathy and detachment is the toolkit lawyers need in order to credibly claim that they have unique access to "the illumination which only immediacy affords and the judiciousness which reality alone can induce." It is therefore an essential part of judges' claim to authority and of law's legitimacy.

Kronman contrasts the qualities of sympathy and detachment with "theoretical extravagance" and further argues that the professional ideal he articulates should be divorced from any instrumental approach to law and should not "be tempted by the false ideal of a legal science."[205] Kronman is surely correct in distinguishing the "educated sensibility" of the legal craft from the technical expertise and rationality of legal science (in either its empirical or its normative side).[206] The temperamental tension between the Aristotelian judge that Kronman anticipates and the social engineer envisioned by Pound suggests that we have no fast-and-easy formula for their accommodation in the person of one lawyer. But, as is true of the tension between sympathy and detachment, we have no reason to believe that a person with the character traits that Kronman rightly celebrates is incapable of also applying value judgments and paying attention to relevant social facts. The realist conception of law celebrates such a mixture of empirical knowledge and normative insight with a devotion to the legal office and sensitivity to the situation type at hand. This mixture may account for the (happy) fact that, notwithstanding the integration of normative and empirical inquiries into mainstream American legal thought, the boundaries between legal discourse and political rhetoric have

---

203. *See* DAGAN, PROPERTY, *supra* note 37, at Part One; Kreitner, *supra* note 15, at 461–78; Rakoff, *supra* note 186, at 219, 222, 225; Frederick Schauer, *Prediction and Particularity*, 78 B.U. L. REV. 773 (1998); Alan Schwartz, *The Default Rule Paradigm and the Limits of Contract Law*, 3 S. CAL. INTERDISC. L.J. 389, 415–19 (1994); *see also infra* Chapter 9.

204. *See* KRONMAN, *supra* note 174, at 72–73.

205. *Id.* at 223–24.

206. *Id.* at 224–25.

not been totally erased, and the understanding of legal reasoning as a some-what distinctive mode of argumentation and analysis remains in place.[207]

IV. On Tradition and Progress

The third constitutive tension of law, according to the realist conception, is already implicit in my discussion in the last two parts, and I will now consider it in more detail. The realist commitment to reason and its complex plan for accommodating scientific and normative insights within a legal profession-alism premised on institutional constraints and practical wisdom imply that the existing doctrine is typically the starting point for analyzing legal ques-tions. Realists, however, are always suspicious about law's power and are care-ful always to distinguish between law and morality. For this reason, they do not essentialize existing doctrine and do not accord every existing rule over-whelming normative authority. In the realist conception of law, the appeal to existing doctrine is not, and should never be, the end of the legal analysis.

For legal realists, then, the notion of legal evolution—the accommodation of tradition and progress[208]—is not merely a sociological observation about law. Rather, legal evolution is part of law's answer to the tension between power and reason and to the challenges of intelligibility and legitimacy. Accordingly, the realist conception of law is profoundly dynamic. Realists reject any legal positivist attempt to understand law in static terms by sheer reference to such verifiable facts as the authoritative commands of a political superior or the collection of rules identified by a rule of recognition.[209] Such a quest for an empirical pedigree is hopeless because law is "a social process, not something that can be done or happen at a certain date."[210] In the realist conception, law is "a going institution" that includes a host of people "running and ruling in courses somewhat channeled, with ideas and ideals somewhat controlled."[211] Therefore, rather than identifying the content of doctrinal rules

---

207. *But cf.* Peller, *supra* note 124, at 1153 (criticizing this predicament as "the domes-tication of much of realist work").

208. Indeed, the realist conception of law denies that tradition and progress are antinomies. *See also* Harold Berman, *The Historical Foundations of Law*, 54 EMORY L.J. 13, 18–19 (2005); Martin Krygier, *Law as Tradition*, 5 LAW & PHIL. 237, 251 (1986).

209. *See respectively* JOHN AUSTIN, THE PROVINCE OF JURISPRUDENCE DETERMINED 14 (H.L.A. Hart ed., 1954) (1832); HART, *supra* note 17, at 107; *see also, e.g.*, RAZ, *supra* note 200, at 40. To be sure, insofar as legal positivism is only "a thesis about legal valid-ity, which is compatible with any number of theses about law's nature"— GARDNER, *supra* note 120, at 33—it is indeed compatible also with the realist conception of law.

210. John Dewey, *My Philosophy of Law*, in MY PHILOSOPHY OF LAW, *supra* note 54, at 73, 77; *see also, e.g.*, GERALD J. POSTEMA, *Justice Holmes: A New Path for American Jurisprudence*, in LEGAL PHILOSOPHY IN THE TWENTIETH CENTURY: THE COMMON LAW WORLD 43, 64–70 (2011); Radin, *supra* note 109, at 295.

211. Llewellyn, *supra* note 54, at 183–84.

at any given moment, a viable conception of law must focus on the dynamics of legal evolution.

Given this non-positivistic tenet of legal realism, some may be tempted to describe realists as early proponents of Dworkin's *Law's Empire*, a temptation that may be further reinforced when we notice the striking similarities between Llewellyn's account of the evolution of law and Dworkin's algorithm for his Herculean judge. This lure should be resisted, however, because the realist voice, as we will see, is quite different from Dworkin's. As recurrently noted, the realist conception of law is not just an early incarnation of currently fashionable legal theories but, rather, a viable alternative to them all.

A. *Between Past and Future*

My inclusion of legal tradition within the realist conception of law may lead some to wonder, given that Holmes, the godfather of legal realism, was the one to issue the well-known dictum deploring the power of legal tradition as a "blind imitation of the past." For Holmes, upholding legal rules whose "grounds have vanished" only because they were "laid down in the time of Henry IV" is "revolting."[212] Such continuity with law's past is objectionable because it "limits the possibilities of our imagination, and settles the terms in which we shall be compelled to think."[213] Although history "must be a part of the study" of law, it should be "the first step toward an enlightened skepticism, that is, . . . a deliberate reconsideration of the worth of [the existing] rules."[214]

Kronman interprets Holmes's dictum as "a call for the rejection of tradition," an attempt to unshackle the law from the authority of the past, replacing this authority with "the timeless authority of reason." To be sure, reason (understood as the judgment of benefits to law's current users) may justify according some degree of binding authority to precedents because of the instrumental benefits of the practice of precedent by way of maximizing utility or guaranteeing equality (or fairness). Yet, for Kronman, even this more moderate approach undervalues the role of tradition in law by underestimating the authority of precedent in law.[215]

I suggest a different interpretation of Holmes's motto. Instead of rejecting tradition, I propose a more moderate reading of his call for an enlightened skepticism, one that seriously addresses his commitment to look at the law

---

212. HOLMES, *supra* note 38, at 187.
213. HOLMES, *supra* note 45, at 211.
214. HOLMES, *supra* note 38, at 186–87; *see also, e.g.,* POSNER, *supra* note 103, at 6, 71–72.
215. *See* Anthony T. Kronman, *Precedent and Tradition*, 99 YALE L.J. 1029, 1036–43 (1990).

as laid down as the first step in every legal inquiry. On my reading, Holmes's problem with blind imitation of the past does not relate to this first step and, therefore, should not be "solved" by repudiating the authority of tradition. Rather, the problem of blind imitation of the past stands for the absence of a second step. Accordingly, the proper remedy is to supplement legal tradition with a program for directing law's future evolution.

Holmes's original intention is, as usual, hard to discern. Fortunately, it is also beside the point of this chapter. My concern is to show that my reading is coherent with some of the main themes of Holmes's realist followers, notably—but not only—Llewellyn.[216] The realist approach seeks to open up a space for a forward-looking perspective within law's respect for tradition. It is best read as a celebration of the common law's Grand Style, described by Llewellyn as "a functioning harmonization of vision with tradition, of continuity with growth, of machinery with purpose, of measure with need," mediating between "the seeming commands of the authorities and the felt demands of justice."[217]

1. Fitness and Flavor

In summarily dismissing the question of whether judges find the law or make it as "meaningless," Llewellyn argues that "judges in fact do both at once." Adjudication for Llewellyn is creative in the sense of "the sharp or loose phrasing of the solving rule" and its "limitation or extension and...direction." But this creativity is considerably constrained by the "given materials which come to [the judges] not only with content but with organization, which not only limit but guide, which strain and 'feel' in one direction rather than another and with one intensity rather than another." Thus, the typical story of the law (at its best) is one of "on-going renovation of doctrine, but touch with the past is too close...the need for the clean line is too great, for the renovation to smell of revolution or, indeed, of campaigning reform." For this reason, judicial decisions are "*found* and recognized, as well as *made*."[218]

More specifically, Llewellyn describes an adjudicatory phenomenon he calls "the law of fitness and flavor." He observes that cases are decided with "a desire to move in accordance with the material as well as within it[,]...to reveal the latent rather than to impose new form, much less to obtrude an outside will." Llewellyn is *not* talking about following precedents, as he is careful to explain that no specific case generates this sense of flavor and fitness. Rather, it is the case law *system* that generates "a demand for moderate consistency, for

216. *See, e.g.,* Leon Green, *The Development of the Doctrine of Stare Decisis and the Extent to Which It Should Be Applied,* 40 Nw. U. L. Rev. 303, 325 (1946).

217. Llewellyn, Common Law Tradition, *supra* note 35, at 37–38.

218. *Id.* at 36; Llewellyn, *supra* note 118, at 361–62.

reasonable regularity, for on-going conscientious effort at integration." The instant outcome and rule must "fit the flavor of the whole"; it must "think with the feel of the body of our law" and "go with the grain rather than across or against it."[219]

This commitment to push the legal envelope as it is found rather than starting always afresh is not a mere derivation from pragmatic reality, which presumes existing rules cannot be abandoned completely.[220] First, the realist conservativism about law—its acceptance of the legal past as both central and authoritative to the legal present[221]—responds to the challenges of predictability and legitimacy. Thus, although judicial creativity is not necessarily limited to borderline cases,[222] tradition-determined lawyers can solve new cases in a way "much in harmony with those of other lawyers," as they are all trained to bring the solution to the new case into harmony with "the essence and spirit of existing law."[223] It is this "juristic method" rather than formalist syllogistic reasoning from preexisting doctrinal concepts or rules that constrains judges and that explains how the bulk of legal material is in fact predictable.[224]

Moreover, law's past is not only an anchor of intelligibility and predictability. Legal realists begin with the existing doctrinal landscape because it may (and often does) incorporate valuable—although implicit and sometimes imperfectly executed—normative choices.[225] They assume, in other words, that because, as we have seen, lawmaking oftentimes combines craft and science, the existing legal terrain represents an accumulated experience and judgment worthy of respect.[226] This approach to legal tradition is not as reverential as Kronman would recommend.[227] And yet, it is a far cry from viewing our legal

219. LLEWELLYN, COMMON LAW TRADITION, *supra* note 35, at 190–91, 222–33; *see also, e.g.*, H. Hamner Hill, *The Way the Law Is*, 8 CAN. J.L. & JURISP. 227, 243 (1995). Alexander and Sherwin are critical of this "reconstructive method." *See* ALEXANDER & SHERWIN, *supra* note 187, at ch. 8. The following paragraphs can be read as a response to their critique.

220. *Cf.* HERZOG, *supra* note 132, at 15.

221. *See* Krygier, *supra* note 208, at 239, 241, 245, 251, 254.

222. LLEWELLYN, COMMON LAW TRADITION, *supra* note 35, at 190.

223. LLEWELLYN, *supra* note 32, at 77.

224. *See* LLEWELLYN, *Impressions of the Conference on Precedent*, *in* JURISPRUDENCE, *supra* note 30, at 116, 126; LLEWELLYN, *supra* note 117, at 250, 260 (arguing only rules whose purpose and reason are clear provide guidance to lawyers and laypeople alike); Llewellyn, *supra* note 83, at 1400 ("If one wants to startle himself with light on how little explicit effective guidance Our Legal System offers the judges...let him look at the judges...not as entrusted with the application of Rules of Law, but as entrusted with the application of juristic method *to* the Rules of Law and *with* them. It is a truer picture."); *see also* Fisher, *supra* note 14, at 276.

225. *See also* HERZOG, *supra* note 132, at 15; Grey, *supra* note 11, at 12.

226. *See* JAMES BOYD WHITE, JUSTICE AS TRANSLATION 91, 95–96, 223 (1990); *cf.* DWORKIN, *supra* note 92, at 211, 213; Grey, *supra* note 11, at 26.

227. Kronman holds that we have a (limited) obligation to respect our legal past for its own sake; just because it is the past we happen to have. This obligation derives from "our participation in the world of culture," which is the source of "our distinctive

past as "just a repository of information" or even as a source of the purely instrumental benefits of maximizing utility or guaranteeing fairness.[228]

2. Justice and Adjustment

Profound respect for law's past is only one side of the realist coin. The other is a focus on the intrinsic dynamism of law. For legal realists, law cannot be understood merely by reference to its static elements (concepts and rules). Law is a doctrinal system in movement, "developed and interpreted [] in continuous flux." Therefore, a viable conception of law must include "also those elements that direct and propel legal development."[229]

Legal realists give two reasons for incorporating this dynamic dimension. The first follows from their critique of the formalist idea of deriving solutions to new cases from preexisting concepts and rules. Realists recognize that the existing doctrinal environment always leaves considerable interpretive leeway. They understand that, because the shape of legal doctrines "is made and remade as its narrative continues to unfold, even apparently surprising lurches can be integrated seamlessly."[230] Thus they accept Pound's claim that legal ideals inevitably play an essential role in the unfolding legal narrative "as the criteria for valuing claims, deciding upon the intrinsic merit of competing interpretations, choosing from among possible starting points of legal reasoning or competing analogies, and determining what is reasonable and just."[231]

The reference to legal ideals as the engine of change is not coincidental, of course. Rather, it captures the essence of the second reason for the realist focus on legal dynamism. Recall that, by integrating power into their conception of law, realists are committed to challenging law constantly, and they are wary of implying that the pace of legal change should always be restrained.[232] With Cardozo, they see law as an "endless process of testing and retesting," which is aimed at removing mistakes and eccentricities and preserving "whatever is pure and sound and fine."[233] This vision of law as a great human

---

identity as human beings." This feature of humanity "liberates us from the narrow temporal constraints to which our ambitions would have otherwise been confined." It also imposes on us a "considerable responsibility of preservation": an obligation "to respect the work of past generations." *See* Kronman, *supra* note 215, at 1052, 1054, 1066–68. Whatever the force of this account regarding other artefacts is, it must be curtailed insofar as law is concerned. The realist conception of law resists, as we have seen, any approach to law that might obscure the role of power and interest in law.

228. *Contra* Kronman, *id.*, at 1032–33.

229. COTTERRELL, *supra* note 60, at 153, 156; *see also* WHITE, *supra* note 226, at 216, 241.

230. HERZOG, *supra* note 132, at 18; *see also id.*, at 15–16; Krygier, *supra* note 208, at 242, 248.

231. Roscoe Pound, *A Comparison of Ideals in Law*, 47 HARV. L. REV. 1, 2–3 (1933).

232. *See* HERZOG, *supra* note 132, at 21–22.

233. CARDOZO, *supra* note 53, at 179; *see also* DWORKIN, *supra* note 92, at 400–13.

laboratory continuously seeking improvement is founded on a spirit of modernist optimism; it relies (as we have seen) on a belief in reason and its ability to react properly to changes in society—constantly providing for social advancement.[234]

This emphasis on the dynamic aspect of law need not undermine the realist claim of rehabilitating legal predictability. Although some measure of unpredictability remains, the realist scheme is still relatively predictable, at least when it is compared with the manipulable and thus indeterminate formalist formulae.[235] The remaining unpredictability, and thus retroactivity, is not necessarily alarming. Insofar as law's evolution is indeed due to its perennial quest for justice, it may help cultivate within the citizenry a desirable attitude of cautious acceptance of the moral propriety of positive law and an anticipation of its moral improvement; a healthy expectation that law should work itself pure.[236]

As usual, it is Llewellyn who best sketches the dynamic dimension of the realist conception of law. For Llewellyn, law involves "the constant questing for better and best law," a relentless "re-examination and reworking of the heritage." Judges have the responsibility to move forward: the "duty to justice and adjustment," which means an "on-going production and improvement of rules."[237] Although "distortion to wrong ends [and] abuse for profit or favor" are part of the life of the law,[238] these are always deemed to be disruptions, which are "desperately bad." And against them there is "in every 'legal' structure...[an implicit] recognition of duty to make good"—not necessarily in every detail, but at the level of "the Whole of the system in net effect and especially in net intent." It is at this level that the law makes "necessary contact with justification" of itself. This quest for justice—the demand of justification—is not just "an ethical demand upon the system (though it is [also] that)." Rather, it is "an element conceived to be always and strongly present in urge," one that cannot be "negated by the most cynical egocentric who ever ran" the legal system.[239]

---

234. *See, e.g.*, Roscoe Pound, *A Survey of Social Interests*, 37 HARV. L. REV. 1, 39, 48 (1943); *see also, e.g.*, Robert Samuel Summers, *Introduction, in* AMERICAN LEGAL THEORY xiii, xiv (Robert Samuel Summers ed., 1992); *cf.* HULL, *supra* note 144, at 30; EDWARD B. MCLEAN, LAW AND CIVILIZATION: THE LEGAL THOUGHT OF ROSCOE POUND xiii–xv (1992).

235. *Cf.* E. Hunter Taylor, Jr., *H.L.A. Hart's Concept of Law in the Perspective of American Legal Realism*, 35 MOD. L. REV. 606, 612 (1972).

236. *See* Hanoch Dagan, *Restitution and Slavery: On Incomplete Commodification, Intergenerational Justice, and Legal Transitions*, 84 B.U. L. REV. 1139, 1173 (2004).

237. LLEWELLYN, COMMON LAW TRADITION, *supra* note 35, at 36, 38, 217.

238. Realists are careful not to fall into the trap of romanticizing law. *But see* Robert W. Gordon, *Critical Legal Histories*, 36 STAN. L. REV. 57, 70 (1984).

239. Llewellyn, *supra* note 83, at 1385; *cf.* Neil MacCormick, *Natural Law and the Separation of Law and Morals, in* NATURAL LAW THEORY 105, 110–13 (Robert P. George ed., 1992).

Indeed, the realist conception of law is both backward looking and forward looking, constantly challenging the desirability of existing doctrines' normative underpinnings, their responsiveness to the social context in which they are situated, and their effectiveness in promoting their contextually examined normative goals. (I deliberately use here the vague notion of "promoting normative goals." Unlike some of the accounts offered by lawyer economists—which tend to focus only on law's material effects—a realist normative analysis seeks to capture the complex ways in which law can facilitate human values. Therefore, it resorts to law's material consequences, to its expressive impact, and to the intricate interdependence of these two effects.[240])

B. The Realist "Chain Novels"

A conception of law as a dynamic justificatory practice that evolves along the lines of fit(ness) and justification has been popularized in recent times by Ronald Dworkin.[241] Although major similarities are discernible between the realist conception of law and Dworkin's conception of law as integrity, the differences between them are equally significant. Just as the endorsement of science or the suspicion of law's power do not turn legal realists into members of the law and economics school or the critical legal studies movement (respectively), the realist understanding of legal evolution cannot be equated with Dworkin's account of law as a chain novel.

I begin with the similarities between the realist conception of law and Dworkin's conception of law. Both understand law as an evolving tradition, a justificatory practice that continually attempts to cast and recast itself in the best possible normative light. Both are exercises in law's optimism, seeking to direct the evolution of law in a way that accentuates its normative desirability. Both understand the quest for justice as integral to law rather than merely an external criterion (as it is according to positivism), or as a test for the validity of law (as it is in natural law theory). In both, normative discourse—an ongoing critical and constructive inquiry of the values underlying the existing doctrine—is thus integrated into legal discourse. In all these respects, the realist conception of law is an important precursor of Dworkin's *Law's Empire*, anticipating Dworkin's account of fit and justification as the two dimensions of legal evolution. (The fact that the debt of Dworkin's theory of law to the realist conception of law has hitherto gone unrecognized—recall Dworkin's own dismissal of realism as nominalism, with which this book began—is one more testimony to the realist legacy's unhappy predicament.)

240. *Cf.* Neil MacCormick, *On Legal Decisions and Their Consequences: From Dewey to Dworkin*, 58 N.Y.U. L. REV. 239, 251–54 (1983).
241. *See* DWORKIN, *supra* note 92, at 52–53, 164–258.

Together with these similarities, the realist account of each of these dimensions significantly differs from Dworkin's. Unlike Dworkin, realists do not treat the dimension of fit(ness) as a global imperative; instead, and in line with their commitment to situation sense, they seek coherence at a far more localized level. Llewellyn explicitly combines the idea of law as an evolving tradition with the realist prescription for contextualism when he claims that the two main keys to wise decisions are "the open quest for situation-sense and situation-rightness" and the "recurrent accounting at once to the authorities as received and to the need for the ever sounder, ever clearer phrasing of guiding for the future."[242] In the contemporary terms set by Raz, Llewellyn's law of flavor and fitness can be interpreted as a prescription for local, rather than global, coherence: an injunction to sustain pockets of coherence that reflect clusters of cases sufficiently similar in terms of the pertinent normative principles that should guide their regulation, and the appropriate weight of those principles, as to suggest that they should be subject to a unified legal framework.[243]

The realists' rejection of global coherence derives from their structural pluralism (explored in Chapters 8 and 9): local, as opposed to global, coherence facilitates the coexistence of a plurality of social contexts governed by distinct and potentially incommensurable moral principles. The realist commitment to structural pluralism, which contrasts sharply with Dworkin's monism,[244] is also part of the reason for the difference between the realist approach to the dimension of justification and Dworkin's rendition of this dimension. For realists, the dimension of justification requires identifying the human values underlying the existing doctrine and the ways in which they can be optimally promoted. This framework does not rely on the (putative) distinction between principles and policies (or rights and public policy) that plays such a core role in Dworkin's jurisprudence.[245]

---

242. LLEWELLYN, COMMON LAW TRADITION, *supra* note 35, at 194; *see also id.* at 44 ("The wise place to search thoroughly for what is a right and fair solution is *the recurrent problem-situation* of which the instant case is *typical*. For in the first place this presses, this drives, toward formulating a solving *and guiding rule*; and to address one-self to the rule side of the puzzle is of necessity both to look back upon the heritage of doctrine and also to look forward into prospective consequences and prospective further problems—and to account to each.").

243. *See* RAZ, *supra* note 74, at 281–82, 294–304. Dworkin's doctrine of "local priority" concedes, to some extent, the significance of context. *See* DWORKIN, *supra* note 92, at 250–54.

244. *See* George. P. Fletcher, *The Right and the Reasonable*, 98 HARV. L. REV. 949, 981–82 (1985).

245. *See* DWORKIN, *supra* note 108, at 82–88. For criticism of this distinction, see, e.g., Kent Greenawalt, *Policy, Rights, and Judicial Decision*, 11 GA. L. REV. 991, 1010–33 (1977); Alon Harel, *Revisionist Theories of Rights: An Unwelcome Defense*, 11 CAN. J.L. & JURISP. 227 (1998).

Furthermore, integrating power into their conception of law pushes realists to be wary of implying that the pace of legal change should always be restrained or that legal normativity is exhausted by the subset of moral principles that are embedded in past legal, political, and particularly adjudicative practices.[246] Although, like many legal theorists, realists pay particular attention to adjudication, they opt for "style of jurisprudence," which goes beyond adjudication to consider the numerous other arenas "replete with lawmaking, law applying, law interpreting, and law developing functions."[247]

One final distinction is in place. The realists' commitment to value pluralism, their distrust of claims by law's carriers that they represent the pure voice of reason, and their view of legal reasoning as an ongoing exercise of persuasion in which confident claims of finding the one right answer are to be viewed with suspicion, all explain the realist caution vis-à-vis judicial review.[248] By contrast, Dworkin is closely associated with the idea that legal questions have one right answer and he is a staunch defender of strong judicial review.[249]

ARE WE ALL REALISTS NOW?

So are we all realists now? If my reconstruction of the realist conception of law in this chapter is convincing, the answer to this question is as clear as it may be surprising. We are not all realists now—even if we set aside those of us who want to revive legal formalism—because, rather than carrying the realist legacy forward, legal scholars of the last decades have torn it apart.[250] The disintegration of legal scholarship during this period robbed the realist conception of law of its most promising lessons.

Contemporary accounts of law's violence, or of its role as a forum of reason, may be richer than the realist accounts of power and reason in law. By the same token, the use of science in legal discourse is today more sophisticated than at the pinnacle of legal realism, and some aspects of the craft of lawyering are better understood now than they were by Llewellyn et al. Finally,

---

246. *Cf.* ROBIN WEST, NORMATIVE JURISPRUDENCE: AN INTRODUCTION 26–27 (2011).

247. Kreitner, *supra* note 66, at 580; *see also* Hanoch Dagan, *Lawmaking for Legal Realists*, LEGISPRUDENCE (forthcoming 2013).

248. *See* POSNER, *supra* note 103, at 121–22; *see also, e.g.,* Thomas C. Grey, *Judicial Review and Legal Pragmatism*, 38 WAKE FOREST L. REV. 473 (2003).

249. *See respectively* DWORKIN, *supra* note 108, at 81–130; RONALD DWORKIN, FREEDOM'S LAW 7–38 (1996). For a harsh (realist) critique, see Roderick M. Hills, Jr., *Are Judges Really More Principled than Voters?*, 37 U.S.F. L. REV. 37 (2002).

250. This process is most conspicuous with respect to law and economics, which "is now professionally recognized as a separate discipline or subdiscipline." R.H. Coase, *Law and Economics at Chicago*, 36 J.L. & ECON. 239, 254 (1993).

contemporary accounts of legal evolution can enrich the sketchy realist thesis about the constitutive dynamism of law.

I do not dismiss or minimize the importance of these (and other) refinements and improvements. But a reconstruction of the realist conception of law raises serious misgivings about this process of specialization and fragmentation. The price of this process is high—indeed, too high—because the realist conception of law implies that debates between law-as-power and law-as-reason, law-as-science and law-as-craft, or law-as-tradition and law-as-progress are futile and harmful, and that any one-dimensional account of law is hopelessly deficient. Law (or any specific legal doctrine or institution) can be properly understood only if we regain the realist appreciation of its most significant feature: its difficult, but inevitable, accommodation of power and reason, science and craft, and tradition and progress. This book attempts to revive just that.

CHAPTER 3

⚭

Between Rationality and Benevolence

The Happy Ambivalence of Law and Legal Theory

OPENING REMARKS

My aim in this chapter is to explore the ambivalence of law and of legal theory toward rationality. The ambivalence I will discuss is one between rationality, narrowly defined as the maximization of an agent's self-interest, and benevolence, broadly understood as behavior that moderates the pursuit of one's self-interest by taking into account the interests of other individuals or of the community as a whole. I will look at two actors who are the central heroes of the legal drama: the subjects of law, more particularly the ordinary people who are the focus of private law, and the carriers of law, centering on judges, on whom legal theory places much of its spotlight.

My first task in this chapter is descriptive. I will show how law assumes its subjects' rationality and also seeks to transcend it. I will also demonstrate how legal theory presents a mirror image of this seeming paradox insofar as judges are concerned: while it expects judges to transcend their self- and group-interest, it suspects that this ideal neither will nor can be perfectly attained. These attitudes may at first glance seem confusing, if not confused: hence my second task, which is to explain and ultimately celebrate these ambivalences. My third and final task is to sketch the complex ways by which law and legal theory face the challenge of sustaining these happy ambivalences. I hope that in describing and justifying these ambivalences and studying the ways they are sustained, I will also both demonstrate their pervasiveness and further refine our understanding of the first constitutive tension of the realist conception of law through the related dualism of rationality and benevolence. This dualism helps explain the importance of the tension between reason and power as part of the realist conception of law.

I. Two Puzzles

Law's conventional story assumes that its subjects are rational maximizers of their self-interest,[1] and that its carriers are benevolent servants of the public good. And yet, at the same time, we can also easily trace within legal discourse the opposite assumptions.

A. Rational but Potentially Benevolent Citizens

I first consider law's conception of its subjects by focusing on private law (the laws of property, contracts, torts, and restitution) because private law structures our daily interactions as individuals more than any other part of our law. Law clearly anticipates a subject who rationally maximizes her self-interest. Subjects with such a disposition need, for example, a proper (legal) incentive if they are to engage in creative activity at a socially desirable level. Without such a legal incentive in place, creative resources may be under-supplied because the expected costs of their production tend to be high, while the costs of their copying, which may turn the copier into a competitor, are rather low. This account underlies one of the conventional understandings of intellectual property law: as a set of carefully designed carrots that encourage creative activity.[2]

By the same token, much of the law of remedies can be analyzed as a legal design aimed at discouraging rational subjects from engaging in activities that are either socially detrimental or incompatible with other people's entitlements. This analysis is obviously acceptable to lawyer-economists, but should also be acceptable to those who hold that our private law entitlements, at least partly, are not grounded in welfarist concerns as long as they acknowledge that many of the potential invaders of such entitlements are rational maximizers of their self-interest. Thus, when the law forces infringers of others' entitlements to disgorge the net profit they have reaped, it is vindicating the latter's right by sending a powerful message to rational people to keep out. By contrast, in some categories of cases, as in the case of patent infringement,

---

1. Or subrational due to difficulties such as imperfect information, cognitive errors, and the like, which are irrelevant to my interest here.
2. *See* ROBERT COOTER & THOMAS ULEN, LAW & ECONOMICS 124–26 (5th ed. 2007).

the law limits recovery to the harm such invasions may cause, or to the fair market value that the invader would have had to pay had he not bypassed the bargaining table. In these types of cases, the law discourages welfare-reducing infringements without dismissing the appeal of efficient ones.[3]

This line of analysis, so familiar to readers of legal scholarship, focuses on the sticks and carrots that law prescribes as the main method for motivating behavior. It thus anticipates as its audience Holmesian bad men. In *The Path of the Law*, Oliver Wendell Holmes endorses the perspective of the bad man who "cares only for the material consequences" of his acts and discounts other reasons for action "whether inside the law or outside of it, in the vaguer sanctions of conscience."[4] The bad man discounts the sheer rhetoric of right and wrong and treats those private law rules, known in the more modern terminology of Calabresi-Melamed as liability rules,[5] as mere taxes added to his activity, lacking independent normative significance: "It does not matter, so far as the given consequence...is concerned, whether the act to which it is attached is described in terms of praise or in terms of blame, or whether the law purports to prohibit it or to allow it."[6] The bad man is, as William Twining explains, "amoral, rational and calculating." He perceives law as "one of the facts of life that he has to cope with as an external force, to be avoided, evaded or perhaps used for his own purposes."[7]

Holmes's bad man analysis, like John Austin's sanction theory of law, was of course severely criticized by H.L.A. Hart. Hart argues that legal norms are taken not only as predictions of judicial action, but also as standards and guides for conduct and judgment, and as bases for claims, demands, admissions, criticism, and punishment. The Holmesian analysis "obscures the fact that, where rules exist, deviations from them are not merely grounds for a prediction that hostile reactions will follow or that a court will apply sanctions to those who break them, but are also a reason or justification for such reaction and for applying the sanctions."[8] This failure to appreciate the normativity of law is significant, insists Hart, because it ignores the "internal point of view" of people who accept the rules and voluntarily cooperate in maintaining them,

3. *See generally* HANOCH DAGAN, UNJUST ENRICHMENT: A STUDY OF PRIVATE LAW AND PUBLIC VALUES (1997), and HANOCH DAGAN, THE LAW AND ETHICS OF RESTITUTION 210–59 (2004), where I extensively discuss other possible measures of recovery as well as some further complications.

4. OLIVER WENDELL HOLMES, *The Path of the Law*, in COLLECTED LEGAL PAPERS 171 (1920).

5. *See generally* Guido Calabresi & A. Douglas Melamed, *Property Rules, Liability Rules, and Inalienability: One View of the Cathedral*, 85 HARV. L. REV. 1089 (1972).

6. HOLMES, *supra* note 4, at 174.

7. William Twining, *Other People's Power: The Bad Man and English Positivism, 1897–1997*, 63 BROOK. L. REV. 189, 209–10 (1997).

8. H.L.A. HART, THE CONCEPT OF LAW 82 (1961); *see also* JOSEPH RAZ, *The Relevance of Coherence*, in ETHICS IN THE PUBLIC DOMAIN 261, 280–81 (1994).

who are usually the majority. From that point of view, "the violation of a rule is not merely a basis for the prediction that a hostile reaction will follow but a *reason* for hostility."[9]

Even Hart recognizes, however, that the "internal point of view" he emphasizes is not law's exclusive perspective. At three points along his fierce critique of any attempt to minimize the accepting attitude of law's subjects, he softens his initial claim of normativity being a necessary and sufficient condition of law. First, Hart concedes that the determinative test as to whether social rules impose obligations—the main difference between rules of grammar or of etiquette and rules of law—is the seriousness of social pressure behind the rules. Second, he acknowledges that:

> [t]he external point of view may very nearly reproduce the way in which the rules function in the lives of certain members of the group, namely those who reject its rules and are only concerned with them when and because they judge that unpleasant consequences are likely to follow violation.

But he insists that these are normally the minority. Finally, Hart restricts the applicability of his theory even further, saying that the internal point of view needs only to characterize the perspective of the official, who must treat the rules as guides for behavior and judgment. The majority of the law's subjects can, but need not, employ this point of view. In their lives, the compulsory power of the law may exhaust its impact.[10]

These concessions by Hart are significant and justified insofar as they go. They show that legal theory should not marginalize law's material consequences, and that power and coercion are constitutive features of law's role in its subjects' lives.[11] They also demonstrate that, at the end of the day, we indeed anticipate the rational maximizer of self-interest as the default recipient of the law. But none of this should lead us to totally dismiss Hart's resistance to conceptualize law's subjects *solely* along the lines of the bad man. Hart is certainly correct in rejecting such a reductionist view of law's conception of its subjects. Indeed, although law never forgets its subjects' rationality, it oftentimes seeks to transcend it and anticipate socially responsible, communitarian, and even altruistic behavior—ideals to which the bad man, "who cares

---

9. HART, *supra* note 8, at 87–88.

10. *Id.* at 84, 88, 113–14. For a similar "whittling down" of the understanding of law as authoritative reasons for action, see generally H.L.A. HART, *Commands and Authoritative Legal Reasons, in* ESSAYS ON BENTHAM: STUDIES IN JURISPRUDENCE AND POLITICAL THEORY 243, 254–68 (1982); *see also* SCOTT J. SHAPIRO, LEGALITY 97 (2011) ("the internal point of view is the attitude of *law acceptance*," so that legal officials need not necessarily be "true believers").

11. *See* Frederick Schauer, *Was Austin Right after All?: On the Role of Sanctions in a Theory of Law*, 23 RATIO JURIS 1, 11–13 (2010).

nothing for an ethical rule which is believed and practiced by his neighbors,"[12] would have responded with cynicism.[13]

Private law again provides numerous examples of doctrines premised, at least to some extent, on the possibility that their subjects would indeed moderate the pursuit of their self-interest through concern for other individuals or for the community as a whole. Realize, for example, that a regime of private property seemingly epitomizing private law in its assumption of self-interested subjects is in fact a type of commons, which means that property law inevitably relies on (some) people's voluntary constraint and cooperation for overcoming the collective action problems inherent in its creation and maintenance.[14] More generally, as Stephen Smith argues, the notion of law's normativity seems plausible given the entrenchment of the social norm of law obedience,[15] which implies that alongside the law cynics, there exist a significant number of "law believers" who treat legal rules "as precisely what they purport to be, namely valid directions as to how they should behave." Indeed, as he insists, "judges and lawmakers who present and explain the law in normative language presumably assume that this language means something to the citizens at whom it is directed."[16] This may explain, for instance, why much of the language of contract law conveys its commitment to facilitate trust and collaboration between strangers.[17] Similarly, law's expectation that its subjects will act in accordance with its normative legal reasons also clarifies why the duties that negligence law imposes are specified in terms of reasonable conduct, implying that persons engaged in risky acts should take into account the interests of those they put at risk.[18]

---

12. HOLMES, *supra* note 4, at 170.

13. I do not argue, of course, that this was the gist of Hart's own critique. Rather, I claim that it is the reason for its intuitive appeal.

14. *See* James E. Krier, *The Tragedy of the Commons, Part Two*, 15 HARV. J.L. & PUB. POL'Y 325, 333 (1992); Carol M. Rose, *Property as Storytelling: Perspectives from Game Theory, Narrative Theory, Feminist Theory*, 2 YALE J.L. & HUMAN. 37, 51 (1990).

15. *See* TOM R. TYLER, WHY PEOPLE OBEY THE LAW 30–37, 40–68 (2006).

16. Stephen A. Smith, *The Normativity of Private Law*, 31 OXFORD J. LEGAL STUD. 1, 8, 27 (2011). Smith also discusses "law akratics": "citizens who sometimes lack the will to do what the law requires despite accepting, in a general way, that they should [do what the law requires]." *Id.* at 17.

17. *See respectively* CHARLES FRIED, CONTRACT AS PROMISE: A THEORY OF CONTRACTUAL OBLIGATION 7–17 (1981); Daniel Markovits, *Contract and Collaboration*, 113 YALE L.J. 1417 (2004). Another example of the ambivalence—and the baseline—discussed in the text comes from law's reluctance to impose duties of rescue versus its relative receptivity of restitution claims by good Samaritans. *See* DAGAN, LAW AND ETHICS, *supra* note 3, at 105.

18. *See* Gregory C. Keating, *Reasonableness and Rationality in Negligence Theory*, 48 STAN. L. REV. 311 (1996); Avihay Dorfman, Private Law and Liberal Solidarity (2008) (unpublished J.S.D. dissertation, Yale Law School).

B. Benevolent but Potentially Self-Interested Judges

Legal theory's portrayal of law's carriers is a mirror image of law's portrayal of the average citizens. Much of legal theory, mostly from its jurisprudential side, conceives of law's carriers as selfless. Namely, law's carriers are conceived as the voice of public-regarding reasons or considered judgments about the common good, as opposed to preferences that reflect their self-interest or the interests of the subgroup to which they belong.[19] But numerous accounts surrounding this "official story," ranging from critical legal studies to political science and economics, are suspicious of judges' alliance with their self- and group-interest and tend to portray them as Holmesian rational maximizers.[20]

Consider first the official canon. Formalists and positivists describe "the standard judicial function [as] the impartial application of determinate exist-ing rules of law in the settlement of disputes."[21] This rather modest version of selflessness, however, is insufficient for post-realist theorists who, justifi-ably, reject the idea that law is or can be a self-regulating system of concepts and rules.[22] These theorists highlight the doctrinal indeterminacy generated by the multiplicity of sources inherent in legal doctrine and thus repudiate the equation of law with doctrine. Instead, they understand law as an ongoing institution,[23] and thus focus their attention on the dynamics of legal evolu-tion, notably adjudication. Judges—especially appellate court judges—tend to be the heroes and heroines of many of these agent-dependent accounts. This traditional optimism of legal theory as to judicial benevolence follows Benjamin Cardozo's vivid description of adjudication as an "endless process of testing and retesting," aimed at removing mistakes and eccentricities and preserving "whatever is pure and sound and fine."[24]

Ronald Dworkin's Herculean judge, who transcends his self-interest and group affiliation, may be the most famous exemplar of this genre.[25] But

19. Notice that although I (deliberately) use the term "reason" in a rather minimalist sense, this sense is still sufficiently distinct from preferences. Reasons are judged by their cogency as per the public interest. Preferences, by contrast, are at bottom about self-interest and are accordingly weighted by the intensity with which they are held. *See* Hanoch Dagan, *Political Money*, 8 ELECTION L.J. 349, 351 (2009).

20. This section is not an exact mirror image of the previous one: although law is internally ambivalent about its subjects (that is to say that it conceptualizes subjects as both rational and benevolent), legal theory is by and large divided between viewing law's carriers as either benevolent or rational, but never both. At first sight law's "inter-nal ambivalence" may seem unprincipled and thus inferior. But I find it preferable to the "external ambivalence" that typifies legal theory. *See infra* Part II.

21. H.L.A. Hart, *American Jurisprudence through English Eyes: The Nightmare and the Noble Dream*, 11 GA. L. REV. 969, 971 (1977).

22. *See generally supra* Chapter 2.

23. K.N. Llewellyn, *My Philosophy of Law*, *in* MY PHILOSOPHY OF LAW 183 (1941).

24. BENJAMIN N. CARDOZO, THE NATURE OF THE JUDICIAL PROCESS 179 (1921).

25. *See* RONALD DWORKIN, LAW'S EMPIRE 259–60 (1986).

Dworkin is not alone in conceptualizing law as "an exhibition of intelligence" and emphasizing "the personal self-effacement" of its carriers.[26] John Rawls argues that the court is "the only branch of government that is visibly on its face the creature of [public] reason and of that reason alone." Justices, in this account, "develop and express in their reasoned opinions the best interpretation of the constitution they can ...." In performing this task, which is "an aspect of the wide, or educative, role of public reason," they resort to "their knowledge of what the constitution and constitutional precedents require" as well as to "the public conception of justice or a reasonable variant thereof." Rawls emphasizes that justices do not "invoke their own personal morality" or "their or other people's religious or philosophical views," which "they must view as irrelevant." The only values to which they can, and should, appeal "are values that they believe in good faith...that all citizens...might reasonably be expected to endorse."[27]

Legal theorists of this optimist tradition are not assuming that judges are superior human beings. Rather, they typically rely on judges' role morality. Thus, Owen Fiss emphasizes that although judges are not unique in their personal characteristics, they do have a "capacity to make a special contribution to our social life ...." This capacity derives from "the definition of the office...through which they exercise power," which "enable[s] and perhaps even force[s] the judge to be objective ...." The crux of the matter, argues Fiss, is "the process that has long characterized the judiciary ...." The judicial process—notably the requirement of judicial independence, the concept of a nondiscretionary jurisdiction, the obligation to listen to all affected parties, the tradition of the signed opinion, and the neutral principles requirement—facilitates judges' benevolence. Fiss seems to be so confident in the self-effacing effects of these procedures of adjudication that he analogizes them to Rawls's original position, thus implying that judges can indeed transcend their self-interest and their group alliances.[28]

Alongside this glorious tradition of judicial benevolence, contemporary legal theory is full of accounts about judges as rational maximizers of their self- or group-interest. Some of these accounts present judges' utility functions in rather mundane terms, as if they are motivated by the desire to maximize pleasure, leisure, influence, the probability of promotion, or their prestige among significant audiences. Others place partisan politics and ideology at the core of judges' pertinent preferences, suggesting that judges maximize these preferences either directly or strategically, that is, while taking

26. ERNEST J. WEINRIB, THE IDEA OF PRIVATE LAW 14–15 (1995).
27. JOHN RAWLS, POLITICAL LIBERALISM 235–36 (1993).
28. OWEN FISS, THE LAW AS IT COULD BE 11, 14, 54–55, 68, 163–64 (2003).

into account the expected actions and possible reactions of other relevant players—other judges, the legislature, or even the public at large.[29]

This contemporary, interdisciplinary literature typically begins with a Jerome Frank–like ridicule of "the myth about the non-human-ness of judges,"[30] and then turns to a painstaking analysis of the pertinent incentives that motivate judges as "all-too-human workers,"[31] namely, as rational maximizers. The different emphases of recent scholars on mundane versus political preferences also echo to some extent the debate between Jerome Frank and Felix Cohen as to the relative significance of personal factors in judicial behavior versus the social forces that mold it.[32] But interestingly enough, these tough-minded portrayals of judges reintroduce at some critical points of the analysis some notion of judicial benevolence, which is why I treat the model of the benevolent judge as the "official story," notwithstanding the voluminous literature contesting it.

The benevolence presupposition comes up, for instance, in Lawrence Baum's critique of the idea that judges are driven by their political preferences. Baum argues that this notion is naïve because political preferences are also, at bottom, driven by ideals about the common good.[33] Thus, he claims that, similar to *Star Trek*'s Mr. Spock, who being half-Vulcan is an altruist, judges in this model are assumed to act "in order to advance the general good." The strategic model, adds Baum, exacerbates this deficiency. It assumes that judges invest "arduous . . . efforts to advance their conceptions of good policy," making "the fully strategic judge seem[] enormously altruistic." But then Baum's own account—that, like Cohen's, emphasizes the impact of the social and professional groups that judges seek to please—also ends up with a somewhat optimistic outlook. This happens when he acknowledges that both the relevant social circles and the legal professional community are saturated with norms that encourage judges to act both "as people who embody virtues such as

---

29. For helpful overviews, see Lawrence Baum, Judges and Their Audiences 5–14, 21–23 (2006); Frank B. Cross, *What Do Judges Want?*, 87 Tex. L. Rev. 183 (2008).

30. Jerome Frank, Courts on Trial: Myth and Reality in American Justice 147 (1949).

31. Richard A. Posner, How Judges Think 7 (2008).

32. *Compare* Jerome Frank, Law and the Modern Mind 108–26 (1930), *with* Felix S. Cohen, *Transcendental Nonsense and the Functional Approach*, 35 Colum. L. Rev. 809, 843–46 (1935).

33. This may be an overstatement. Although political preferences are preferences about convictions (namely, political causes we care about), they are still similar to other preferences more directly related to people's interests. The reason is that, rather than reflecting the cogency or the importance of specific convictions, these sometimes-intense preferences reflect their holders' passions about these convictions, which is irrelevant to their status qua reasons.

impartiality that they associate with good judges" and "as [being] committed to the law and skilled in its interpretation."[34]

Richard Posner—who argues that judicial behavior is best explained by studying "what judges want," and that "they want the same basic goods that other people want, such as income, power, reputation, respect, self-respect, and leisure"—ends up with an even rosier account of the judicial utility function. What motivates judges the most, he concludes, is "a taste for being a *good* judge," which "requires conformity to the accepted norms of judging." Judges, says Posner, or at least "[m]ost judges, like most serious artists, are trying to do a 'good job,' with what is 'good' being defined by the standards for the 'art' in question," either because they are motivated by a "desire for self-respect and for respect from other judges and legal professionals," or because of "the intrinsic satisfactions of judging."[35]

II. Justified Complexity

Law's ambivalence on both counts is well justified because people, both citizens and judges, are indeed both self-interested and potentially other-regarding and community-seeking. Many scholars have of course noted for years the reductionism of the rational maximizer of the self-interest model.[36] Recently, Yochai Benkler added an updated synthesis of studies from such diverse fields as experimental economics, evolutionary biology, psychology of motivation, and organizational sociology, in addition to the more familiar literature on common property and online collaboration and social software design. Benkler concludes that "human beings have diverse motivational-behavioral profiles." More specifically, he reports that in most experiments:

> [A]lmost one-third indeed behave as predicted by selfish *homo economicus*. But more than half act cooperatively. Many are active reciprocators—respond kindly and cooperatively to cooperating others, and punish, even at a cost to themselves, those who behave uncooperatively. Others cooperate unconditionally, whether because they are true altruists or solidarists, or because they simply prefer to cooperate and do not measure what others are doing.

34. *See* BAUM, *supra* note 29, at 18, 90, 106; *see also* Frederick Schauer, *Incentives, Reputation, and the Inglorious Determinants of Judicial Behavior*, 68 U. CIN. L. REV. 615, 615–17, 619–21 (2000).

35. POSNER, *supra* note 31, at 11–12, 60–61, 371.

36. *See, e.g.*, BEYOND SELF-INTEREST (Jane J. Mansbridge ed., 1990); Russell B. Korobkin & Thomas S. Ulen, *Law and Behavioral Science: Removing the Rationality Assumption from Law and Economics*, 88 CALIF. L. REV. 1051, 1126–43 (2000).

Furthermore, "[n]ot everyone falls neatly...into one or the other of these categories. The distribution of behaviors is not smooth, but has modes around what a selfish actor would do and what a cooperator or reciprocator would do." Finally, Benkler observes that, whether these differences are "innate, acquired, or mixed," the evidence "supports the proposition that these behavioral patterns are also situational"; namely, they can be affected by the pertinent institutional context.[37]

The ambivalence of law and legal theory documented above should be understood with this human heterogeneity in mind. More specifically, given this complexity, both the baseline assumptions of law regarding judges and citizens, as well as the fact that their corresponding opposites always accompany the portrayals of these heroes of the legal drama, are well justified. Thus, notwithstanding the truism that judges are human, the somewhat romantic canon of legal theory is justified as a baseline because it is part of a cultural and institutional structure that strengthens our expectations that judges will transcend their self- and group-interest and will serve the public good. Legal theorists as well as ordinary citizens should, by and large, remain indifferent between judges' intrinsic pursuit of the common good and their instrumental desire for the high regard of their peers and friends. What should matter most for us all is that judges behave as if they were benevolent Vulcans, trying to be good judges, devoting time and effort to carefully and impartially deciding cases, and developing the law so that it will indeed vindicate people's rights and promote the public good.[38]

Law's opposite baseline regarding its subjects being rational maximizers of their self-interest is also easy to understand and justify. Although liberals realize that true autonomy requires collective goods[39] that often require people to behave benevolently, a liberal society committed to individual autonomy must assume and, as far as possible, must also ensure that these communal goods and pursuits are aspects of individual self-fulfillment.[40] Neither the associations to which we belong nor the other-regarding commitments we undertake should erase our individual identity. Associations and commitments may be constitutive of people's identity, but each one should be able to decide whether and for how long to remain within them. This is true because of the crucial role that geographical, social, familial, and political mobility play in

37. *See* Yochai Benkler, *Law, Policy, and Cooperation, in* GOVERNMENT AND MARKETS: TOWARD A NEW THEORY OF REGULATION 299, 300, 304, 309–10 (2010).

38. *See* Lynn A. Stout, *Judges as Altruistic Hierarchs*, 43 WM. & MARY L. REV. 1605, 1609–10, 1625–26 (2002).

39. *See* JOSEPH RAZ, THE MORALITY OF FREEDOM 193, 198–207 (1986).

40. *Cf.* ANDREW MASON, COMMUNITY, SOLIDARITY AND BELONGING: LEVELS OF COMMUNITY AND THEIR NORMATIVE SIGNIFICANCE 23, 58–59 (2000).

the preservation of individual freedom,[41] and also because, at least partly, the value of such other-regarding commitments and collective associations is due to the fact that they are realized through voluntary choice—if not *ex ante*, then at least *ex post*.[42] Thus, a broad assumption of rationality sets an appropriate baseline for a society committed to allow its citizens to pursue their own individual conception of the good.

But neither baseline should exhaust our attitude toward law's carriers and law's subjects, and, therefore, their "underground" accounts are also significant. Thus, it is justified to be suspicious of the ability and inclination of judges to transcend their self- and group-interests, and it is therefore imperative to constantly remember that the ideal of selfless adjudication is a benchmark that is seldom perfectly attained. Legal theory should be aware of the complacent portrayal of adjudication as purely a public-regarding institutional service and constantly guard against such self-serving (and at times self-deluding) judicial judgments. Challenging the canon's romantic account is particularly important given the subtle ways in which law's power manifests itself. Law's coerciveness is not exhausted by the obvious fact that, unlike other judgments, those prescribed by law's carriers can recruit the state's monopolized power to back up their enforcement. It also has manifestations that are far more elusive, founded on institutional and discursive means that tend to downplay at least some of the dimensions of law's power. Among the most notable are the institutional division of labor between "interpretation specialists" (read: judges) and the actual executors of their judgments, as well as our tendency to "thingify" legal constructs and accord them an aura of obviousness and acceptability.[43]

Similarly, membership in constitutive communities and commitments to other-regarding causes are indeed crucial components of individual autonomy and even of personal identity. Hence, it is important for the law to facilitate not only market-like interactions between rational maximizers of self-interest, but also types of interpersonal relationships typified by communitarian and other-regarding norms. A legal regime that is solely premised on the model of rational maximizers of self-interest defines our obligations qua citizens and qua community members as exchanges for monetizable gains. To be sure, as I noted above, law can and should acknowledge the virtues of impersonal norms

---

41. *See* Leslie Green, *Rights of Exit*, 4 LEGAL THEORY 165, 176–77 (1998); Michael Walzer, *The Communitarian Critique of Liberalism*, 18 POL. THEORY 6, 11–12, 15–16, 21 (1990).

42. *Cf.* Kenneth L. Karst, *The Freedom of Intimate Association*, 89 YALE L.J. 624, 632, 637 (1980).

43. *See* Cohen, *supra* note 32, at 811–12, 820–21, 827–29; ROBERT COVER, *Violence and the Word*, *in* NARRATIVE, VIOLENCE, AND THE LAW 203 (Martha Minow et al. eds., 1992); Robert W. Gordon, *Unfreezing Legal Reality: Critical Approaches to Law*, 15 FLA. ST. U. L. REV. 195, 212–14 (1987); Louis L. Jaffe, *Law Making by Private Groups*, 51 HARV. L. REV. 201 (1937); *see also supra* Part I.B.2.a of Chapter 2.

that liberate individuals from personal ties and obligations. Nonetheless, it should avoid allowing these norms to override those of the other spheres of society. Law participates in the constitution of some of our most coopera- tive human interactions, prescribing the rights and obligations of spouses, partners, co-owners, neighbors, and members of local communities. Imposing impersonal and alienated norms on these divergent spheres ignores and may even threaten these spheres of human interaction and would thus undermine both the freedom-enhancing pluralism and the individuality-enhancing mul- tiplicity crucial to the ideal of autonomy.[44]

III. Sustaining Fragile Ambivalences

Herein lies the challenge confronting law: Given the heterogeneity and mal- leability of human nature, how does law sustain its ambivalence? On both fronts—regarding law's subjects as well as its carriers—law needs to accom- modate these seemingly contradictory pictures and resist collapsing into the poles of naïve utopianism or hopeless cynicism. Law can, and at its best indeed does, avoid this dangerous binarism. Both the law of the people and the law of our judges do so by subtly utilizing the fact that some people tend to behave benevolently, at least in the right institutional settings. This allows law and legal theory to use a mixture of material and expressive means in order to construct and maintain spheres of human interaction that are governed by varying degrees of concern for others. For judges qua judges, this is the way law constructs the institution of adjudication, which is their vocational home; for the rest of us, this underlying strategy guides the construction of valuable options for association and organization that law offers without overwhelming us with the unacceptable alternative of overreaching universal benevolence.

Consider the law of property, which prescribes the entitlements peo- ple have vis-à-vis one another and society as a whole with regard to scarce resources. Property law constructs various property institutions that fittingly illustrate this broad description. Each property institution combines aspira- tional expressive doctrines seeking to tinker with people's preferences and protective safety nets addressing the potential risk of failure in this benevo- lent transformation, that is, the risk of defection and potentially devastating opportunism.[45] The default arrangement in liberal societies, namely, individ- ual ownership or fee simple absolute, is not very ambitious about people's benevolence. Although it must rely, as I have noted, on some voluntary con- straint and cooperation, property law also sets material disincentives against

---

44. *See infra* Chapter 8.
45. *See generally* HANOCH DAGAN, PROPERTY: VALUES AND INSTITUTIONS Parts I & III (2011).

violation and, in proper cases, is not shy of applying them rather sharply.[46] But the fee simple absolute is only one property institution, and the repertoire of property institutions includes others that are or can be more ambitious.

Michael Heller and I typified one important cluster of such property institutions that includes, for example, marital property, co-ownership, condominiums, partnerships, and close corporations as belonging to a family we call "the liberal commons." A liberal commons is a family of property institutions that enables a "limited group of owners to capture the economic and social benefits from cooperative use of a scarce resource, while also ensuring autonomy to individual members who retain a secure right to exit." Each of these property institutions encourages people to come together to create limited-access and limited-purpose communities dedicated to shared management of a scarce resource. Each offers "internal governance mechanisms to facilitate participatory cooperation and the peaceable joint creation of wealth, while simultaneously limiting minority oppression and allowing exit." The mechanisms of these diverse property institutions vary, as does the degree of their "benevolence ambition." But they all recognize, at least to some extent, the intrinsic value of interpersonal trust and cooperation, and therefore provide complex platforms for fostering such communities without sacrificing the liberal commitment to exit.[47]

A similar combination prevails in the institution of adjudication. Even Baum and Posner, who insist on presenting judges as rational maximizers of self-interest, admit that this unique institutional setting facilitates good judging. As scholars from both this and the canonical tradition recognize, this setting relies on a subtle mixture of cultural messages that seek to generate a role-morality that tinkers with judges' preferences, and protective sets of incentives: sticks in the form of public and professional critique together with carrots by way of judicial legacy. No one has formulated this complexity better than the great legal realists Karl Llewellyn and Felix Cohen.

Llewellyn and Cohen forcefully claimed that the judicial ethos, epitomized by the adversary process and the judicial opinion and reinforced by the rituals of the formal legal process, directs judges to be open, deeply introspective and thoughtful, inquisitive of new ideas, and responsive to reason. Indeed, for them, these structural characteristics of the judicial office have a way of channeling judges into "service of the whole."[48] These features turn the legal arena into a forum in which the participants' normative and empirical

46. *See* Edwards v. Lee's Adm'r, 96 S.W.2d 1028 (Ky. 1936) (restitutionary damages); Jacque v. Steenberg Homes, Inc., 563 N.W.2d 154 (Wis. 1997) (punitive damages).

47. Hanoch Dagan & Michael A. Heller, *The Liberal Commons*, 110 YALE L.J. 549, 553 (2001); *see also* Hanoch Dagan & Michael A. Heller, *Conflicts in Property*, 6 THEORETICAL INQUIRIES. L. 37 (2005).

48. KARL N. LLEWELLYN, THE COMMON LAW TRADITION: DECIDING APPEALS 46–48 (1960).

horizons are constantly challenged by conflicting perspectives. They thus encourage lawyers, notably judges, to develop a comprehensive vision that is "a distinguishing mark of liberal civilization."[49] Hence, at its best, legal professionalism makes lawyers "experts in that necessary but difficult task of forming judgment . . . in terms of a Whole, *seen whole*."[50]

Yet, because they realize that judges, like the rest of us, have interests and preferences that cannot be wholly set aside when they take the bench, these legal realists would have undoubtedly rejected the comparison between judges and Rawlsian impartial representatives, as well as the accompanied portrayal of adjudication as a purely public-regarding institutional service. Law, they insisted, should be separated from morality in order to "hold the responsibility for working toward the Right and the Just within the hard legal frame . . . to *de*fuse and *de*confuse the merely authoritative . . . from the Just or the Right, and to get into spotlighted pillory so much of Law as has no business to be Law . . . ."[51] Indeed, unchecked, law may serve "to perpetuate class prejudices and uncritical moral assumptions which could not survive the sunlight of free ethical controversy,"[52] hence the realist commitment to constantly challenge existing law and critically examine its carriers' utterances. At the same time, these legal realists never reduced law to "brute power," nor did they dismiss the judges' reliance on an "element of recognition" so that it is indeed "in tune with the net requirements of the Entirety."[53]

CONCLUDING REMARKS

Instead of summarizing my claims, I want to conclude this chapter with a comment that accords with the interdisciplinary emphasis of the Lectures Series for which this chapter was originally written. Most of the time, when legal academics talk about interdisciplinarity, they mean using a theoretical discipline from the social sciences or from the humanities for the analysis of law.[54]

---

49. Felix S. Cohen, *Field Theory and Judicial Logic, in* The Legal Conscience: Selected Papers of Felix S. Cohen 121, 125 (Lucy Kramer Cohen ed., 1960).

50. Karl N. Llewellyn, *American Common Law Tradition, and American Democracy, in* Jurisprudence: Realism in Theory and Practice 282, 310 (1962); *see also* Katharine T. Bartlett, *Feminist Legal Methods*, 103 Harv. L. Rev. 829, 880–87 (1990); *supra* Part III.B.1 of Chapter 2.

51. K.N. Llewellyn, *The Normative, the Legal, and the Law-Jobs: The Problem of Juristic Method*, 49 Yale L.J. 1355, 1372 (1940).

52. Cohen, *supra* note 32, at 840.

53. Llewellyn, *supra* note 51, at 1367, 1399; *see also id.* at 1364, 1370, 1372–73, 1381–83, 1398–99.

54. *See, e.g.*, Richard A. Posner, *The Decline of Law as an Autonomous Discipline: 1962–1987*, 100 Harv. L. Rev. 761, 779 (1987).

The intellectual openness to law's neighboring disciplines is certainly imperative.[55] The subtext implicit in these pronouncements, however, whereby no significant theoretical lesson intrinsic to law that is important for legal theory could also be potentially enriching to these neighboring disciplines, is both wrong and unfortunate. This is obviously a broad issue that I will not attempt to discuss here (it is the subject of Chapter 4). But I hope that my foray into the way law and legal theory conceptualize the human subjects they address demonstrates at least two of the potential contributions of legal research to the social sciences, as identified by Chris McCrudden.

First, although economics and sociology often accept legal rules and concepts "as a datum, as fact, unproblematic, and one-dimensional," legal research shows, McCrudden claims, that legal norms and concepts are "likely to be complex, nuanced and contested."[56] As we have seen, this complexity is true not only regarding law's obvious products—rules and concepts—but also regarding the human nature that law reflects.

Second, and even more significantly, McCrudden argues that many social scientists fail to appreciate the role that law plays "in the social and economic phenomena they are attempting to analyze." Law, he maintains, never "simply reflect[s] social context, but also shapes it," and "many of the ideas and categories through which we understand the world are in part legally determined."[57] The role of rationality and benevolence in the lives of both citizens and judges is no exception. Therefore, legal research cannot content itself with the undoubtedly important and challenging task of adjusting legal doctrines to the social scientific findings regarding the pertinent actors' motivational behavioral profiles. Rather, we must always also ask what is the normatively desirable human attitude for the pertinent setting and whether law and legal theory can prescribe institutional arrangements that nurture such an attitude.[58]

55. *Contra* Ernest J. Weinrib, *Can Law Survive Legal Education?*, 60 VAND. L. REV. 401, 429 (2007). For a critique of Weinrib isolationist conception of legal academia, see Hanoch Dagan, Law as an Academic Discipline, *available at* http://ssrn.com/abstract=2228433.

56. Christopher McCrudden, *Legal Research and the Social Sciences*, 122 L.Q. REV. 632, 647–49 (2006).

57. *Id.* at 648–49.

58. I use the word "nurture" here deliberately in order to flag the possible role not only of law but also of legal theory and legal education in generating the proper attitudes about our institutions.

CHAPTER 4

⚬◌⚬

The Character of Legal Theory

With ROY KREITNER

OPENING REMARKS

Is legal theory worth talking about? Worth studying? Does it make sense to imagine legal theory as a distinctive academic endeavor? Or does legal theory always collapse, either into a different academic discipline on the one hand, or into a variety of professional discourse on the other? These questions about legal theory are not new. At least since legal realists discredited the formalist vision of legal theory as an autonomous discipline governed by three characteristic intellectual moves (classification, induction, and deduction) legal scholars have grappled ambivalently with the idea of law as an academic discipline. Of course, not all legal scholars address these questions, and almost nobody addresses *only* these questions. There is a great deal of normal science in the legal academy, and most of the production of legal scholars is not especially reflexive in nature. But when they have reflected on what legal theory might mean, scholars have often minimized its potential in two ways: some have abandoned the notion of a *legal* theory and opted to borrow a theoretical discipline from the social sciences or from the humanities. Others have discarded the idea of legal *theory* by highlighting the practical wisdom of lawyers and celebrating law as a craft.[1]

Both types of responses contributed immensely to the academic analysis of law. But both, explicitly or implicitly, disparaged too quickly the enterprise of a post-formalist legal theory, which is irreducible to any other discipline.

---

1. *See* Anthony Kronman, *Jurisprudential Responses to Legal Realism*, 73 CORNELL L. REV. 335, 337–38 (1988).

This has resulted in a disciplinary malaise of the legal academy. In academia, disciplinary malaise can quickly evolve into crisis, and an increasing fragmentation of (American) law schools to "mini-departments" of other disciplines cautions that we would be wise to be mindful. But at the same time, tormented soul-searching seems somewhat awkward given the thriving industry of distinctly legal theories of, for example, property, regulation, international relations, and human rights, at least according to the understanding of the concept of legal theory this chapter advances.[2]

The mission of this chapter is to describe legal theory as an enterprise robust enough to justify separate naming. Legal theory focuses on the work of society's coercive normative institutions. It studies the traditions of these institutions and the craft typifying their members while at the same time continuously challenging their outputs by demonstrating their contingency and testing their desirability. In performing the latter tasks, legal theory necessarily absorbs lessons from law's neighboring disciplines. But at its best, legal theory is more than a sophisticated synthesis of relevant insights from these friendly neighbors because of its pointed attention to the classic jurisprudential questions regarding the nature of law, notably the relationship between law's normativity and its coerciveness and the implications of its institutional and structural characteristics.

Before turning to elaborate on these features in Part II, Part I of this chapter offers an outline of the three other important discourses about law. Although the first two—law and policy and sociohistorical analysis of law—both represent the three dots after "law and...," (i.e., the interdisciplinary analyses of law), they are sufficiently distinct to warrant separate treatment. The third discourse—craft—is obviously different from the first two. Sketching these three genres of legal scholarship is instrumental for our task here because analyzing the ways in which legal theory is different from these other modes helps characterize legal theory. It is also important because it invites the remarks of Part III concerning the interrelationship between these four members of the family of legal discourses.

I. A Topology of Discourses about Law

A. *Law and Policy*

The familiar approach of law and policy begins with Oliver Wendell Holmes's prescription that legal reasoning should be concerned with providing reasons

---

2. *Cf.* J.M. Balkin, *Interdisciplinarity as Colonization*, 53 WASH. & LEE L. REV. 949, 965 (1996).

that refer to the social ends of law—to "considerations of social advantage"[3]—and that "those who make and develop the law should have those ends articulately in their minds."[4] This focus, Holmes predicted, is bound to extract legal discourse from its solitude: jurists will have to study "the ends sought to be attained and the reasons for desiring them"[5] and thus utilize lessons from bordering disciplines, such as criminology and political economy. This prediction explains, of course, his illustrious dictum that "the black-letter man may be the man of the present, but the man of the future is the man of statistics and the master of economics."[6]

It is in this spirit that Roscoe Pound called for "'team-work' between jurisprudence and the other social sciences." Pound insisted that jurists must take account of the "social facts" to which various legal institutions apply, evaluate the "the actual social effects of legal institutions and legal doctrines," and choose among competing alternatives according to the desirability of the actual consequences of their realization. This emphasis on the social effects of law and on the means for producing these effects, Pound argued, needs to be made as the interpretive strategy of courts, as the proper way for preparing legislation within the legislative branch, and as an important focus of legal history.[7] The famous "Brandeis brief" provides an early epitome of this vision, as it recruited social science to legal advocacy by incorporating empirical findings of social scientists in a formal legal presentation.[8]

As these early manifestations of law and policy imply, students of these schools view legal rules and other forms of law as "most essentially[,] tools devised to serve practical ends," and thus insist that "rules and other varieties of law, once created, ought to be interpreted, elaborated, and applied in light of the ends they are to serve."[9] As Felix Cohen succinctly described, law

---

3. OLIVER WENDELL HOLMES, *The Path of the Law, in* COLLECTED LEGAL PAPERS 167, 184 (1920).

4. OLIVER WENDELL HOLMES, *Law in Science and Science in Law, in* COLLECTED LEGAL PAPERS, *id.* at 210, 238–39.

5. HOLMES, *supra* note 3, at 195. In the wake of Rudolf von Jhering, Holmes developed his ideas of tying law to social purposes. *See, e.g.,* RUDOLF VON JHERING, LAW AS A MEANS TO AN END 325–47 (Isaac Husik trans., 1999) (1877).

6. HOLMES, *supra* note 3, at 187.

7. Roscoe Pound, *The Scope and Purpose of Sociological Jurisprudence,* 25 HARV. L. REV. 489, 510, 512–16 (1912); *see also, e.g.,* KARL N. LLEWELLYN, *Some Realism about Realism, in* JURISPRUDENCE: REALISM IN THEORY AND PRACTICE 42, 70–73 (1962).

8. *See* Brief for Defendant in Error, Muller v. Oregon, 208 U.S. 412 (1908), *in* AMERICAN LEGAL REALISM 237 (William W. Fisher III et al. eds., 1993); N.E.H. HULL, ROSCOE POUND AND KARL LLEWELLYN: SEARCHING FOR AN AMERICAN JURISPRUDENCE 29 (1997); *see also, e.g.,* Phoebe C. Ellsworth & Julius G. Getman, *Social Science in Legal Decision-Making, in* LAW AND THE SOCIAL SCIENCES 581, 582–610 (Leon Lipson & Stanton Wheeler eds., 1986) (describing varied uses of social sciences by appellate and trial courts).

9. ROBERT SAMUEL SUMMERS, INSTRUMENTALISM AND AMERICAN LEGAL THEORY 20–21 (1982).

and policy shifts legal discourse "away from the attempt to systematize and compare" legal doctrine or "from concern with the genesis and evolution" of law and toward "a study of the consequences...in terms of human motivation and social structure"[10] and away from the lawyer–craftsman standards of "legal beauty or finesse" toward "concrete human values" and "the effects of law upon human desires and feelings."[11]

For many legal scholars, this shift is a matter of degree. But at its extreme version, policy swallows law. Thus, as early as 1934, Edward Robinson described law as "an unscientific science" and urged lawyers to become scientific. Robinson claimed that "legal science has imposed a constant drag upon the adventurous spirit of the times." He described the practice of precedent— "the principle that the concurrence of a judge with his predecessors is a direct test of the validity of his decision"—as "a habit of mind in which a stupidity may be perpetuated on the grounds that it is well-established." He vigorously criticized this "conservative logic" and argued that the only way of "attaining an improved set of values as to what courts ought to do" is by "going through a period during which we thoroughly discredit many of the things courts have been thought to do." In this view, lawyers—especially academic lawyers— should become genuine social engineers; for such engineering to be successful, legal scholarship should apply social scientific methods for the practical solution of sociolegal problems.[12]

At times, it seems that some contemporary branches of law and policy faithfully fulfill Robinson's legacy. In its extreme manifestation, law and policy takes the methodology of another discipline (typically economics) to explain legal doctrine or to call for its reform with no reference, explicit or implicit, to the concept of law or to the possible constraints of law's constitutive characteristics.[13] It was from this perspective that George Priest claimed that "legal scholarship has become specialized according to the separate social sciences" so that a law school should be structured as "a set of miniature graduate departments in the various disciplines." Given this dominance of such other disciplines, Priest claimed that it is difficult to justify "why law is a subject worthy of study at all," and he furthermore denied even the

---

10. FELIX S. COHEN, *Transcendental Nonsense and the Functional Approach, in* THE LEGAL CONSCIENCE: SELECTED PAPERS OF FELIX S. COHEN 33, 56 (Lucy Kramer Cohen ed., 1960).

11. FELIX S. COHEN, *Modern Ethics and the Law, in* THE LEGAL CONSCIENCE, *id.* at 17, 31–32.

12. Edward S. Robinson, *Law—An Unscientific Science*, 44 YALE L.J. 235, 236–39, 256, 264 (1934).

13. Richard Posner even defines legal theory along these lines as "the study of the law...'from the outside,' using the methods of scientific and humanistic inquiry to enlarge our knowledge of the legal system." Richard A. Posner, *The Decline of Law as an Autonomous Discipline: 1962–1987*, 100 HARV. L. REV. 761, 779 (1987).

utility in "extensive knowledge of the intricacies of legal doctrine and legal argument."[14]

B. *Sociohistorical Analyses of Law*

Although the label of the second grouping of legal discourses—sociohistorical analyses of law—is unfamiliar, sociohistorical analyses have distinctly different characteristics from doctrinalist legal science and from the law and policy approaches discussed above. And despite the wide range of methodologies involved, there are certain common features that justify grouping these types of analyses together.

First, sociohistorical analyses see law as a subject matter or as a field of inquiry distinct from scholarship internal to law. To the twenty-first century American reader, this point may seem obvious, but one should remember how starkly this distinguishes such analyses from traditional legal science. Recall that at its height, legal science—especially in its most developed (German) version—viewed scholarly production as a crucial aspect of the law itself, whether as a formal source or as a binding guide to interpret posited norms. As John Merryman and Rogelio Pérez-Perdomo famously described this vision, "The teacher-scholar is the real protagonist of the civil law tradition. The civil law is a law of the professors."[15] Although law and policy approaches do not go so far, they are often framed in terms that blur the boundaries between scholarship and legal practice, leading to what Edward Rubin described warily as a "unity of discourse."[16] Sociohistorical analyses, in contrast, constantly (and some might say obsessively) draw attention to a sharp distinction between their own academic discourse—including its language, method, audience, and goals—and the instrumental orientation they associate with practical legal discourse.[17]

---

14. George L. Priest, *Social Science Theory and Legal Education: The Law School as University*, 33 J. LEGAL EDUC. 437, 437, 438–39, 441 (1983). Later, Priest added that interdisciplinarity does not imply the neglect of legal doctrine, but even his later writings testify that by "interdisciplinary research," Priest in fact meant research that uses a methodology of another discipline. *See* George L. Priest, *The Growth of Interdisciplinary Research and the Industrial Structure of Legal Ideas: A Reply to Judge Edwards*, 91 MICH. L. REV. 1929, 1936 (1993).

15. JOHN HENRY MERRYMAN & ROGELIO PÉREZ-PERDOMO, THE CIVIL LAW TRADITION: AN INTRODUCTION TO THE LEGAL SYSTEMS OF EUROPE AND LATIN AMERICA 56 (3d ed. 2007); *see also* GEORGE P. FLETCHER & STEVE SHEPPARD, AMERICAN LAW IN A GLOBAL CONTEXT: THE BASICS 36 (2005).

16. Edward L. Rubin, *The Practice and Discourse of Legal Scholarship*, 86 MICH. L. REV. 1835, 1859 (1988).

17. *See* Meir Dan-Cohen, *Listeners and Eavesdroppers: Substantive Legal Theory and Its Audience*, 63 U. COLO. L. REV. 569, 579–89 (1992); *see also* Austin Sarat & Jonathan Simon, *Cultural Analysis, Cultural Studies, and the Situation of Legal Scholarship*, in CULTURAL ANALYSIS, CULTURAL STUDIES, AND THE LAW: MOVING BEYOND LEGAL REALISM 1, 3–6 (Austin Sarat & Jonathan Simon eds., 2003).

A second, related feature of sociohistorical analyses is that they typically eschew any normative or reformist impulse and thus bracket the typical perspective of much legal scholarship that concentrates on solving concrete legal problems or existing social problems through law. For some scholars who use sociohistorical analyses, this distance from a normative perspective requires an apologetic posture.[18] For others, it is a point of pride.[19] The distance from the normative perspective is a matter of degree (and dispute). Thus, some scholars see a total divorce from the normative perspective as a precondition for quality scholarship[20] while others suggest that bracketing direct normative questions will eventually lead back to normative inquiry with new perspectives.[21] But almost all sociohistorical analyses suspend direct normative inquiry in large measure.

The third feature of sociohistorical analyses is a sense of reflexivity. Analyses of this sort are constantly folding back onto themselves, pouring attention on categories such as legal consciousness and on the role of the scholar in shaping consciousness. This type of reflexivity may have been born of the jurisprudential conflicts between legal realists and their predecessors—conflicts that forced the actors into self-conscious positions on legal scholarship itself. Generations later, such analyses were part of what gave critical legal studies much of its energy,[22] but the reflexive mode has spread well beyond critical legal studies. Paul Kahn's voice is indicative: "The only way out of the limitless claims of the hermeneutic circle is self-reflexive. That is, we must be able to take the categories of experience as a subject of reflection even as we deploy them."[23]

These three features—distinguishing scholarship from practice, suspending normative inquiry, and reflexivity—are not necessarily present in every sociohistorical analysis. Taken together, however, they roughly mark out a style of legal scholarship readily identifiable in today's academy, and when taken to

---

18. One can think of any number of legal history articles that conclude with normative speculations that seem to have little grounding in the work that preceded them.

19. At the extreme, the normative perspective may be held up to ridicule. *See* Pierre Schlag, *Normative and Nowhere to Go*, 43 STAN. L. REV. 167, 167–68, 170–77 (1990).

20. PAUL W. KAHN, THE CULTURAL STUDY OF LAW: RECONSTRUCTING LEGAL SCHOLARSHIP 18 (1999).

21. MEIR DAN-COHEN, RIGHTS, PERSONS, AND ORGANIZATIONS: A LEGAL THEORY FOR BUREAUCRATIC SOCIETY 1–4 (1986).

22. For mature versions of critical legal studies analyses that concentrate on what it means for legal academics to develop their particular styles of scholarship and argumentation, see generally DUNCAN KENNEDY, A CRITIQUE OF ADJUDICATION (1997); ROBERTO MANGABEIRA UNGER, WHAT SHOULD LEGAL ANALYSIS BECOME? 63–78 (1996).

23. Paul W. Kahn, *Freedom, Autonomy, and the Cultural Study of Law*, in CULTURAL ANALYSIS, *supra* note 17, at 154, 177.

their logical endpoint, they raise serious doubts about the very possibility of legal theory:

> [L]egal study unavoidably becomes a program for the reform of law. With this, the line separating the scholar from the object of his or her study disappears. The study of law turns out not to be an intellectual discipline at all; it is a part of the practice that was to be the very object of study. From the very beginning, the study of law is co-opted by legal practice. The independence of the discipline will never be possible unless the understanding deployed in theoretical inquiry can be distinguished from the reason deployed in legal practice. Such a distinction in the forms of reason is neither readily available nor easily achieved.[24]

C. Law as Craft

Alongside policy and sociohistorical studies, a third genre of legal discourse identifies law as craft.[25] Aristotelian in its inspiration, this group of studies focuses attention on law's shared professional norms.

Two strands of legal scholarship seek to explore and give meaning to this inward-looking focus.[26] One such strand is procedural, studying the institutional structure of (common law) adjudication as the epitome of virtuous legal dispositions and as the core of law's legitimacy. Thus, Llewellyn claims that the legal ethos—which is epitomized in the adversary process and the judicial opinion and is reinforced by "[t]ime, place, architecture and interior arrangement, supporting officials, garb, [and] ritual"—directs judges to be "[o]pen, truly open, to listen, to get informed, to be persuaded, to respond to good reason."[27] More recently, Owen Fiss highlighted a number of significant institutional features: the requirement of judicial independence, the concept of a nondiscretionary jurisdiction, the obligation to listen to all affected parties, the tradition of the signed opinion, and the neutral principles requirement.[28]

---

24. KAHN, *supra* note 20, at 18.

25. For an extended elaboration, see Brett G. Scharffs, *Law as Craft*, 54 VAND. L. REV. 2245, 2274–322 (2001).

26. For the third strand, dealing with normative coherence, thus integrating craft with policy, see Part II.B, *infra*. Coherence of the doctrinal type is not included in the topology of this part because, aside from the more technical aspects of the law, a reference to coherence—like other formalist strategies—is question begging. *See* Hanoch Dagan, *Codification, Coherence, and Priority Conflicts*, *in* THE DRAFT CIVIL CODE FOR ISRAEL IN COMPARATIVE PERSPECTIVE 149, 151–52 (Kurt Siehr & Reinhard Zimmermann eds., 2008).

27. KARL N. LLEWELLYN, THE COMMON LAW TRADITION: DECIDING APPEALS 46–47 (1960).

28. *See* OWEN FISS, THE LAW AS IT COULD BE 163 (2003); *see also id.* at 11–12, 14, 54–55, 68; JOHN RAWLS, POLITICAL LIBERALISM 235–36 (1993); Lon L. Fuller, *The Forms and Limits of Adjudication*, 92 HARV. L. REV. 353, 365 (1978).

The structural characteristics of the judicial office, Llewellyn and Cohen argued, have a great power to lead judges to consider the needs of the whole.[29] They consider law an area in which the participants, most particularly judges, are constantly challenged by conflicting perspectives, thus (potentially) broadening their normative and empirical horizons.[30] Hence, at its best, legal professionalism (and, in this view, legal theory at its best) makes lawyers "experts in that necessary but difficult task of forming judgment without single-phase expertness" by considering the needs of the whole.[31]

The second inward-looking strand focuses on the skill of lawyers—judges, practitioners, and legal academics—to capture the factual subtleties of different types of cases and to adjust the legal treatment to the specific characteristics of each of these categories. Herman Oliphant, for example, celebrated the traditional common law strategy of employing narrow legal categories, which help to produce "the discrimination necessary for intimacy of treatment," holding lawyers close to "the actual transactions before them" and thus encouraging them to shape law "close and contemporary" to the human problems they deal with. This strategy facilitates one distinct comparative advantage of lawyers (as opposed to, say, economists and political philosophers) in producing legal norms: their unmediated access to actual human situations and problems in contemporary life. When law's categories are in tune with those of life so that an "alert sense of actuality checks our reveries in theory," lawyers enjoy "the illumination which only immediacy affords and the judiciousness which reality alone can induce."[32] Of course, Oliphant's is just one particular (and particularly optimistic) view of thinking like a lawyer. Attention to law as rhetoric or discourse may reach conclusions quite opposed to the view of lawyers as enjoying illumination or unmediated access to human situations.[33]

Anthony Kronman, writing in the same inspirational mode as Oliphant, argues that instilling attentiveness to context into legal discourse helps to

---

29. LLEWELLYN, *supra* note 27, at 48.

30. COHEN, *Field Theory and Judicial Logic, in* THE LEGAL CONSCIENCE, *supra* note 10, at 121, 125.

31. LLEWELLYN, *American Common Law Tradition, and American Democracy, in* JURISPRUDENCE, *supra* note 7, at 282, 310; *see also, e.g.,* Katharine T. Bartlett, *Feminist Legal Methods,* 103 HARV. L. REV. 829, 880–87 (1990).

32. Herman Oliphant, *A Return to Stare Decisis,* 14 A.B.A. J. 71, 74–76 (1928). Joseph Raz's analysis of the phenomenon of distinguishing cases brings home a similar point. *See* JOSEPH RAZ, THE AUTHORITY OF LAW: CHAPTERS ON LAW AND MORALITY 183–97 (1979).

33. Thus, based on a close linguistic analysis of the language employed in teaching first-year contracts, Elizabeth Mertz concludes that thinking like a lawyer requires initiation into a tradition of thinking that places limits on law's democratic aspirations. *See* ELIZABETH MERTZ, THE LANGUAGE OF LAW SCHOOL: LEARNING TO "THINK LIKE A LAWYER" 4–11, 207–23 (2007). Deciding between the likes of Oliphant and Mertz is not the task of this chapter. The point is to show that analyses of the rhetoric of law have a wide range of valence and methodologies. For an additional view of the limitations that

nourish some of the legal profession's most significant qualities. Kronman conceptualizes these qualities in terms of sympathy and detachment: the uneasy combination of compassion—enabling lawyers to imagine themselves in their clients' position (or, for judges, in that of the litigants)—and independence, coolness, and reserve that are prerequisites for the ability to pass judgment on the situation's merits. This combination of sympathy and detachment is, for Kronman, the professional toolkit of lawyers and the crux of law's authority and legitimacy.[34]

At times, writers in this mode of discourse seem to argue that their accounts exhaust what law, properly speaking, is all about. It follows, they claim, that legal scholarship should focus on studying the structures (including substantive doctrine and procedure) of law as well as the character traits that are most conducive to practical wisdom. Scholars like Owen Fiss, Brett Scharffs, and James Boyd White have developed a perspective that recognizes the content of law as immanent in practical legal materials while simultaneously according legal scholarship an important role.[35] Kronman goes even further: he contrasts the qualities of sympathy and detachment with "theoretical extravagance." He argues that the professional ideal he articulates is one of practical wisdom—"wisdom about human beings and their tangled affairs"— that is a human excellence, a disposition associated with certain temperamental qualities rather than any form of technical expertise. Therefore, Kronman insists that law's professional ideal should be divorced from any instrumental approach to law and not be "tempted by the false ideal of a legal science."[36]

II. Characterizing Legal Theory

Notwithstanding law's proud career as part of the modern university, post-realist legal academia faces a serious disciplinary challenge. As we have seen, the collapse of doctrinalism as a credible academic paradigm triggered two diametrically opposed strategies: assimilating law into "stronger" disciplines, and turning inward in an attempt to strengthen the porous boundaries between law and its neighboring disciplines.[37] I have claimed that both these strategies are unsatisfactory.

legal rhetoric imposes, see MARIANNE CONSTABLE, JUST SILENCES: THE LIMITS AND POSSIBILITIES OF MODERN LAW 8–44 (2005).

34. ANTHONY T. KRONMAN, THE LOST LAWYER: FAILING IDEALS OF THE LEGAL PROFESSION 72–73, 113–21, 223–24, 360, 362, 375 (1993).

35. *See* Brett G. Scharffs, *The Character of Legal Reasoning*, 61 WASH. & LEE L. REV. 733, 734–43 (2004); James Boyd White, *An Old-Fashioned View of the Nature of Law*, 12 THEORETICAL INQUIRIES L. 381, 402 (2011).

36. KRONMAN, *supra* note 34, at 223–25.

37. *Cf.* Armin Krishnan, What Are Academic Disciplines? Some Observations on the Disciplinarity vs. Interdisciplinarity Debate 48–50 (NCRM Working Paper, Economic

Law's assimilation into the social sciences and the humanities generated an influx of new insights about law and rejuvenated its academic exploration. But the assimilationist strategy tends to fragment the interdisciplinary lessons of law, and ultimately poses a real threat to the identity of law as an academic discipline. If indeed law has no theoretical core—if law is "a parasitic discipline"[38]—law schools are destined to become (or remain) loose coalitions of distinct and fragmented subdisciplines, whose only common denominator is their interest in law.[39] Internal analyses of law, by contrast, have difficulties distinguishing legal scholarship from high-skilled performance by nonacademic members of the legal profession.[40] More theoretical attempts for guarding the autonomy of legal academia are not more successful. Thus, although Ernest Weinrib's subtle analysis, which I cannot address in this chapter (but discuss and criticize elsewhere), elucidates the unique justificatory burden generated by the distinctive characteristics of adjudication,[41] it unacceptably blinds itself to the broader social ramifications entailed by any significant legal pronouncement.[42]

Legal theory compensates for the limitations of both external and internal analyses of law. This part describes the added value of legal theory and explains why it deserves a separate naming. There are two interconnected aspects to the distinct character of legal theory: the attention it gives to law as a set of coercive normative institutions, and its relentless effort to engage, incorporate, and synthesize the lessons of the other discourses about law.

A. Coercive Normative Institutions

Legal theory is typically structured—explicitly or (much more frequently) implicitly—around the central and persistent questions of jurisprudence, interrogating the law as a set of coercive normative institutions.[43] This understanding of law typifies many jurisprudential schools with some (such as John

and Social Research Council [ESRC] National Centre for Research Methods, Mar. 2009), *available at* http://eprints.ncrm.ac.uk/783/1/what_are_academic_disciplines.pdf.

38. *See* Anthony Bradney, *Law as a Parasitic Discipline*, 25 J.L. & SOC'Y 71 (1988).

39. *See* David E. Van Zandt, *Discipline-Based Faculty*, 53 J. LEGAL EDUC. 332, 334–35 (2003).

40. *See* Douglas W. Vick, *Interdisciplinarity and the Discipline of Law*, 31 J.L. & SOC'Y 163, 187 (2004).

41. Ernest J. Weinrib, *Can Law Survive Legal Education?*, 60 VAND. L. REV. 401 (2007).

42. *See* Hanoch Dagan, Law as an Academic Discipline, *available at* http://ssrn.com/abstract=2228433.

43. Another important way of looking at law is through its functions. In this context, one may think of law in terms of its role in resolving disputes, channeling and coordinating its subjects' conduct, distributing entitlements and obligations, and expressing values. Legal theory is obviously interested in all of these functions as well as in their (rather intricate) interplay.

Austin) emphasizing law's coercive dimension and others (such as H.L.A. Hart) highlighting its normativity.[44] This section relies on the realist conception of law, which offers, as we have seen in Chapter 2, a powerful articulation of the idea that power and reason are equally essential to law while concurrently appreciating the difficulties of their cohabitation.[45] Furthermore, the realist account of law carries another important lesson that also informs the title of this section: in understanding law as an ongoing institution, realists view law as an enterprise that cannot be reduced to its constituent parts. Consequently, jurisprudence must go beyond adjudication to consider the numerous other arenas that are replete with lawmaking, law-applying, law-interpreting, and law-developing functions.[46]

An important clarification is nonetheless in order. The main goal in this chapter is to forward an argument for the importance of legal theory as a genus, and legal realism is just one—albeit particularly important—species of that genus. As far as this chapter is concerned, there is no stake in converting readers to legal realism. For example, although realism's constant balancing of reason and power recommends it as a legal theory, other legal theories could have a completely different take on the relationship between reason and power. Kantian legal theories (or natural law theories), for example, take the possibility of coercion as a mandate for reason to be the sole motivator in law (i.e., for there to be law, all coercive power must be subjugated to reason).[47] Some Marxist theories, on the other hand, maintain that although law exhibits an internally consistent and reasoned framework, the entire mode of reason flows from and is dependent on (economic) power (i.e., in actuality, law's reason serves power).[48] These theories are completely different from legal realism, but they are obviously part of legal theory. In the end, legal theorists will argue about which legal theories are useful, elegant, thought provoking, true, dangerous, or anything else; as should be clear by now, the very terms of reference for what would make a legal theory good or valuable are quite up for grabs. The following reminder of the legal realist analysis of power and reason in law (which is discussed at some length at Part II of Chapter 2) is just an example of what legal theory might offer. Again, I use legal realism—specifically: the

44. *See* JOHN AUSTIN, THE PROVINCE OF JURISPRUDENCE DETERMINED 9–33 (1832); H.L.A. HART, THE CONCEPT OF LAW 55–59 (1961).

45. For a source less familiar in American legal theory but equally adamant about the uneasy cohabitation of power and normativity (or what he calls force and norm), see VON JHERING, *supra* note 5, at 239–62.

46. *See* NEIL K. KOMESAR, IMPERFECT ALTERNATIVES: CHOOSING INSTITUTIONS IN LAW, ECONOMICS, AND PUBLIC POLICY 3–13 (1994).

47. For an extended discussion along these lines, see ARTHUR RIPSTEIN, FORCE AND FREEDOM: KANT'S LEGAL AND POLITICAL PHILOSOPHY 4–29 (2009).

48. This is one interpretation of the classic work on Marxist jurisprudence. *See* EVGENY BRONISLAVOVICH PASHUKANIS, THE GENERAL THEORY OF LAW & MARXISM 63–64 (Barbara Einhorn trans., 2002) (1924).

realist analysis of power and reason in law—merely as an illustration and not as the only legal theory that is useful and important in and of itself.

Realists justify their preoccupation with coerciveness in two steps. The first, obvious part of the argument is that unlike other judgments, those that law's carriers prescribe can recruit the state's monopolized power to back up their enforcement. But the second, more subtle part of the argument is just as important, and it rests on the institutional and discursive means that downplay some of the dimensions of law's power. These built-in features of law— notably, the institutional division of labor between "interpretation specialists" and the actual executors of their judgments together with our tendency as lawyers and even as citizens to accord legal constructs an aura of naturalness and acceptability—render the danger of obscuring law's coerciveness particularly troubling. They explain the realists' wariness of the trap entailed in the blurring of law's coerciveness.

But realists also reject as reductive an alternative image of law that portrays it as naked power or pure interest. They insist that law is also a forum of reason, and that modes of legal reasoning often function as constraints on the choices of legal decision makers. Law is not *only* about interest or power politics; it is *also* an exercise in giving reasons. Furthermore, because so much is at stake in reasoning about law, legal reasoning ought to be urgent and rich, attentive, careful, and serious. The question of how rich legal reasoning will be is often a function of how hard people are willing to work in undermining unreflective understandings of what the law is or must be.[49] Reasons are appeals to a host of values in an attempt to justify law's coercion. Reasons may be articulated at varying levels of abstraction from the general proposition down to the argument contextually tailored for a particular situation of application. Reasons also range from the wholly substantive to the technical.[50]

If we recognize this range of registers for reasoned argument, it would appear bizarre to equate normative reasoning with parochial interests or arbitrary power. In legal theory, normative reasoning must aspire to appeal beyond the parochial or the arbitrary even as legal theory invites the analyses that expose some instances of existing argumentation as covers for interest. Analyses that give up on the aspiration to reasoned persuasion are problematic to the extent that they relinquish responsibility: the responsibility of legal

---

49. *See* Duncan Kennedy, *A Left Phenomenological Alternative to the Hart/Kelsen Theory of Legal Interpretation, in* LEGAL REASONING: COLLECTED CHAPTERS 153, 158–61 (2008).

50. At times, reasons could devolve to aesthetics as most claims do for a rule on the basis of doctrinal coherence. Aesthetic reasons for legal rules are not usually good reasons, but it is clear that they are still reasons, and, other things being equal, elegant wording is preferable to clumsy wording even assuming no functional or normative difference. Of course, *other things* are never actually equal.

theory to offer possibilities of critique of status quo power arrangements and the option of marshalling the law for morally required social change.

Legal theories of institutions, forms of reasoning, or particular doctrines take these lessons seriously. Because reasoning about law entails a host of consequences affecting people's interests and the distribution of social power, legal theory is frequently suspicious of the reasons given by law's carriers, and it invites criticism of law's means, ends, and (particularly distributive) consequences.[51] This stage often uses insights of sociohistorical analyses of the law. But the critique of legal doctrine often leads legal theory to a reconstructive stage guided by the dynamic understanding of law as a great human laboratory continuously seeking improvement, an "endless process of testing and retesting"[52] as part of an interminable quest for more just societies. At this stage in particular, important inputs come into play from various law and policy schools (including, of course, those schools that question the legitimacy of resorting to policy as opposed to considerations of principle).

Furthermore, legal theorists often incorporate an institutional perspective in their analysis.[53] At its best, legal theory overcomes jurisprudential tunnel vision that sees the legal universe through judicial eyes. Instead of an adjudication-centered perspective, legal theory expands its view to the set of institutions through which law is created, applied, or otherwise becomes effective. Some of the institutions upon which legal theory lavishes attention actually enforce norms (e.g., courts, prosecutors, and administrative agencies); some institutions are hierarchical and rule based with readily identifiable agents involved in norm obedience (e.g., corporate counsel and tax advisors); and some are webs of social norms, including the norm of deference to the symbolic power of law. The core of the institutional vision is an image of law as an ongoing enterprise that is not usefully reduced to its constituent parts. Analyses of discrete parts are crucial to institutional knowledge, but understanding the complete phenomenon requires a nonreductive account.

---

51. Legal theorists have this response to the characteristic features of practitioners and judges' communications as strategic and insincere. *See* Dan-Cohen, *supra* note 17, at 571–74. Dan-Cohen claims that the only adequate remedy for this is "that substantive legal theory...not participate in a dialogue in which judicial opinions or other official pronouncements count as interlocutors." *Id.* at 590. For a persuasive response to this provocative claim, see Robert Post, *Legal Scholarship and the Practice of Law*, 63 U. COLO. L. REV. 615, 618–25 (1992).

52. BENJAMIN N. CARDOZO, THE NATURE OF THE JUDICIAL PROCESS 179 (1921); *see also* RONALD DWORKIN, LAW'S EMPIRE 400–13 (1986).

53. For a survey of recent institutionalist work, see Victoria Nourse & Gregory Shaffer, *Varieties of New Legal Realism: Can a New World Order Prompt a New Legal Theory?*, 95 CORNELL L. REV. 61, 85–90 (2009).

B. *Synthesizing the Other Discourses*

Legal theory seeks to shed light—either explanatory, justificatory, critical, or reformist—on society's coercive normative institutions. To perform these tasks, it often resorts to insights from the other discourses about law. But as Part III.A explained, the synthetic spirit of legal theory is not just a matter of methodological inclination; rather, the appreciation of the nature of law as a set of coercive normative institutions justifies—indeed, mandates—it.[54]

Legal theorists resort to sociohistorical analyses of the law as well as to comparative law (a traditional tool of academic lawyers) because they can offer contextual accounts that help explain the sources and the evolution of the legal terrain. Sociohistorical analyses and comparative law are also instrumental in opening up the legal imagination by undermining the status quo's (implicit) claim of necessity and revealing the contingency of the present. At times, they can help unearth competing legal possibilities and provide hints as to the possible ramifications of their adoption.

Law and policy is obviously helpful in figuring out the real-life ramifications of current law. This task, which is important both to understand the law and to evaluate it, often relies on social scientific methods (from economics, psychology, sociology, anthropology, and political science), both empirical and theoretical. Insofar as this stage of research is aimed at assessing the normative desirability of law, it typically leads to a second stage that looks at law's goals and thus resorts to guidance from the evaluative neighboring disciplines, notably ethics and political philosophy. And where legal theorists aim at reconstruction—at designing alternatives and comparing their expected performances—they typically use both social scientific tools and normative ones.[55]

Law as craft is no less vital for legal theory than the two other discourses about law. As with many human practices, deep understanding of the evolution and dynamics of law requires some inside information that only law as craft can provide. Similarly, a robust acquaintance with law's institutional, structural, and discursive characteristics is also necessary to appreciate the potential of alternative legal reforms and to caution us against programs that are insufficiently sensitive to law's typical and recurrent limitations. Thus, more so than their counterparts in the social sciences and the humanities who write about law, legal theorists often synthesize, explicitly or implicitly, these critical dimensions into their accounts. They are also sensitive to the subtle

---

54. For a refreshing recognition of the significance of such synthesis by a legal philosopher and a legal economist, see Daniel Markovits & Alan Schwartz, *The Myth of Efficient Breach: New Defenses of the Expectation Interest*, 97 VA. L. REV. 1939 (2011).

55. This distinction is rough and solely methodical; it does not mean to imply that social science can actually be value-free or devoid of normative underpinnings.

differences between various legal fields and legal institutions. One manifestation of the significance of law and craft for legal theory is legal theory's tendency to be less abstract than the philosophical, economic, or other theories
with which it interacts.

Legal theorists who recognize the possibilities of synthesizing these languages of legal scholarship might not be overly concerned with the dismissal
of the legal tradition as unscientific[56] or by the fear of intellectual co-optation
by legal practice.[57] The range of starting points for analysis is immense. For
example, some legal theorists will begin with existing doctrine or proposals
for legal reform, convinced that a starting point in the actual arrangements
governing some aspect of life is recognition of the social basis of the law.[58]
Others will begin with a general analytical problem and may not discuss particular doctrines in much detail at all.[59] Others still might begin with an abstract
question but extensively use doctrine to illustrate or test their claims.[60] Legal
theory comes in many flavors, from the apologetic to the radical, and (of
course) at varying levels of quality. One can hope that theorists will examine
legal doctrines or institutions with both a critical eye and a reconstructive
spirit while utilizing the insights of all three discourses about law in the ways
just described. And one can similarly hope that legal theorists will not shy
away from reaching a conclusion that nothing short of radical transformation
may be required for law to be acceptable.[61]

Thus conceived, legal theory combines lessons from interfacing disciplines
of the social sciences and the humanities, but is irreducible to any of them. By
the same token, although legal theory acknowledges the significance of the
internal insights of law as craft, it has no aspiration of closure. Rather than
seeking to establish law as an autonomous academic discipline, it celebrates its
own embeddedness in the social sciences and the humanities.[62] Furthermore,

56. *See supra* text accompanying note 12.
57. *See supra* text accompanying note 24.
58. *See, e.g.*, Anne L. Alstott, *Equal Opportunity and Inheritance Taxation*, 121 Harv.
L. Rev. 469, 472–73 (2007).
59. For an example complete with a definition of legal theory, see Dan-Cohen, *supra*
note 21.
60. *See, e.g.*, Eyal Zamir & Barak Medina, Law, Economics, and Morality
79–104 (2010).
61. Indeed, legal theory is not limited to the happy middle; genuine insight often
comes from what some perceive as extremes. Although such insights might require
domestication for implementation through law, we would still hope to see the
insights themselves arise and develop in legal theory. *Cf.* Robin West, Normative
Jurisprudence: An Introduction (2011).
62. This position may be controversial in itself: legal theory can be conceived as a sub-
system with the kind of autonomy described by autopoiesis. A detailed argument with
systems theorists is beyond the scope of this chapter, but it is important to note that
the conflict is actually minimal. Systems theorists believe that systems are cognitively
open but operatively closed. For the purposes of this chapter it suffices to note that
because legal theory (as imagined here) does not actually have an operative mode, its

although the synthetic enterprise of legal theory sounds (and indeed is) academically ambitious, it is, or at least can be, highly relevant to the practice of judges and practicing lawyers, at least insofar as they are interested in explaining, justifying, or reforming the law. In this sense, legal theory may help to reduce the gap between legal academia and the legal profession.[63] It also sets up an attractive vision of legal education. As Llewellyn insisted, studying law as a liberal art by combining "[t]echnique, the intellectual side, the spiritual—the true, the beautiful, the good"—is the best practical training as it accords students "vision, range, depth, balance, and rich humanity," which are the key for effective and good practical work.[64]

III. The Family of Legal Discourses

Legal theory, as characterized in this chapter, is both inherently self-confident and intrinsically tormented. These seemingly contradictory dispositions may explain why good legal theory does not simply accept the surroundings of the other discourses about law in patient resignation but in fact doggedly seeks out interactions with those surroundings.

The self-confidence of legal theory springs from its internalization of the complexity of law and a belief that only an engagement with complexity can generate useful accounts of legal phenomena. If what typifies law is indeed the institutional cohabitation of power and reason, and if this core feature of law necessitates a synthesis of the type described above, then any one-dimensional account of law—or any one-dimensional account of any specific legal doctrine or practice—is, by definition, partial and deficient. This conviction leads legal theorists to a principled antipurist position.[65] This position is further strengthened for legal theorists of the evaluative (justificatory or reformist) type because the responsibility in potentially affecting people's

---

cognitive openness is all that is at stake in the current formulation of embeddedness. *See* NIKLAS LUHMANN, LAW AS A SOCIAL SYSTEM 76–141 (Fatima Kastner et al. eds., Klaus A. Ziegert trans., 2004).

63. *See* Harry T. Edwards, *The Growing Disjunction between Legal Education and the Legal Profession*, 91 MICH. L. REV. 34, 41–42 (1992). For a persuasive platform of cooperation between legal academia and the bar, see Robert W. Gordon, *Lawyers, Scholars, and the "Middle Ground,"* 91 MICH. L. REV. 2075, 2098 (1993).

64. Llewellyn, *The Study of Law as a Liberal Art, in* JURISPRUDENCE, *supra* note 7, at 375, 376, 394. *See also, e.g.,* Kathleen M. Sullivan, *Foreword: Interdisciplinarity*, 100 MICH. L. REV. 1217 (2002).

65. *Cf.* Christopher McCrudden, *Legal Research and the Social Sciences*, 122 L.Q. REV. 632, 645 (2006) (arguing the "methodological pluralism" that typifies "current legal scholarship" demonstrates "a mature openness to other disciplines that demonstrates a welcome self-confidence").

lives forces upon them a duty to doubt as well as a duty to decide, and one cannot discharge these obligations from any single perspective on law.[66]

But alongside its self-confidence, an almost constitutive discomfort typifies legal theory. This disposition derives from the fact that in most dimensions of law, legal theory is positioned somewhere midway between the other discourses about law,[67] and it is thus always exposed (albeit to a moderate degree) to the professional hazards of their practitioners. Thus, on the one hand, legal theory typically puts less emphasis on law's coerciveness and the risks of its collapse to brute politics than do sociohistorical analyses. Therefore, it is subject to the risk of lack of critical reflectivity that haunts both law and craft and (to a lesser degree) law and policy (because they rarely pay attention to these dimensions). On the other hand, by distancing itself to some extent (that is, more than law as craft) from legal doctrine and from jurists' internal point of view, legal theory may be insufficiently attuned to law's distinctiveness vis-à-vis other social, economic, and cultural institutions. Similarly, although legal theory is more responsive than both sociohistorical analyses and law as craft to the normative dimension of law and to its potential role as an instrument for social change, legal theory is typically less reform minded than law and policy and thus may be subject—at least to an extent—to the risks of either romantic conservatism or ivory-tower playfulness.

The core convictions underlying legal theory require legal theorists to navigate these unstable middle positions. They imply that legal theory will generally rely on pragmatic judgments as to the optimal degree of suspension from the practice of law and as to the optimal mix of sociohistorical and normative perspectives that should be called in for its analysis. Although there is no reason to disparage the enterprise because of the imprecision of such judgments, there is always good reason for not being complacent about them. The environment of the other discourses not only provides legal theory with essential inputs; each of them also serves as a potential source of critique toward excesses or shortcomings in striking this delicate and sensitive balance. The critiques are obviously different from each other; indeed, at times, they may be diametrically opposed. Legal theorists, whose accounts often serve as bridges among these opposing positions, can rely on the critical attitudes of the other members of the family of legal discourses as checks on what may be the most challenging task of a solid legal theory: properly accommodating the

---

66. *See* Alan Schwartz, *Two Cultural Problems in Law and Economics*, 2011 U. ILL. L. REV. 1531, 1532; Joseph William Singer, *Normative Methods for Lawyers*, 56 UCLA L. REV. 899, 910–11 (2009); Eyal Zamir, *Towards an Integrative Legal Scholarship*, 4 HAIFA L. REV. 131, 142–43 (2008).

67. One exception to this rule is the institutional one, to which legal theory seems to be the most sensitive, whereas law as craft is the least sensitive (with law and policy and sociohistorical analyses taking midway positions).

insights of sociohistorical analyses of law, of law and policy, and of law as craft into workable, theoretical frameworks that rely on a robust understanding of law as a set of coercive normative institutions.

CONCLUDING REMARKS

I conclude this chapter not with any truly conclusive statement but rather with a reflection on three implications one might draw from this chapter's exercise in characterization. The three implications deal with the relationship between law and other academic disciplines, the institutional structure of the legal academy, and advanced legal education.

Many people involved in the legal academy experience a certain discomfort about the academic status of legal scholarship. A recurring thought seems to be that there are two alternatives: adopt an external academic discipline (e.g., economics, sociology, psychology, or philosophy) or relinquish academic or scientific pretensions and delve more deeply into practical professionalism. But those alternatives offer a false choice. Legal theory, distinctive in its emphasis on the significance of synthesis and its focus on coercive institutional normativity, should be understood as a distinctive academic alternative. The strong version of this claim is this: legal theory has—just as other academic fields have—generated a language with which the initiated can advance more nuanced arguments than would be available to lay audiences. The language is far from impenetrable, but it does require training to gain facility with it, and it does allow for a deepening of inquiry.[68]

The second implication touches on the structure of the legal academy as a community of scholarship. Law faculties are collections of people and are prone to combination and division. Sometimes those divisions are generational; at times they may be thematic; often they seem to be methodological; and sometimes they map onto institutional or more characteristic politics. Nothing in this chapter suggests a way to overcome such divisions—indeed, they may be valuable overall to prevent boredom (and boring scholarship).

---

68. Why would one want a deeper and more nuanced inquiry? Well, part of that desire must be based simply on a will to know, and possibly aesthetic aspirations that determine that deeper and more nuanced knowledge is more satisfying. However, there are also more instrumental ways to think of the value of depth and nuance. One issue is that depth and nuance are avenues for innovation, for new ways of seeing, or for overcoming the kinds of roadblocks to thinking that often arise from stale polarizations from arguments that have reified into "positions." This too can be understood as a pragmatic benefit (for better, more convincing results), or an existential benefit of a chance to experience something new, or a political benefit in the sense that self-governance is heightened when choice is better informed. Again, this is only meant to suggest; a serious discussion of the phenomenology of legal academia is way beyond the scope of this chapter.

However, the account of this chapter suggests that although the development of high-powered other-discipline(s)-based academic associations and peer-review journals is important, it is likewise imperative to develop parallel institutional venues that can similarly nurture legal theory, both in general and respecting the various branches of the law. It also implies that legal theory is a place where the divisions between the various genres of legal scholarship do not simply divide but rather become the focus of discussion. This observation is most pertinent regarding methodological differences: the discussion of legal theory brings the specialist partway out of a form of isolation and forces an engagement with additional perspectives and agendas. In its strongest form, the implication would be that although people in the law school could do anything in the way of scholarship, they would also have to *speak* legal theory if not with native proficiency then at least as a second language.[69]

This brings us to the third implication of this chapter, dealing with advanced legal education. If the core claim of this chapter about legal theory is correct, then the legal academy should not rely too heavily on other disciplines to train its scholars.[70] There is certainly room for many philosophers, economists, historians, and practitioners from other neighboring disciplines on law faculties. However, a reliance on other fields for advanced training may mean that many people who join law faculties will have to learn the language of legal theory on the fly. To the extent that legal theory has content, then legal theory itself should be part of the toolkit imparted to the aspiring legal academic. In other words, legal academics should have a background in legal theory—they should study it as a field. And the way to do that seems to be to develop and support PhD (or other research-based advanced degree) programs in law.[71]

Reflecting on these three implications brings us back to the nature of this chapter's attempt to generalize about legal theory. This chapter is an exercise in figuring out what legal theory is and what it could be. In doing so, we are not involved in a maximization project that calls for an advanced algorithm.

---

69. Requesting participants in a social practice to command a language that is deemed core for that practice raises a risk of creating a hegemonic discourse that might marginalize unorthodox languages. But given the secure positions of the other discourses about law and their intrinsic significance to legal theory, applying this request to legal theory does not entail such a risk. To the contrary, rather than silencing disputes, a broad recognition of the importance of having legal theory as a common language is likely to trigger a fruitful—and probably quite fierce—debate as to its precise characteristics.

70. *Cf.* Mattias Kumm, *On the Past and Future of European Constitutional Scholarship*, 7 I-CON 401, 410–12 (2009).

71. For one example, which both Roy Kreitner and I have spent considerable energy supporting, see *The Zvi Meitar Center for Advanced Legal Studies*, TEL AVIV U. BUCHMANN FAC. L., http://www.law.tau.ac.il/Eng/?CategoryID=191 (last visited Mar. 16, 2013).

Rather, the project is more like an appeal to character, and thus its title has a double meaning. On the one hand, there is a descriptive project of characterizing existing and future legal theory. But on the other hand, this chapter tries to draw out a type of participant, a character in a particular institutional drama. If you are persuaded, perhaps you already identify with that character.[72] If not, I hope the character of legal theory is at least interesting enough for further engagement.

72. *See* Jerry Frug, *Argument as Character*, 40 STAN. L. REV. 869, 873 (1988).

CHAPTER 5

⌘

The Limited Autonomy
of Private law

OPENING REMARKS

The relationship between private law adjudication (typified as the bipolar encounter between plaintiff and defendant) and social values usually associated with much broader settings (such as the pursuit of distributive justice by state legislation) is a perennial concern of legal theory.[1] This topic, which brings to the forefront the supposed schism between the internal perspective on law (discussed in previous chapters in terms of craft) and its external implications (evaluated or reconfigured using insights from the humanities and the social sciences), has become particularly acute in recent years due to two important developments, one internal and one external to legal theory. The internal one is that two important paradigms have reached the "state of the art" stage in their development: the economic analysis of law, viewed as the ultimate instrumental approach to private law, and neo-Kantian formalism, viewed as the ultimate anti-instrumental understanding.[2] The external development concerns Europeanization and globalization processes, which highlight the practical importance of a choice between the voices of private law autonomy and the instrumentalization of private law for such purposes as promoting competition and trading in a common market.[3] The core disagreement between autonomists and instrumentalists, and the sole focus of my inquiry here,[4] revolves around

1. *See* Nils Jansen & Ralf Michaels, *Private Law and the State: Comparative Perspectives and Historical Observations*, 71/2 RABELSZ 345, 358–92 (2007).
2. *See infra* text accompanying notes 6–7.
3. *See* Ralf Michaels & Nils Jansen, *Private Law beyond the State? Europeanization, Globalization, Privatization*, 54 AM. J. COMP. L. 843 (2007).
4. At times, the debate between autonomists and instrumentalists takes an institutional form. I discuss this aspect—although not exactly in these terms—in Part III of Chapter 9.

the question of which values should inform the content of the rules of private law: autonomists argue that our collective or public values—the very values that instrumentalists invoke—have no legitimate role to play in private law.

My claim in this chapter is that neither autonomist theory nor its instrumentalist counterpart provides a satisfactory account of private law. Autonomist theory is, I will argue, implausible. Private law is founded on a perfectionist view of society and hence cannot claim to be indifferent to social values. (As we will see, nothing in this claim implies that the values underlying private law are identical to those guiding public law, or that only one set of values underlies private law in its entirety—quite the contrary.) But the failure of private law autonomy need not mean the endorsement of unlimited instrumentalism. Autonomists are correct in emphasizing the normative significance of the bipolar structure of private law litigation. Furthermore, they are right when stating that by ignoring this feature of private law, instrumentalism may undermine private law's integrity and legitimacy.

These two propositions yield the main conclusion of this chapter: the normative infrastructure of any private law doctrine should be responsive both to (minor) bipolarity requirement on the one hand, and to social values appropriate to the pertinent category of human interaction on the other. This conclusion demonstrates again the significance of the legal realist insight that law is necessarily about both science and craft. It also shows that a proper understanding of private law requires, as legal realism prescribes, to investigate the ways in which these external and internal perspectives on law can be accommodated, rather than focusing on only one perspective, to the exclusion of the other. (To clarify: the responsiveness to social values is limited to the task of prescribing private law rules, namely, justifying private law entitlements. My claim should not be confused with the discredited contention that in evaluating individual cases judges should make ad hoc judgments based on these values.) In what follows, I try to defend this conclusion and demonstrate some of its applications and implications for three specific doctrinal issues: marital property, monetary remedies for breach of entitlements, and right of entry (into property), addressed in Parts II, III, and IV.

I. Neither (Wholly) Autonomous, nor (Purely) Instrumental

A. *Instrumentalists versus Autonomists*

Private law theory can be told as a story of the competition between two accounts of the relationships between private law and social values. On one side of this watershed are the instrumentalists. At its bluntest, instrumentalism stands for the proposition that private law is merely one form of regulation. Private law is, in this view, indistinguishable from other regulatory regimes, either in the type of aims it can promote or in the means it can legitimately use in order to achieve them.[5] Thus, for instance, nothing prevents private law from pursuing such aims as condemning antisocial behavior or promoting the interests of parties other than the plaintiff and the defendant. Similarly, punitive—and not only compensatory—damages are free game for private law, if their use is helpful for a pertinent purpose. In short, blunt instrumentalism perceives civil suits as one "mechanism whereby the state authorizes private parties to enforce the law."[6]

Private law autonomists are on the other side of this divide. Proponents of this position argue that no social purpose or social value, even if ostensibly desirable otherwise, can legitimately inform private law. Private law, in this view, is a realm with its own inner intelligibility, isolated from the social, economic, cultural, and political realms. This isolation derives from the bilateral logic of private law adjudication understood as a unique forum for the vindication of infringed rights. As such, private law must comply with the injunction of correlativity, requiring both that the reasons underlying the plaintiff's right be the same as the reasons that justify the defendant's duty, and that these very reasons also explain the specific remedy inflicted on the defendant. The commands of correlativity, in this view, are so robust that they leave no space for any other (social) value.[7]

In what follows, I claim that autonomists are correct to oppose a full-blown instrumentalization of private law, but too often exaggerate the implications of this insight. I will also argue that many so-called public values do, and in fact should, inform private law without undermining the normative significance of its bipolarity. In this sense, then, private law can never be autonomous from the state whose values it is supposed to promote. (Notice that here, as elsewhere in this chapter, "state" should be read as synonymous with "public" or "collective," rather than with "government" or "national."[8]) These claims will prove compatible rather than conflicting with some of private law's

---

5. Expectedly, the distinction between private law adjudication and public law regulation is particularly blurred in some law and economics accounts of the common law. *See, e.g.,* RICHARD A. POSNER, ECONOMIC ANALYSIS OF LAW 383–85 (6th ed. 2003).

6. Edward L. Rubin, *Punitive Damages: Reconceptualizing the Runcible Remedies of Common Law*, 1998 WIS. L. REV. 131, 154.

7. *See, e.g.,* ERNEST J. WEINRIB, THE IDEA OF PRIVATE LAW 3–14, 212, 214 (1995); Ernest J. Weinrib, *Restitutionary Damages as Corrective Justice*, 1 THEORETICAL INQUIRIES IN LAW 1, 3–5, 37 (1999).

8. For this helpful distinction, see Gunther Teubner, *State Policies in Private Law? A Comment on Hanoch Dagan*, 56 AM. J. COMP. L. 835 (2008); Christiane C. Wendehorst, *The State as the Foundation of Reasoning in Private Law*, 56 AM. J. COMP. L. 567 (2008); *see also infra* note 28.

most characteristic features, notably its heterogeneity. Furthermore, nothing in my argument necessitates the collapse of the private–public distinction, although my account does require a rephrasing of its foundations.

B. *Striking a Middle-Ground*

Private law is not just a means for normative regulation. Rather, intrinsic to private law are features that constrain the types of rules it can legitimately promulgate. The reason is that private law—as law more generally—is a coercive mechanism, which means it must also be a justificatory practice.[9] For private law, this means that judges should be able to justify to defendants all aspects of their state-mandated power. Private law autonomists—notably Ernest Weinrib[10]—are particularly helpful in elucidating the justificatory burden of private law adjudication as a bilateral interaction between a particular plaintiff and a particular defendant in which one party's triumph is the other's defeat. As they insist, private law should be able to justify to defendants both the identity of the beneficiary of any liability imposed on them and the exact type and degree (or magnitude) of that liability. The correlativity requirement answers exactly this concern insofar as it insists that the defendant's liability and remedy correspond to the plaintiff's entitlement.

Such correlativity indeed captures the distinction between private law and regulation, and is thus essential to the integrity of private law. But the correlativity between plaintiff's entitlement and defendant's liability should not obscure the rich social fabric that serves as the inevitable context for the parties' relationship. Thus, contrary to the autonomists' thesis, correlativity need not mean that private law has, or should have, an inner intelligibility decipherable without recourse to social values. Quite to the contrary, private law can neither be explained nor justified in isolation from the social values that determine its initial entitlements.

The canonical, if at times implicit, strategy for deriving the thesis of private law autonomy from correlativity is to rely on the idea of property. Property, in this view, serves as a benchmark requiring no reference to collective (or state) values: whereas voluntary changes in the distribution of property obviously cannot generate any legitimate grievance, involuntary changes both justify owners' complaints and specify the appropriate remedial response.[11]

9. On the dialectical relation between law's coercion and its nature as a justificatory practice, see *supra* Part II of Chapter 2.

10. *See supra* note 7.

11. *See* Weinrib, *supra* note 7, at 6–7, 12, 24; *see also, e.g.,* Ross B. Grantham & Charles E.F. Rickett, Enrichment and Restitution in New Zealand 485 (2000); Peter Benson, *Contract as Transfer of Ownership*, 48 Wm. & Mary L. Rev. 1673 (2007).

Property is indeed a key, and perhaps even *the* key, concept of private law. But the reference to property cannot resolve the debate. As an essentially contested concept,[12] property is open to competing interpretations and permutations.[13] There is no inevitable content to property, and the choice among its competing configurations entails significant distributive consequences: each additional stick in the owner's bundle of rights, and any expansion of an existing stick, is ipso facto a burden on nonowners.[14] Thus, no arbitration among the different available conceptions of property is possible without some normative apparatus.[15] Property is not a panacea that can miraculously detach private law from social values.[16] The doctrinal choice among competing theories of property—each of which may well be robust enough to serve as a benchmark—is itself implicated in, and is a construction of, social values. Therefore, reliance on the concept of property only obscures the distributive and expressive implications of this choice,[17] thus undermining the most fundamental commitment of private law: to be a justificatory practice.

To be sure, neo-Kantian autonomists have advanced theories of property that purport to support a division of labor between a private law, which is strictly libertarian, and a robust welfare state, which remedies the resultant threat of dependence.[18] But as I show elsewhere, the public law of tax and redistribution is unlikely to supplement private law with rules adequately remedying the injustices of a libertarian private law, if not in terms of distribution at least in terms of interpersonal dependence. The realities of interest group

---

12. *See* Walter Bryce Gallie, *Essentially Contested Concepts*, 56 PROCEEDINGS OF THE ARISTOTELIAN SOCIETY (New Series) 167 (1956).

13. *See, e.g.*, JOSEPH WILLIAM SINGER, ENTITLEMENT: THE PARADOXES OF PROPERTY 7 (2000).

14. *See* Wesley Newcomb Hohfeld, *Fundamental Legal Conceptions as Applied in Judicial Reasoning*, 26 YALE L.J. 710 (1917); Joseph William Singer, *The Legal Rights Debate in Analytical Jurisprudence from Bentham to Hohfeld*, 1982 WIS. L. REV. 975. Nothing in the text should be interpreted as supporting the view that property is just a "laundry list" of substantive rights with a limitless number of possible permutations. *See* HANOCH DAGAN, PROPERTY: VALUES AND INSTITUTIONS pt. I (2011).

15. The need for a normative defense of private law's distributive implications is not premised on any claim or presupposition that the reasons for its structure are distributive. *Contra* Ernest J. Weinrib, *Restoring Restitution*, 91 VA. L. REV. 861, 876 (2005) (reviewing HANOCH DAGAN, THE LAW AND ETHICS OF RESTITUTION (2004)). Rather, it is founded on their critical ramifications on people's lives.

16. *Cf.* James Gordley, *The Purpose of Awarding Restitutionary Damages: A Reply to Professor Weinrib*, 1 THEORETICAL INQUIRIES IN LAW 39, 41, 45, 48 (1999); Robert L. Rabin, *Law for Law's Sake*, 105 YALE L.J. 2261, 2270 (1996); Kenneth W. Simons, *Justification in Private Law*, 81 CORNELL L. REV. 698, 737 (1996); Stephen A. Smith, *The Idea of Private Law*, 112 LAW Q. REV. 363, 365 (1996).

17. *Cf.* CRAIG ROTHERHAM, PROPRIETARY REMEDIES IN CONTEXT: A STUDY IN THE JUDICIAL REDISTRIBUTION OF PROPERTY RIGHTS (2002).

18. *See* ARTHUR RIPSTEIN, FORCE AND FREEDOM: KANT'S LEGAL AND POLITICAL PHILOSOPHY chs. 3, 4 & 9 (2009); ERNEST J. WEINRIB, *Poverty and Property in Kant's System of Rights*, *in* CORRECTIVE JUSTICE 263 (2012).

politics in the promulgation of tax legislation render egalitarian tax regimes (such as one based on Rawls's difference principle) a matter of political theory rather than of empirical reality. This difficulty is intrinsic to the concept of democracy, which respects people's preferences and not only their principles. Furthermore, because our understandings of the responsibilities of owners and the limits of what we perceive to be their legitimate interests are influenced by our legal conception of ownership, an extreme libertarian private law regime might undermine social solidarity and dilute people's responsiveness to claims from distributive justice. Finally, treating the propertyless as passive recipients of welfare and mere beneficiaries of the public duty to support the poor entrenches their dependent, subservient status rather than their dignity and independence. Shifting dependence from the context of private law to that of the individual's relationship with the state via the welfare bureaucracy does not solve the problem and, indeed, might actually exacerbate it.[19]

The reliance of property on social values is particularly clear for those who accept the realist conception of property I defend in my book, *Property: Values and Institution*[20] (and describe in somewhat more detail than here in Part IV of Chapter 8 of this book). In this view, property is an umbrella for a set of institutions (property institutions) that bear family resemblances. The meaning of property—the contents of an owner's entitlements—varies with the divergent categories of social settings in which it is situated as well as with the categories of resources that are subject to property rights. At least ideally, property institutions both construct and reflect the ideal ways in which people interact in a given category of social contexts (e.g., market, community, family) and with respect to a given category of resources (e.g., land, copyright, patents). Thus, some property institutions are structured along the lines of the Blackstonian conception of property as "sole despotic dominion."[21] These institutions are atomistic and competitive, and they vindicate people's negative liberty. In other cases, such as that of marital property[22] (where ownership is a locus of sharing), a much more communitarian view of property may dominate. And in yet many other cases along the spectrum between strangers and spouses there are shades and hues: cases where both liberty and community are of the essence, and the applicable property configuration includes both rights and responsibilities.

The implausibility of isolating private law from social values does not render correlativity vacuous; it does not, in other words, collapse private law into just another form of regulation. After all, as Weinrib correctly insists,

19. *See* DAGAN, *supra* note 14, at 63–66.
20. *See* DAGAN, *supra* note 14.
21. WILLIAM BLACKSTONE, 2 COMMENTARIES ON THE LAWS OF ENGLAND *2 (University of Chicago ed., 1979) (1765–69).
22. *See infra* Part II.

taking correlativity seriously precludes assertions that the plaintiff's right is simply the "analytic reflex" of the defendant's duty (or vice versa).[23] Yet, understanding that correlativity is situated within a thick layer of social values does require a more modest formulation of the correlativity injunction.

In this formulation, correlativity prescribes that it is not enough for a plaintiff to demonstrate the desirability of the state of affairs that would result if the type of complaint she raises were to generate the remedy sought. Rather, a private law plaintiff has an additional justificatory burden: to give reasons people in her predicament should be entitled to extract from people in the defendant's category the kind of remedy she now requires. This additional hurdle is obviously crossed in some cases, as in the paradigmatic case of an injured plaintiff seeking a remedy from a defendant who negligently caused her harm. But some cases are more challenging as, for instance, when the defendant can plausibly ask "why me?" (why should she be forced to be the agent of remedying the plaintiff's unjustified harsh predicament?), or "why you?" (why should the plaintiff be allowed to invoke the state's machinery to remove an unjust privilege that the defendant currently holds?). Moreover, even if the plaintiff has good answers to both questions, she still needs to justify her entitlement to the specific measure of recovery she seeks to impose on the defendant.

Insofar as our social values inform our ideals regarding the relationship between the plaintiff category and the defendant category (as, for example, spouses, neighbors, co-owners, members of the same community, transactors, competitors, or drivers and pedestrians), they can—indeed, should—also inform the answers to this set of questions. Social values that are credibly relevant to these normative inquiries—"internal" social values—define the *ex ante* entitlements of the litigating parties and hence their legitimate expectations from one another. They thus serve as the foundation of the parties' bilateral relationships. Therefore, such social values are importantly different from other "external" values or public policies whose guidance is more problematic to private law because they impose on the parties goals that are alien to their bipolar relationship.

Weinrib goes further by also requiring that the reasons for the parties' entitlements—and not only the entitlements themselves—are correlative, namely that these reasons themselves are entirely internal to the parties' relationship.[24] But this additional requirement of relational reasons is excessively demanding and unwarranted. The bipolar form of private law is only one (important) object of the justificatory burden prompted by each application of state coercion. Therefore, although cases in which the reasons for the parties' entitlements are correlative are indeed easier cases (insofar as the integrity

23. WEINRIB, *supra* note 7, at 124.
24. *See* Weinrib, *supra* note 15, at 869–74.

of private law is concerned), this does and should not imply that they are the only cases. Nor should we a priori assume that even if the reasons are not correlative their implications with respect to the parties' entitlements will not be sufficiently convergent. In other words, private law's bipolar form should not be entitled to exclusivity in determining the types of normative considerations we must take into account; it should not be allowed to overwhelm our justificatory inquiry. Hence, no fast-and-easy way is available for determining the limits of private law. Each type of case requires a careful account of the reasons for and against recognizing the plaintiff's entitlement vis-à-vis the defendant. These very reasons, it is important to add, are of the kind autonomists try to exclude from private law, namely whether law's endorsement of such claims supports or distorts the ideal construction of the type of relationship under consideration, and whether using private law in this way is both necessary and overall conducive to the public purpose at hand.

Three clarifications may be in order at this point. First, although the practical implications of this additional inquiry are limited, they are by no means trivial. Indeed, because I take seriously the requirement that the plaintiff give reasons why someone in her predicament should be entitled to extract from someone such as the defendant the kind of remedy she now requires, my position does not collapse into blunt instrumentalism. Thus, the conclusion in some cases is that allowing a private law claim of the sort required would be unjust, even when likely to bring about a desirable state of affairs. And yet, a complaint in private law may still, at times, justifiably involve the interests of numerous other potential plaintiffs, so that the actual plaintiff serves as a so-called private attorney general.[25] Likewise, it may justifiably target many or all members of a group who have profited from a risky activity in which the plaintiff was injured.[26] Neither feature should *necessarily* prevent the complaint from proceeding if the justificatory burden of showing the desirability of allowing it in its private law form is, on balance, properly met.[27]

---

25. On the concept of private attorney general, see, e.g., William B. Rubenstein, *On What a "Private Attorney General" Is—and Why It Matters*, 57 VAND. L. REV. 2129 (2004).

26. As in cases seeking market-share liability, see Sindell v. Abbott Labs., 607 P.2d 924, 935–38 (1980).

27. *Cf.* Alice Erh-Son Tay & Eugene Kamenka, *Public Law—Private Law*, in PUBLIC AND PRIVATE IN SOCIAL LIFE 67, 89 (S.I. Benn & G.F. Gaus eds. 1983). As an aside, notice that at times special attention is called to reasons for *not* allowing a private law claim and not just to reasons *for* allowing it. Thus, for example, enforcing certain competition rules may admittedly be furthered by providing not only regulators (and consumers) but also competitors with a cause of action. *See* Ofer Grosskopf, *Protection of Competition Rules via the Law of Restitution*, 79 TEX. L. REV. 1981 (2001). But such an instrumentalist use of private law may be unfortunate overall if it facilitates bypassing the discretion of public officials, insofar as such discretion is aimed at continuously adjusting a policy of enforcing these rules so as to optimally serve the public interest.

Second, in a Comment on the previous published version of this chapter, Gunther Teubner refers to the ideal construction of the type of relationship under consideration as "the 'living legal relation' between the actors involved...their social interaction and...the broader social system in which their concrete relation is embedded." Teubner makes a sharp contrast between "state policies and public values" on the one hand and "the inner normativity of diverse social institutions" on the other. In Teubner's view, the former have no role in private law, whereas the latter is all-important. Thus, he identifies private law's central role as the juridification of "diverse processes of decentralized spontaneous norm-formation in civil society" and the constitutionalization of "the autonomy of many diverse social configurations."[28] Insofar as Teubner seeks to emphasize the importance of private law's heterogeneity, I happily agree, as is evident from my realist conception of property mentioned above and further elaborated in my celebration in Chapter 8 of private law's pluralism. Furthermore, as long as it is clear, as Teubner states later in his Comment, that the internal values of these private law institutions are themselves (at least partly) public and collective, I also by and large accept his insistence that external arguments can play a role if and only if they are compatible with these internal values.

Finally, realizing that the injunction to comply with the prescription of correlativity is only one, albeit important, component of private law's justificatory burden implies that correlativity may at times be outweighed by stronger competing normative concerns. Thus, there may be classes of cases in which the interest of third parties *is* part of the justificatory premise for the parties' entitlements even though allowing such external reasons admittedly creates a justificatory deficit.[29] Given the forward-looking consequences of any significant legal pronouncement, law's carriers are also necessarily responsible to other parties who may be affected even if this responsibility is less pressing (because it is somewhat remote) than their responsibility toward the plaintiff and defendant categories. As Weinrib recently acknowledged, "[i]n adjudication, a court combines these two dimensions by projecting its own omnilateral authority onto the parties' bilateral relationship [] thereby extend[ing] the significance of its decision beyond the specific dispute, making it a norm for all members of the state." Weinrib, however, considers that the implications of this forward-looking dimension of adjudication are modest: they are

---

28. Teubner, *supra* note 8, at 841–42.

29. An important example of this possibility in contemporary restitution law is the expansion of the doctrine governing self-regarding conferral of benefits to the innovative pattern of governments' restitution claims against injurious industries for preventive and ameliorative costs spent due to the wrongs of these industries. *See* Hanoch Dagan, *Just and Unjust Enrichments*, in THE GOALS OF PRIVATE LAW 423, 442–43 (Andrew Robertson & Tang Hang Wu eds., 2009).

exhausted by two requirements—"publicness" (namely, "exhibiting justifications for liability that are accessible to public reason") and "systematicity"
(i.e., "acting within its competence as an adjudicative body" and making "[t]he
principle of the decision...cohere with the entire ensemble of similarly binding decisions").[30] Given the significance of these forward-looking effects of
adjudication, however, limiting the implications of the practice of precedent
in this fashion is puzzling. It is hard to see why judges should have no *substantive* duty to justify their decisions to those who will be subject to them, even
if those affected are not participating in the judicial drama at hand. In other
words, although the default position of private law should be that only internal values can legitimately shape its rules, this presumption can be overcome
in the face of stronger competing normative concerns that call for the incorporation of external values to a particular private law doctrine.

To conclude: private law is structured as a drama between plaintiff and
defendant. Therefore, autonomists rightfully claim that if it is to retain its
nature as a justificatory practice, this feature of private law requires paying
special attention to the correlativity between the defendant's liability and the
plaintiff's entitlement. This concession, however, does not entail the dissoci-
ation of private law from our public values. Quite to the contrary, the pivotal
role of private law in defining our mutual legitimate claims and expectations
in our daily interactions undermines the legitimacy of a private law regime
that ignores these values. For this reason, the parties' *ex ante* entitlements,
from which this correlativity must be measured, are best analyzed by reference to our social values.[31]

C. The Private–Public Distinction

Before I move on to the three examples that I hope will demonstrate as well
as justify these abstract claims, I need to address briefly one of the typical
battlegrounds between autonomists and instrumentalists: the private–public distinction. Here, as elsewhere, their positions tend to be diametrically
opposed. Devoted autonomists vigorously guard the division between private
and public law, insisting that these are two distinct legal domains, obeying
different logics and guided by different regulative principles.[32] By contrast,
staunch instrumentalists—and critical legal scholars tend to be the bluntest

---

30. Ernest J. Weinrib, *Private Law and Public Right*, 61 U. TORONTO L.J. 191, 196–98
(2011).
31. *Cf.* JAMES GORDLEY, FOUNDATIONS OF PRIVATE LAW: PROPERTY, TORT, CONTRACT,
UNJUST ENRICHMENT 11 (2006); Peter Cane, *Distributive Justice and Tort Law*, 2001
N.Z.L. REV. 401.
32. *See, e.g.,* NIGEL E. SIMMONDS, *The Decline of Juridical Reason, in* DOCTRINE AND
THEORY IN THE LEGAL ORDER 121, 128, 130–31 (1984); WEINRIB, *supra* note 7, at
204–31.

here—ridicule the private–public distinction as an arcane residue of legal for-malism.[33] The instrumentalist recommendation is simply to ignore this dis-tinction and consider private law as that part of public law that happens to regulate relations between private parties.[34]

Not surprisingly, I find both these positions lacking. Autonomists are mis-taken, as the recourse of both public and private law to a social values founda-tion implies that the private–public distinction is far from airtight and by no means natural or conceptually inevitable. Even more significantly, this conti-nuity between private and public law means that private law, just like public law, should not be immune to a distributive analysis. Private lawyers, like their public brethren, should (also) invariably consider the distributive implications of the rules they advocate or apply.[35]

For good normative reasons, however, the law should retain the separate legal construction of horizontal and vertical social interactions.[36] The bipolar-ity of private law, then, is not the only characteristic challenging the collapse of private into public law, and such a radical move is also resisted by valid social values. Thus, some of our most important normative commitments—to freedom-enhancing pluralism and individuality-enhancing multiplicity—jus-tify adhering to, and indeed facilitating, the differentiation between the private and the public so as to fracture and multiply human authority.[37] Fundamental principles of democratic governance also justify imposing on public authori-ties particularly demanding obligations of trust, which are inappropriate to most (although not necessarily all) private actors.[38] The private–public dis-tinction serves as a means for entrenching these expectations and the ideals for which they stand.

With these theoretical observations at hand, I turn now to the three exam-ples I intend to use as case studies, demonstrating that the account of private

33. *See, e.g.*, Duncan Kennedy, *The Stages of the Decline of the Public/Private Distinction*, 130 U. PA. L. REV. 1249 (1982).

34. *See, e.g.*, MARK KELMAN, A GUIDE TO CRITICAL LEGAL STUDIES 102–09 (1987); Karl E. Klare, *The Public/Private Distinction in Labor Law*, 130 U. PA. L. REV. 1358, 1384, 1417–20 (1982). For early incarnations of this view, see, e.g., HANS KELSEN, PURE THEORY OF LAW 280–83 (Max Knight trans., 1967); Morris R. Cohen, *The Basis of Contract*, 46 HARV. L. REV. 553, 589 (1933).

35. *See, e.g.*, HANOCH DAGAN, UNJUST ENRICHMENT: A STUDY OF PRIVATE LAW AND PUBLIC VALUES (1997); Gregory C. Keating, *Rawlsian Fairness and Regime Choice in the Law of Accidents*, 72 FORDHAM L. REV. 1857 (2004); Anthony Kronman, *Contracts and Distributive Justice*, 89 YALE L.J. 472, 501 (1980).

36. Nothing in this claim implies the homogeneity of either side of the private–public divide. In particular, preserving the private–public distinction (as reformulated herein) does not impinge upon or undermine the heterogeneity of private law.

37. *See* DON HERZOG: HAPPY SLAVES: A CRITIQUE OF CONSENT THEORY 156, 166–68, 173–75 (1989).

38. *See* Nicholas Bamforth, *The Public Law—Private Law Distinction: A Comparative and Philosophical Approach*, in ADMINISTRATIVE LAW FACING THE FUTURE: OLD

law sketched above provides a better explanatory framework than both the autonomist and the instrumentalist alternatives.

II. Marital Property

Marital property, an issue I have discussed at length elsewhere,[39] will serve well as the first example. It shows the kind of internal social values necessary for providing a credible understanding of existing law. It also demonstrates the types of external public concerns that should probably not be allowed to define the *ex ante* entitlements of the litigating parties.

The starting point for any modern discussion of marital property law (at least in liberal democracies) must be the rule of equal division upon divorce. Although this is a relatively late rule in marital property law, we can now hardly think of marital property law without equal division, which is probably the feature least contested by courts, commentators, and lay people alike, at least on theoretical grounds.[40] It is therefore surprising that the underlying justification for equality is far from settled.

The main justification offered for this rule fits the autonomist conception of private law because it does not refer to, let alone rely on, any social vision of the ideal marriage. Rather, it rests on an understanding of private law as a realm of interaction between autonomous individuals holding absolute property rights. It also invokes the contribution theory that, in the Lockean tradition, stands for pre-legal notions of justice.[41] Equal division, in this view, simply reflects an accurate valuation of both spouses' contribution, taking into account nonmarket work and interpersonal support.[42]

But this seemingly appealing explanation is factually implausible. The nonmarket contribution and the interpersonal skills of the spouse with less market power would not, ordinarily, equalize the significant differences in market

CONSTRAINTS AND NEW HORIZONS 136, 138 (Peter Leyland & Terry Woods eds., 1997).

39. *See* DAGAN, *supra* note 14, at ch. 9.

40. *See, e.g.*, Marsha Garrison, *The Economic Consequences of Divorce: Would Adoption of the ALI Principles Improve Current Outcomes?*, 8 DUKE J. GENDER L. & POL'Y 119, 124 (2001).

41. *See* STEPHEN BUCKLE, NATURAL LAW AND THE THEORY OF PROPERTY 149–52 (1991); STEPHEN R. MUNZER, A THEORY OF PROPERTY 255–56, 285–87 (1990). The text should not be read as an endorsement of Locke's tormented account of property, which has been extensively and persuasively criticized. *See, e.g.*, GOPAL SREENIVASAN, THE LIMITS OF LOCKEAN RIGHT IN PROPERTY (1995); WALDRON, *supra* note 20, at 137–252.

42. *See, e.g.*, AMERICAN LAW INSTITUTE, PRINCIPLES OF THE LAW OF FAMILY DISSOLUTION: ANALYSIS AND RECOMMENDATIONS § 4.09, at 735 (2000); MARY ANN GLENDON, THE NEW FAMILY AND THE NEW PROPERTY 63 (1981).

power pervading social life.[43] To be sure, the intuition to equalize marital contributions taps into a deep truth of marriage: it would be inappropriate for
one spouse to think of the other as an unequal partner, as a free rider in the
collective enterprise. But this truism is not based on a meaningfully objective
calculation. In other words, although both spouses are certainly expected to
contribute to the marital community, desert is not the foundation of equal
division. Indeed, equal division stands *against* any sort of investigation into
the interior functioning of the marital community to determine individual
desert. Fifty percent is the number that best demonstrates that no party is
more entitled to the marital assets than the other.

   This more plausible understanding of equal division, the most fundamental and indisputable rule of marital property law, relies on an ideal conception
for the institution of marriage. I maintain that equal division can be readily
justified as a manifestation of the ideal of marriage as an egalitarian liberal
community. In this perfectionist vision, a commitment to marital community
wherein spouses share without reference to individual desert combines with
a concern for non-subordination and the protection of individual autonomy
through, primarily, free exit.[44]

   More precisely, the ideal of marriage as an egalitarian liberal community
perceives marriage as reflecting a plural subject that generates the potential
for intimacy, caring and commitment, and meaningful self-identification.
The projects of marriage, including the common management of resources,
facilitate these virtues by providing opportunities for an intensive, long-term
fusion of the couple. This (partial) fusion forms the basis for the sharing
principle. Sharing both the advantages and difficulties of a joint life, infus-
ing costs and benefits with an intersubjective character, and rejecting any
strict accounting based on individual merit, is the linchpin of the marital community. But although the marital ideal is inherently communal, it is
also bounded by a commitment to autonomy as free exit and to equality as
non-subordination. No-fault divorce, the legal manifestation of spouses' right
to exit, is an important feature of the ideal marriage because it clearly distinguishes between marital communities as good for spouses and marital communities as exercises in self-denial. The legal right to free exit is a prerequisite
of a self-directed life, a precondition of the ability to form, revise, and pursue
our own ends. This right is particularly important in marriage because, in the
liberal conception, the communal goods of marriage are all part of the good
life for individuals, not a legal duty they must bear regardless of its continuing
appeal. Furthermore, the legal right to free exit is an important means for the

---

43. This is also why another proposed explanation, relying on the spouses' hypothetical consent, is dubious. *See* DAGAN, *supra* note 14, at 212.
44. The following paragraphs summarize the thesis developed in DAGAN, *supra* note
14, at ch. 9.

continuing reaffirmation of the spouses' plural identity. Finally, like autonomy, equality is also a constraint and a core feature of the ideal of marriage. It is a constraint because disparity in the control and possession of the goods of marriage (the most pervasive human engagement) leads to subordination, which systematically and pervasively denies the importance of one spouse and threatens his or her basic personhood. It is a core feature of the ideal of marriage because subordination is a threat to the communal nature of marriage itself: hierarchy, exploitation, and oppression subvert intimacy, caring and commitment, and meaningful self-identification.

An important challenge to a marital property law that seeks to follow this ideal of marriage is to provide institutional guarantees of gender equality to support the community of marriage in a liberal context of free exit. Equal division is one important means for this aim, although, in an environment of pervasive gender inequality, it is certainly not sufficient. Equal division treats each party identically and thus erases, for the duration of marriage, men's greater power to gather resources in the market. Moreover, equal division of existing marital assets most clearly sends a message of ownership: the award is not a social welfare handout, but an entitlement. Finally, not only does equal division vindicate equality and thus also equal exit, but it also serves as a locus of plural identity uniquely appropriate for the marital community. Equal division spreads the benefits and the risks of sharing behavior equally between the parties, thus transforming personal pursuits into joint endeavors.

To understand spouses' claims for 50 percent of the marital estate as expressing the ideal view of marriage as an egalitarian liberal community is to recognize the decisive place of social values in shaping this important doctrine of private law. And yet, it would be both wrong and misleading to use this example to justify private law instrumentalism or evoke concern among guardians of the integrity of private law.

To see why, compare our case with Augustus' use of matrimonial law for population policy,[45] an example rightfully deemed obnoxious. (As Nils Jansen and Ralf Michaels report, this use occurred "only shortly before . . . a principle of public utility eroded all individual liberty . . . and became the guiding measure of all law under the absolutistic, personal domination of the late [Roman] emperors."[46]) The reason it so obviously represents an abuse of private law is that the promotion of a population policy cannot plausibly inform the entitlements of spouses against one another. This is not a logical but rather a normative claim about the legitimacy of even considering the issue of population policy when constructing the legal framework governing the spouses' relationship. Why should a spouse who infringes a governmental population policy be accountable to the other? In fact, such a liability would easily make the

45. Jansen & Michaels, *supra* note 1, at 364.
46. *Id.*

parties' relationship appear less attractive. By contrast, the ideal of marriage as an egalitarian liberal community does not impose external goals on the parties' bipolar relationship, meaning goals that are alien or even potentially subversive to their relationship. The ideal of marriage as an egalitarian liberal community is what defines, or should define,[47] the spouses' *ex ante* entitlements and hence their bilateral legitimate expectations. This ideal entails a property configuration very different from the monistic Blackstonian model that autonomists assume pervades private law. Once translated into legal doctrine, however, the ideal of marriage as an egalitarian liberal community is simply the foundation of the bilateral relationships within the marital community rather than an intrusive public policy.

The ideal of marriage can serve as an instance of an "internal social value," and population policy as one of an "external social value" that threatens to have an illegitimate impact from outside on the spouses' relationship. Yet there are also hard cases of social values that fail to fit clearly on one or another side of the divide. Consider the question of whether divorce law should address the issue of gender discrimination. On its face, the challenge of gender imbalances is a clear example of a social purpose external to the marital community and thus worth addressing only in an instrumentalist understanding of private law. But gender inequality is not a problem merely for women individually but also for the institution of marriage, as serious disparities between the post-divorce financial status of men and women[48] give men greater bargaining power within the marriage, raising the specter of subordination.[49]

If men and women entered and left marriage equally able to earn an income in the market, the rule of equal property division would be perfectly consistent with the vision of egalitarian marriage. But although equal division sends a message of equal entitlement and partially neutralizes men's greater market power vis-à-vis the resources of the marital community, it falls short of adequately addressing this challenge.[50] This predicament implies that a noninstrumental marital property law, guided by the ideal of marriage as an egalitarian

---

47. As the text implies, understanding marital property law as grounded in the ideal of marriage as an egalitarian liberal community yields suggestions for reform, both regarding the scope of the marital estate and its governance during an intact marriage. See DAGAN, *supra* note 14, at 214–16, 223–27 (endorsing a broad definition of the marital estate that encompasses any changes effected during the tenure of marriage in the spouses' earning capacity, and a recognition of both spouses' interests in the marital estate as present and vested during the marriage rather than as mere expectancies that are only meaningful upon divorce).

48. See, e.g., LENORE J. WEITZMAN, THE DIVORCE REVOLUTION: THE UNEXPECTED SOCIAL AND ECONOMIC CONSEQUENCES FOR WOMEN AND CHILDREN IN AMERICA 323–56 (1985).

49. See SUSAN MOLLER OKIN, JUSTICE, GENDER, AND THE FAMILY 147 (1989).

50. See Martha L. Fineman, *Implementing Equality: Ideology, Contradiction and Social Change*, 1983 WIS. L. REV. 789, 827–30.

liberal community, should offer an inevitably imprecise remedial response mitigating the devastating consequences of gender inequality for marriage without imposing its entire burden on spouses (mostly, men).

This is the role of the recent practice of rehabilitative alimony.[51] Rehabilitative alimony does not require former husbands to equalize their wives' financial situations for the remainder of their lives. Such a requirement would impose a prohibitive exit tax on men, undermining not only the autonomy of spouses but also the community as a whole, constituted as it is of voluntary attachments. Rather, rehabilitative alimony is expressly aimed toward self-sufficiency, giving women the tools to overcome their market disadvantages. Its purpose is merely to cover the education or training of spouses with a smaller income to enable them to support themselves better after divorce.[52] These awards are inherently time-limited, so that their impact on exit is restricted. To be sure, rehabilitative alimony does place some of the burdens of gender discrimination on the alimony-paying spouse, but this is hardly unfair because he too benefits from the arrangement. To the extent that he desires the unique goods arising from communal marriage, he benefits from lessening the threat that gender inequality poses to genuine community. A limited alimony obligation enables him to participate in and benefit from a good marriage without unduly compromising his autonomy.

III. Monetary Remedies

My second example of the way social values inform private law without undermining its distinctive features also builds on my previous work.[53] This example shows more particularly that even goals ostensibly public (and thus unlikely to legitimately affect the parties' bilateral relationship) fit, if properly analyzed, into the logic of correlativity[54]—suggesting that the practical implications of correlativity may well be far more modest than autonomists imply.

The current issue is the choice of monetary remedies for the infringement of entitlements in such cases as trespass, conversion, or the breach of various types of intellectual property rights. Prevailing doctrine reveals a variety of measures of recovery depending on the type of resource at stake.[55] Thus,

---

51. For a critique of other attempts to explain rehabilitative alimony, see DAGAN, *supra* note 14, at 220–21.

52. *See* John C. Williams, Annotation,*Propriety in Divorce Proceedings of Awarding Rehabilitative Alimony*, 97 A.L.R.3D 740, 743–44 (1980).

53. DAGAN, *supra* note 35.

54. *Cf.* Peter Cane, *Corrective Justice and Correlativity in Private Law*, 16 OXFORD J.L. STUD. 471, 481–82 (1996).

55. This was first noted in Daniel Friedmann, *Restitution of Benefits Obtained through the Appropriation of Property or the Commission of a Wrong*, 80 COLUM. L. REV. 504, 512–13, 556–57 (1980).

concerning some resources, the sheer infringement of the plaintiff's right triggers a rather severe measure of recovery that allows her to choose between the fair market value of the resource, or its unauthorized use, and the net profit gained by the defendant. In American law, this is the case respecting infringements of the plaintiff's rights to her identity, physical integrity, or land. On the other hand, the invasion of other types of resources triggers pecuniary recovery only if the defendant employed improper means: the sheer appropriation of trade secrets or pre-contractual expectations triggers no liability. In between these poles, there are several other interesting points. Thus, the infringement of copyright allows the plaintiff to choose between the fair market value of the copyright at issue and a proportional part of the defendant's profits. The infringement of patents, however, allows a plaintiff only the recovery of fair market value.[56]

As I show elsewhere,[57] this diversity of recovery measures regarding various resources is neither chaotic nor unprincipled, but reflects the extent to which a community perceives them to be constitutive of their possessor's identity. The more closely a resource is attached to its holder's identity, the greater the degree of protection accorded to it, and vice versa. For our purposes, focusing on profits and fair market value—the two measures of recovery most frequently used in such cases—should suffice. The measure of profits discourages potential invaders from circumventing the bargaining process and appropriating the protected interest without first securing its holder's consent. Thus, the measure of profits deters nonconsensual invasions. Entitling the resource holder to any net profit the invader may have acquired from the appropriation effectively undoes the forced transfer. Therefore, a profits remedy implies that transfers are legitimate only by obtaining the plaintiff's consent *ex ante*, thereby vindicating her control over the breached entitlement. Prescribing a remedy of fair market value is significantly different. Fair market value is what the defendant would presumably have had to pay to the plaintiff had he not circumvented the bargaining process, even if we take the plaintiff's consent to the transfer for granted. As a remedy, it does not deter appropriations; at times, it may even encourage them. In the absence of a better proxy, fair market value measures an entitlement's objective level of well-being or utility to its holder.[58] Fair market value aims to secure for the plaintiff (merely) the value of the utility that the appropriated resource embodies. Thus, an award of fair market value vindicates the plaintiff's well-being.

Autonomists, who struggle to justify the existing doctrinal heterogeneity, are particularly troubled by deterrence. They perceive deterrence as a public

---

56. For a fuller account, see DAGAN, *supra* note 35, at ch. 4.
57. *Id.* at ch. 2.
58. "Objective" is used here in the sense that the protected utility does not include any psychological utility an owner may produce merely by control over the resource.

purpose, perhaps the most paradigmatic public purpose, which cannot be accommodated within the correlative nature of private law justifications.[59] Properly analyzed, however, the choice between the compensatory measure of fair market value and the deterring measure of profits does not implicate any purpose extrinsic to the parties' relationship. Rather, it requires choosing between two types of entitlements that define this very relationship. The profits measure reflects and reverses a breach of the plaintiff's entitlement to control the resource, whereas the fair market value reflects and reverses a breach of her entitlement to the well-being embodied by the resource. The claims to control and well-being are inherent in the plaintiff's entitlement. These claims entail the applicable measures of recovery in the very strict way that correlativity requires.

Thus, where the law applies the libertarian model of rights and seeks to vindicate the control of a resource holder, it should effectively deter potential infringements by entitling the plaintiff to profits from conscious infringements. Tailoring the remedial response to the standard of effective deterrence need not be construed as an attempt to use the event of the wrong to try to make the world a better place in the future. Rather, a deterring measure of recovery—the *ex post* parallel to injunctive relief—is entailed by law's commitment to take the plaintiff's control seriously, to demonstrate to the defendant that infringing the plaintiff's entitlement is not something he could gain from.[60] In other words, where a profits measure of recovery is appropriate, deterrence is entailed by an entitlement to control and is thus intrinsic to the parties' relationship. By contrast, where the only legitimate claim of the plaintiff to the resource is to the well-being it embodies, she is (only) entitled to the fair market value of its use or alienation. When the entitlement is utilitarian, even an intentional circumvention of the market should not trigger any additional recovery. If we are not to legislate by definitions, we must acknowledge that both alternatives as well as other possible measures of recovery and their corresponding rationales are possible and, at least on their face, legitimate for any type of infringement (for instance, of proprietary and nonproprietary interests alike). A normative discussion, which refers to the ideal reconstruction of the relationship of the type of parties under consideration, is needed to choose among these options.

Furthermore, insofar as control and well-being are concerned, the autonomists' dichotomous distinction between the relationship of particular parties on the one hand, and our social values on the other, is misleading. The fear of imposing external social values on a defendant, who thereby becomes an

---

59. *See* Weinrib, *supra* note 7.

60. This is why, where the risk of under-enforcement is serious and systemic, the law should—and frequently does—apply a multiplier. *See infra* note 66 and accompanying text.

instrument for society's broader goals, is here groundless. These goals, the social visions respecting the parties' relationship, will inevitably define their initial entitlements.[61] It is only by reference to these choices that the injunction to correlate the defendant's liability and remedy to the plaintiff's entitlement is intelligible and normatively desirable.

This analysis, however, does not imply that correlativity allows any type of public concern to guide the law of remedies. Consider rare cases in which private law allows a plaintiff to recover the entire gross proceeds the defendant captured from infringing the plaintiff's entitlement, forbidding the plaintiff to deduct the costs he has in fact incurred in obtaining them. Correlativity explains why this pecuniary remedy is indeed rare. The recovery of the proceeds measure does more than vindicate the resource holder's control. It also expresses society's condemnation of the invader's antisocial behavior, as evident in the punitive forfeiture of part of the defendant's own estate. But condemnation is mostly external to the parties' relationship.[62] Social condemnation cannot be easily condensed into the scope of the plaintiff's entitlement, and we usually have no reason to think that the plaintiff is also entitled to society's disapproval of the defendant's behavior. Quite the contrary: absent a significant countervailing reason,[63] the law is justified in sticking to its convention of endowing only state officials with the authority to condemn, stigmatize, and punish.[64] Allowing private law plaintiffs to take over the task of social condemnation would have (at least in most cases) distorted our ideal construction of the relationship between wrongdoers and their victims as well as undermined the very public purpose of social condemnation.

This constraint is important but rather limited because, as noted, as long as the public purpose (or social value) is capable of legitimately informing the *ex ante* definition of people's entitlements, it is not external to the parties' relationships. Because entitling individuals to society's condemnation is problematic, punishment should generally have no role in private law. Entitling them to the well-being embedded in their resource or to control over it (or to both), however, is perfectly sensible. Both compensation and deterrence, then, are proper goals of private law's pecuniary remedies.

---

61. *Cf.* Ariel Porat, *Questioning the Idea of Correlativity in Weinrib's Theory of Corrective Justice*, 2 THEORETICAL INQUIRIES IN LAW 161, 172, 174 (1999).

62. Ernest J. Weinrib, *Punishment and Disgorgement as Contract Remedies*, 78 CHI.-KENT L. REV. 55, 90–91 (2003).

63. As the text implies, I am not claiming that no such reasons could be adduced. *See, e.g.*, Dan M. Kahan, *Privatizing Criminal Law: Strategies for Private Law Enforcement in the Inner City*, 46 UCLA L. REV. 1859 (1999).

64. *See, e.g.*, CESARE BECCARIA, ON CRIMES AND PUNISHMENT 58 (Henry Paolucci trans., Bobbs-Merrill 1963) (1764) ("[T]he right to inflict punishment is a right not of an individual, but of all citizens, or of their sovereign."); ROBERT NOZICK, ANARCHY, STATE, AND UTOPIA 138 (1974) ("[T]he victim occupies the unhappy special position of victim and is owed compensation, [but] he is not owed punishment.").

This conclusion further emphasizes the limited nature of the constraint posed by the injunction of correlativity, because it means that correlativity does not necessarily rule out all forms of aggravated damages from private law. Thus, because correlativity endorses compensation as an important goal of private law remedies, it also allows aggravated damages addressing the aggravated injury inflicted on the plaintiff by the defendant's malevolence, which injures her feelings of dignity and self-worth.[65] Similarly, because correlativity accepts deterrence as a legitimate goal of private law remedies, it allows a seemingly confiscatory portion of a monetary award if calculated in a way that confirms the plaintiff's control, given systematic and significant probability of under-enforcement (of her own right!).[66] In both cases, aggravated damages properly respond to the defendant's wrong by establishing the plaintiff's entitlement to (respectively) well-being and control.

IV. A Right to Entry

Limits on the right of individual or group property owners to exclude, either by refusing to sell or lease or by insisting that nonowners do not physically enter their land, are usually discussed in terms of the legitimacy or desirability of allowing external public law concerns to infiltrate private law.[67] This is an admittedly important question, but one that I wish to suspend. Instead, the following pages address the limits of exclusion from the perspective of private law per se, and ask whether private law allows, or even requires, some scope for nonowners' right to entry. Although my discussion here is fairly general, it is informed by three types of cases in which existing law limits exclusionary practices and recognizes nonowners' right to entry: common-interest communities law, landlord–tenant law, and the law of public accommodations.

In one quite obvious sense, the prevailing framework for analyzing these cases as involving the impact of public law challenges the autonomy of private law. In another sense, however, it fits the autonomists' understanding of private law, as both opponents and proponents of the approach that allows such impact (implicitly) assume that the right to entry is anathema to private law. This (implicit) presupposition is probably premised on the Blackstonian understanding of property that, as noted, is associated with the autonomist position. But this understanding, again as noted, is unable to do the work ascribed to it because the entitlements configuration of each property

---

65. *See* Weinrib, *supra* note 62, at 91, 98; *see also* Amir Nezar, Note, *Reconciling Punitive Damages with Tort Law's Normative Framework*, 121 YALE L.J. 678 (2011).

66. *See* Hanoch Dagan & James J. White, *Governments, Citizens, and Injurious Industries*, 75 NYU L. REV. 354, 420–22 (2000).

67. *See, e.g.*, Kevin Gray & Susan Francis Gray, *Civil Rights, Civil Wrongs and Quasi-Public Space*, 1 EUR. HUM. RIGHTS L. REV. 46 (1999).

institution from which correlativity is measured is always determined by the pertinent social values. Therefore, in order to determine whether a right to entry exists at all and, if so, what is its scope, we need to reflect on the pre-scriptions of the pertinent social values and their possible accommodation within the correlativity structure typical to private law. This exercise shows that an a priori dismissal of the right to entry is by no means entailed by the relevant values. Quite the contrary, at least some of these values—some of the very justifications of the property institutions at hand—point to substan-tial, albeit well-circumscribed, limits of the owners' right to exclude, as well as to important reasons for allowing entry to nonowners.[68] The convergence of these normative conclusions explains why, in some cases, the right to entry can, and indeed should, be recognized as a necessary outgrowth of private law rather than as an embarrassing aberration. (I use the term "convergence of normative reasons" advisedly. As we will see, these reasons are not rela-tional, so that they would not qualify under the account of correlativity of staunch autonomists. Nevertheless, as I hope to show, their convergence is thick enough to justify the responsiveness of the [correlative] entitlements of property owners and potential entrants.)

Despite the diversity of the property institutions at stake, all implicate three important values: autonomy, personhood, and community. None of these values sanction an absolute right to exclude; furthermore, to varying degrees, they even positively require curbing such a right and recognizing the right to entry of nonowners.[69]

Although autonomy appears to be the most obvious property value sup-porting a rigid right to exclude, in fact, it does not. As a general, right-based justification of property, the idea that personal autonomy requires individual property rights implies that every human being is entitled to some property or, more precisely, entitled to the property needed to sustain human dignity.[70]

---

68. *Cf.* Joseph W. Singer, *No Right to Exclude: Public Accommodations and Private Property*, 90 Nw. U.L. Rev. 1283, 1303, 1466 (1996).

69. Other contexts, where the property value of welfare (or utility) is prominent, are also likely to be amenable to a similar conclusion. Generally, allocating the entitlement to determine the time and terms of a resource's use with its owner is efficient but may, in some cases, do a disservice to social welfare if the law were to strictly sanction an owner's refusal to sell or lease (generally or to a certain subset of potential entrants). One such well-known category of cases involves instances where high transaction costs, caused by the number of parties involved or by their placement in a bilateral monopoly, is likely to preclude efficient transactions. *See* Guido Calabresi & A. Douglas Melamed, *Property Rules, Liability Rules, and Inalienability: One View of the Cathedral*, 85 Harv. L. Rev. 1089, 1094–95 (1972). In such cases, correlativity applies quite straight-forwardly because when welfare is the justification of property, it would *ex ante* curtail the right to exclude when this right is likely to be welfare-reducing, while prescribing the corresponding rights to entry when they are welfare-enhancing.

70. *See* Jeramy Waldron, *Homelessness and the Issue of Freedom*, in Liberal Rights 309 (1993); Joseph William Singer, *Rent*, 39 B.C.L. Rev. 1, 39 (1997).

Furthermore, even if we focus on property's role in protecting people's negative rather than positive liberty, no absolute right to exclude necessarily follows. Indeed, private property protects people's independence and security because it tends to decentralize decision-making power. Its protective effect, then, is not universally significant but rather particularly important to those who are either part "of the non-organized public... or of a marginal group with minor political clout."[71] The combination of these positive and negative aspects (the special significance of providing nonowners access to property on the one hand, and the inverse relation between an owner's wealth and power and the importance of safeguarding her right to exclude on the other hand) points to categories of cases in which the nonowners' claim to entry rather than the owners' claim to exclude derives from our commitment to autonomy.[72]

Similar and possibly more pointed conclusions emerge from the analysis of the personhood value of property. Whereas ownership of a fungible property plays a purely instrumental role in an owner's life, holders of constitutive resources are personally attached to their properties insofar as they reflect their identity, because such resources are external projections of their personality.[73] Hence, the same property value that is particularly strict about curtailing a nonowner's demand to enter (purchase, lease, use, or physically enter) a constitutive resource, may be almost indifferent regarding a fungible resource. In some cases, the position of the personhood value of property is virtually reversed: when a resource is fungible for its owner but constitutive for another (say: its long-term lessee), the personhood value of property is particularly suspicious of the owner's claim to exclude that particular other.[74]

Finally, consider the property value of community. Property institutions can, and often do, create an institutional infrastructure that facilitates the long-term cooperation necessary for successful communities fostering human flourishing.[75] Community, by definition, requires some demarcation from the broader society, and thus some measure of practical and symbolic exclusion.[76] But not every type of exclusion is sanctioned. The ways property serves community cover a wide spectrum, ranging from close-knit cultural communities

---

71. DAGAN, *supra* note 14, at 92.

72. *See also* Joseph William Singer & Jack M. Beermann, *The Social Origins of Property*, 6 CAN. J.L. & JURISP. 217, 228, 242–45 (1993); *cf.* Sophia Moreau, *What Is Discrimination*, 38 PHIL. & PUB. AFF. 143 (2010).

73. For a synthesis of the philosophical and social-scientific literature on the subject, see DAGAN, *supra* note 35, at 38–42.

74. *See* Margaret Jane Radin, *Residential Rent Control*, 15 PHIL. & PUB. AFF. 350 (1986). For another argument for the right to entry based on the Hegelian account of the personhood theory of property, see William N.R. Lucy & Francois R. Barker, *Justifying Property and Justifying Access*, 6 CAN. J.L. & JURISP. 287, 309–17 (1993).

75. *See generally* DAGAN, *supra* note 14, at ch.8.

76. *See* Gregory S. Alexander, *Dilemmas of Group Autonomy: Residential Associations and Community*, 75 CORNELL L. REV. 1, 37–39, 51–52 (1989); Clayton P. Gillette, *Courts, Covenants, and Communities*, 61 U. CHI. L. REV. 1375, 1394–95 (1994).

to much thinner ones, where co-ownership is itself a significant medium for creating shared community values.[77] Both types of situations prescribe only specific types of reasons legitimizing exclusion. One end of the spectrum authorizes exclusion if, and only if, exclusion is required to preserve the community's *ex ante* distinction from the surrounding society (as when segregation is practiced by a minority group to preserve its distinctive culture and way of life), *and* is indeed necessary to sustain a prosperous proprietary community.[78] At the other end of the spectrum, involving a community partly constituted by the property structure, limitations on entry are even more restricted and justified only insofar as they either prevent inclusion of "bad cooperators" likely to jeopardize the success of the commons property, or enhance shared cooperative values that are a necessary condition of such success.[79] The community value of property is not only reluctant to sanction broad exclusionary practices but, in some cases, even positively requires entry. Our entire citizen body is also an important human community, so that preserving open boundaries between subcommunities, at least to some extent, also serves the property value of community.[80]

Without pretending to offer a comprehensive account of any one of the doctrines at stake, the current state of the law can be shown to be roughly in accord with these theoretical observations. The law of common-interest communities, for instance, justifiably polices exclusionary practices of residential communities insofar as they are used against, rather than by, cultural minority groups,[81] and when exclusionary practices unreasonably limit the mobility of the excluded persons and thus their autonomy.[82] Similarly, landlord–tenant law vigorously protects the right to exclude in intimate settings, where the personhood value of the owner (potential landlord) trumps any possible interest of potential tenants. Yet, it reverses this rule and recognizes a rather capacious right to entry where the lessor is a commercial entity, in particular where the refusal to rent is contemptuous (namely, related to conspicuous features of the potential lessee's identity).[83] Finally, public accommodations law also reflects the proper adjustment of the content of ownership concerning a place that is mostly instrumental for its owner but functions as a locus

---

77. *See* Elinor Ostrom, *Community and the Endogenous Solution of Commons Problems*, 4 J. THEORETICAL POL. 343, 347–50 (1992).

78. *See* Eyal Benvenisti, *"Separate but Equal" in Allocating Israeli Land for Residency*, *in* LAND LAW IN ISRAEL: BETWEEN PRIVATE AND PUBLIC 547, 553–65 (Hanoch Dagan ed., 1999) [Heb.].

79. *See* DAGAN, *supra* note 14, at 47.

80. *See* Kevin Gray, *Equitable Property*, 47(2) CUR. LEGAL PROBS. 157, 213 (1994).

81. *See, e.g.*, Roderick M. Hills, Jr., *You Say You Want a Revolution? The Case against the Transformation of Culture through Antidiscrimination Laws*, 95 MICH. L. REV. 1588, 1592–614 (1997).

82. *See* Gillette, *supra* note 76, at 1437–39.

83. *See generally* Fair Housing Act, 42 U.S.C. 3601 (2006).

of opportunities for personal development[84] and significant socialization for other members of the public.[85] In other words, this persistent doctrine[86] prescribes a right to entry that is determined by a fine-tuned balance between the owner's reduced personhood interest and key autonomy and community interests of potential entrants.

In all three bodies of law, nonowners who fall within categories of cases in which the law recognizes a right to entry can typically justify the imposition of this burden on defendants vulnerable to such claims. Such potential plaintiffs can surely face the question of why they should be entitled to a remedy, and why the said remedy should enforce their entry. But they can also face the additional justificatory burden of private law, and explain why the defendants at hand—common-interest associations, lessors, and owners of public places such as hotels, restaurants, or shopping malls—should be the ones who carry the burden. At times, the reason is straightforward, as when potential defendants enjoy a local monopoly in the relevant area. But the scope of legitimate entitlements to force entry is not limited to these extreme instances: it also includes cases that do not involve a monopoly but, due to the convergence of local owners' attitudes in a certain area, make a nonowner's right to entry virtually meaningless without the power to curtail these owners' exclusionary practices.

CONCLUDING REMARKS

Private law is unique due to the correlativity of defendant's liability and plaintiff's entitlement. This characteristic seemingly entails the radical autonomy of private law, making the language of social values intrusive and inappropriate for private law discourse. As is often true of first impressions, however, this one too is misleading. The entitlements prescribed by private law, the very baselines from which correlativity is measured, must be determined by, or at least examined against, our collective values. There are, to be sure, limits to the kinds of public values that any particular plaintiff can invoke, and not every social interest can be legitimately enlisted as a foundation for a plaintiff's entitlement to extract a specific remedy from a specific defendant, but we have no a priori litmus test for the legitimacy of such an exercise. Even the determination of whether a putative value is extrinsic to the parties' relationship requires detailed deliberation on our ideal vision of the pertinent category of interpersonal relationships and on the reasons for and against

---

84. *See* Gray, *supra* note 80, at 173–74.
85. *See* Singer, *supra* note 68, at 1476.
86. For the history of this doctrine, see Gray & Gray, *supra* note 67, at 80–100; Singer, *supra* note 68.

allowing an arguably desirable state of affairs to be brought about by a private law claim.[87] Indeed, although institutions personifying the state, such as legislatures or courts, may be more or less present in private law discourse, our collective values will always be there.[88]

87. Therefore, we cannot rule out a priori that the use of consumer law for furthering market competition and trade could be justified without violating correlativity. *But cf.* Jansen and Michaels, *supra* note 1, at 355–56 (arguing that it "can be understood only from an instrumentalist point of view.").

88. As the text implies, I believe that from a qualitative and substantive—as opposed to quantitative and institutional—perspective, globalization need not, indeed should not, make a difference to private law. Private law was, is, and should remain the law governing various types of horizontal spheres of relationships deserving of critical, interpretive respect. Thus, globalization may affect the level of institutions that should shape the future development of private law—it may require that some *trans*national body scrutinize its content vis-à-vis our *global* collective ideals about the important social institutions governed by its rules. But this does not, or at least need not and should not, change the interpretive discourse that characterizes private law at its best, as I have attempted to demonstrate in this chapter.

CHAPTER 6

cᴧɔ

Legal Realism and the Taxonomy
of Private Law

OPENING REMARKS

The revival of academic interest in taxonomy is one of Peter Birks's most significant achievements and a key element of his distinguished legacy.[1] Birks
was passionate about taxonomy: "Better understanding of law," he wrote,
"depends upon a sound taxonomy of the law." Without proper academic attention to taxonomy, he warned, "the common law will dissolve into incoher-
ence." Birks's concerns about taxonomy were rooted in his endorsement of
legal positivism. Legal taxonomy owes its significance, in his view, to its role
in the facilitation of the learning and application of positive rules. In order
to pursue these important purposes, legal rules should be properly organized
because information "which cannot be sorted is not knowledge."[2]

This chapter may be an unwelcome defense of the significance of legal
taxonomy. It may be unwelcome because it starts from a very different jurisprudential premise than the one shared by most of the scholars interested in
taxonomy who, like Birks, tend to be positivists.[3] The jurisprudential underpinnings of this chapter are of course realist; and realism, at least in the account
of this book, is antithetical to legal positivism.[4] The profound realist critique
of legal positivism is, as I argue in Part I, quite damaging to the positivist

1. This chapter was originally written for a collection of essays in memory of Peter
Birks.
2. Peter Birks, *Introduction, in* ENGLISH PRIVATE LAW li (2000).
3. Or formalists, which is actually not the same. *See* Ernest J. Weinrib, *The Juridical
Classification of Obligations, in* THE CLASSIFICATION OF OBLIGATIONS 37, 37 (Peter
Birks ed., 1997).
4. *Contra* Brian Leiter, *Legal Realism and Legal Positivism Reconsidered*, 111 ETHICS
278 (2001).

rationale of legal taxonomy. But legal realism, at least in the charitable reading this book offers, does not look down on taxonomy. Quite the contrary, as I show in Part II, there are good (read: legal realist) reasons for considering legal taxonomy significant.

Identifying these reasons is important not only to show that realists can and should care about taxonomy, but also because it points to some prescriptions about the taxonomic enterprise that, unsurprisingly, are quite distinct from the way taxonomy is envisioned from a positivist (or doctrinalist) perspective. I present the preliminary elaboration of these prescriptions in Part III, in the spirit of Birks's call for a "taxonomic debate among scholars." Indeed, it was Birks who characteristically urged us to continue engaging in this question, hoping that "with vigorous debate, the best hypotheses available now will be modified or replaced."[5] The realist program for legal taxonomy presented here, then, may not be unwelcome after all.

I. Debunking Doctrinalist Taxonomies

Contemporary friends of legal taxonomy emphasize the usefulness, indeed the inevitability, of classification for the purpose of gaining knowledge of law. With Birks, they insist that "[t]here is no body of knowable data which can subsist as a jumble of mismatched categories. The search for order is indistinguishable from the search for knowledge."[6] Thus, for example, Stephen Smith, a proud defender of the legal taxonomy project in its doctrinalist rendition, argues that "[t]o make good decisions courts need to distinguish like from unlike; to understand the law scholars need to do the same thing. When lawyers and scholars argue about how a case should be decided, or about the meaning of a particular rule, they are in large part arguing about how to classify the case or the rule."[7]

Insofar as these claims stand for the proposition that reasoning in general, and thus legal reasoning more particularly, must rely on certain concepts that necessarily involve some classificatory work and requires some organization of the body of legal rules in order to make them accessible to legal actors, they are indeed undisputable truisms.[8] But both Birks and Smith go further than this. Birks engaged in, and Smith vehemently defended, a specific and indeed particularly doctrinalist method of classification, resorting to "the sort of

---

5. Birks, *supra* note 2, at li.

6. Birks, *Preface*, *in* ENGLISH PRIVATE LAW, *supra* note 2, at xxxi–xxxii.

7. Stephen A. Smith, *Taking Law Seriously*, 50 U. TORONTO L.J. 241, 244 (2000).

8. *See, e.g.*, Jay M. Feinman, *The Jurisprudence of Classification*, 41 STAN. L. REV. 661, 710 (1989); Peter Jaffey, *Classification and Unjust Enrichment*, 67 MODERN L.REV. 1012, 1013 (2004); Emily Sherwin, *Legal Taxonomy*, 15 LEGAL THEORY 25, 40 (2009); Weinrib, *supra* note 3, at 54.

categories that judges use when deciding cases, that legislators employ when making law, and that lawyers use when arguing before courts. In other words, these are categories such as 'tort,' 'contract,' 'unjust enrichment,' 'equity,' and so on."[9] Recourse to existing doctrinal categories fits well with the perception of taxonomy as a means for gaining knowledge. If indeed, as doctrinalists like to claim, the taxonomy of the law is analogous to cartography—if legal classification is on a par with mapping[10]—it makes perfect sense to take the existing legal terrain as the fixed data that needs to be organized.

Legal realism upsets this seemingly straightforward program. Recall that for legal realists law is a doctrinal system in movement: as the shape of legal doctrine "is made and remade as its narrative continues to unfold... even apparently surprising lurches can be integrated seamlessly."[11] Therefore, law cannot be understood merely by reference to its static elements (its existing rules); understanding the doctrinal materials at any given moment as the things to be classified misses the inherent dynamism of the law. This means that the analogy of legal taxonomy to cartography is mistaken and even misleading. Cartography assumes stability in the geographical features to be mapped; it implies that there is "a fixed and immutable topography 'out there' waiting to be accurately charted." But law is constantly changing. Therefore, "no map is ever likely to be produced that can, at one and the same time, explain the past and act as a means for predicting the future."[12]

The doctrinalist version of legal taxonomy is not only misguided because it fails to account for the dynamism of law. It is also perilous, because it contributes unduly to one of the most important professional hazards of doctrinalism identified by realists: the "thingification" of legal concepts. As Felix Cohen argued, this innocuous practice is risky because of the lawyerly tendency to essentialize contingent legal categories as if they somehow transcend human choice and represent a non-modifiable part of our natural or ethical environment.[13] This risk is serious because such thingification tends to render legal constructs obvious and acceptable, thus immunizing them from proper justification. This risk is particularly high with respect to private law, which

---

9. Smith, *supra* note 7, at 246.

10. *See, e.g.*, Birks, *supra* note 2, at xxxv.

11. Don Herzog, Poisoning the Minds of the Lower Orders 18 (1998); *see also id.*, at 15–16; Martin Krygier, *Law as Tradition*, 5 Law & Phil. 237, 242, 248 (1986).

12. Stephen Waddams, Dimensions of Private Law: Categories and Concepts in Anglo-American Legal Reasoning 12–13, 226 (2003); Roscoe Pound, *Classification of Law*, 37 Harv. L. Rev. 933, 942–43 (1924); Geoffrey Samuel, *Can the Common Law Be Mapped?*, 55 U. Toronto L.J. 271, 286, 290, 295 (2005).

13. *See* Felix S. Cohen, *Transcendental Nonsense and the Functional Approach*, 35 Colum. L. Rev. 809, 811–12, 820 (1935); *see also* Joseph Bingham, *What Is the Law?*, 11 Mich. L. Rev. 1, 12 (1912); Jeremy Waldron, *"Transcendental Nonsense" and System in the Law*, 100 Colum. L. Rev. 16, 51 (2000).

structures our daily interactions and tends to blend into our natural environment.[14] Not surprisingly, then, legal realists focus on exposing the contingency of the concepts and rules of property, contract, and tort law, in an attempt to expose the hidden ways in which law applies its power.

Cohen's critique about the "thingification" of property is a prime example. Courts justify the protection of trade names on the grounds that, if people create a thing of value, they are entitled to protection against deprivation, because a thing of value is property. "The vicious circle inherent in this reasoning," explains Cohen "is plain. It purports to base legal protection upon economic value, when, as a matter of actual fact, the economic value of a device depends upon the extent to which it will be legally protected." This flawed legal reasoning obscures the coercive and distributive effects of law. What courts actually do in these cases is to establish "inequality in the commercial exploitation of language," thus creating and distributing "a new source of economic wealth or power." Traditional doctrinalist discourse shields these decisions from normative critique and is thus tantamount to "economic prejudice masquerading in the cloak of legal logic." Unchecked, law may serve "to perpetuate class prejudices and uncritical assumptions which could not survive the sunlight of free ethical controversy."[15]

Geoffrey Samuel is thus right on target when he criticizes the project of doctrinalist legal taxonomy, which confusingly treats "[c]ontracts, torts, ownership, rights or whatever" as "phenomena waiting to be observed and rationalized by independent observers." Because, in fact, these "are notions created by a particular group of 'scientists' who in effect impose them on social reality," taxonomic hypotheses in law cannot be verified (or falsified) by correspondence to external facts. The taxonomic scheme we use in law does not merely organize our legal knowledge.[16] Rather, our legal taxonomy necessarily participates in our construction of that knowledge and thus in the ongoing evolution of law.[17]

14. *See, e.g.*, Robert W. Gordon, *Unfreezing Legal Reality: Critical Approaches to Law*, 15 FLA. ST. U. L. REV. 195, 212–14 (1987).

15. Cohen, *supra* note 13, at 814–18, 840; *see also* Louis L. Jaffe, *Law Making by Private Groups*, 51 HARV. L. REV. 212 (1937).

16. *Contra* Peter Birks, *Equity in the Modern Law: An Exercise in Taxonomy*, 26 MELBOURNE U.L. REV. 1, 9 (1996).

17. Geoffrey Samuel, *English Private Law: Old and New Thinking in the Taxonomy Debate*, 24 OX. J. LEGAL STUD. 335, 341, 362 (2004); *see also* MARTHA MINOW, MAKING ALL THE DIFFERENCE: INCLUSION, EXCLUSION, AND AMERICAN LAW 3, 4, 8 (1990); WADDAMS, *supra* note 12, at 2–3, 14–15, 21–22, 226–27; Feinman, *supra* note 8, at 663; Pound, *supra* note 12, at 937–38; J.E. Penner, *Basic Obligations, in* THE CLASSIFICATION OF OBLIGATIONS, *supra* note 8, at 91, 91; Samuel, *supra* note 12, at 286; *cf.* ROGER COTTERRELL, THE POLITICS OF JURISPRUDENCE 85–87 106–109 (1989).

II. The Functions of Taxonomy

Realists, as noted, dispute the cogency of doctrinal legal taxonomy and, furthermore, warn against its overly conservative potential implications. This position is at times mistaken for an advocacy of ad hoc judgments and thus a dismissal of the significance of legal classifications, rendering the title of the last part of this chapter—realist taxonomies—an ostensible oxymoron. But legal realism (at least if charitably interpreted) in fact rejects the dubious nominalistic approach to law and recognizes the importance of legal categories and thus of legal taxonomy.[18]

Legal realists acknowledge that law's use of categories, concepts, and rules is unavoidable[19] and even desirable, and that in most cases many legal reasoners should simply follow rules.[20] (This is why realists take pains to improve rules, relying—as Part III of Chapter 2 explains—on empirical data, normative commitments, and situation sense.) Indeed, as I claim in Chapters 2 and 9, legal realism should not be interpreted as the enemy of rule-based decision making, as long as we remember that the (limited) stability of rules at any given moment relies on, and is thus contingent on, a convergence of lawyers' background understandings and not on the determinacy of the doctrine as such. Furthermore, properly interpreted, realism also disavows "rule-sensitive particularism," which allows judges to depart from rules whenever the outcome of the particular case at hand so requires, while taking into account both substantive values and the value of preserving the rule's integrity. Rather, legal realists merely insist that, at least some legal actors, notably judges of appellate courts, should occasionally use new cases as triggers for an ongoing refinement of rules. These are opportunities to revisit the normative viability of existing rules qua rules and to reexamine the adequacy of legal categorization.

Furthermore, legal taxonomy is not merely a necessary pursuit but also one that is worthwhile, indeed laudable. In other words, although we should resist any attempt to essentialize law's existing categories, we should acknowledge their potentially desirable role in the law.

---

18. *Cf.* Andrew Altman, *The Legacy of Legal Realism*, 10 LEGAL STUD. FORUM 167, 171–72 (1986); Todd D. Rakoff, *The Implied Terms of Contract: Of "Default Rules" and "Situation Sense," in* GOOD FAITH AND FAULT IN CONTRACT LAW 191, 216 (Jack Beatson & Daniel Friedmann eds., 1995).

19. The unavoidability of using categories in thinking about law follows, of course, from the unavoidability of using categories in thinking in general.

20. Rules authoritatively settle disputes, thus securing the moral benefits of coordination, expertise, and efficiency. *See* LARRY ALEXANDER & EMILY SHERWIN, THE RULE OF RULES 12–15 (2001); *see also, e.g.,* Frederick Schauer, *The Generality of Law*, 107 W. VA. L. REV. 217, 224–34 (2004).

For realists, law's existing categories are typically the starting point of any analysis of legal questions. Lawyers can assume (until proven wrong) that the current categorization incorporates valuable, although implicit and sometimes imperfectly executed, normative choices. This conservative assumption derives not only from the pragmatic reality that existing categories cannot be abandoned completely, but also from a recognition that they represent an accumulated judicial experience that is worthy of respect. This respect follows from the realist celebration of the common law's commitment to continuity, discussed in Part IV of Chapter 2. It also derives, even more specifically, from the important functions realists ascribe to legal categories, which I discuss below.[21]

Each legal category (or subcategory) targets, in its own way and with respect to some intended realm of application, a set of human values that can be promoted by its constitutive rules. As such, legal categories consolidate people's expectations regarding core types of human relationships so that they can anticipate developments when entering, for instance, a common interest community, or, for that matter, invading other people's rights. Thus, a set of fairly precise rules or informative standards must govern each legal category of this type so as to enable people to predict the consequences of various future contingencies and to plan and structure their lives accordingly.[22] Furthermore, legal categories also serve as a means for expressing law's normative ideals for these types of human interaction (think, for instance, of crimes [as opposed to torts], or of marriage or contract). For this reason, legal taxonomy performs a significant expressive and cultural function. Both roles—consolidating expectations and expressing law's ideals—require some measure of stability: to form effective frameworks of social interaction and cooperation, law can recognize a necessarily limited (and relatively stable) number of categories.[23]

These functions of legal taxonomy explain, at least to some extent, the distinctions between private law and other parts of the law, the distinctions between the various fields within private law, and the more minute distinctions between subcategories within these fields. Exploring these differences in any detail is surely far beyond the scope of this short chapter, but a brief sample will hopefully suffice for a sketchy demonstration of these points.

---

21. For an elaborate discussion in the context of property law, see HANOCH DAGAN, PROPERTY: VALUES AND INSTITUTIONS Part One and Part Three (2011).

22. As should be clear by now, a realist approach does not undermine law's predictability; in fact, it reinforces it. At least relative to the hopeless indeterminacy of pure doctrinal analysis that, as noted, is caused first and foremost by the multiplicity of doctrinal sources, a contextual normative inquiry can secure a much more stable, and thus predictable, legal equilibrium.

23. *See infra* Part II of Chapter 9.

Consider first the distinction between private law and public law.[24] As many realist and post-realist authors have shown, the private–public distinction is far from airtight and, more significantly, is by no means natural or conceptually inevitable. For realists, this continuity between private law and public law means that private lawyers, like their public brethren, should invariably consider the distributive implications of the rules they advocate or apply.[25] Good reasons still remain, however, for respecting the differences between private and public law. Some of these reasons, which were the focus of Chapter 5, relate to the unique justificatory burden judges face when adjudicating a bilateral interaction between a particular plaintiff and a particular defendant in which one party's triumph is the other's defeat. Other reasons are even more general; they relate to the significance of retaining the separate ways in which the law constructs horizontal as opposed to vertical social interactions. Some of our most important normative commitments justify adhering to, and indeed facilitating, some such differentiation between the private and the public in order to fracture and multiply human authority.[26] Furthermore, fundamental principles of democratic governance justify imposing on public authorities particularly demanding obligations of trust, which are inappropriate with respect to most (although not necessarily all) private actors. By contrast, in defining "the rights and duties of [persons] as they relate to one another," private law should pay unique attention to the social norms pertaining to such interaction.[27] The private–public distinction may serve as a means for entrenching these expectations and the ideals for which they stand.

By the same token, there are good (read: realist) reasons for the division of private law into separate fields. There are, for example, important and rather fundamental, normative distinctions between contracts and torts. At least from the viewpoint of the important value of autonomy, the purposes of contracts and torts are distinctly different.[28] Contracts are usually understood as conventional frameworks of voluntary promises, which the law enforces

---

24. I believe that an analysis analogous to the one I offer regarding the private–public distinction applies to the distinction between private law and criminal law. *Cf.* Paul H. Robinson & John M. Darley, *The Utility of Desert*, 91 Nw. U.L. Rev. 453, 479–82 (1997).

25. *See, e.g.*, Hanoch Dagan, Unjust Enrichment: A Study of Private Law and Public Values (1997); Dagan, *supra* note 22, at chs. 2 & 5.

26. *See* Don Herzog: Happy Slaves: A Critique of Consent Theory 156, 166–68, 173–75 (1989).

27. John C.P. Goldberg, *The New Private Law*, 125 Harv. L. Rev. 1640, 1640 (2012) (Goldberg suggests that realists are skeptical about these ideas).

28. Even the economic analysis of the law, which is of course preoccupied with another important value—social welfare—acknowledges the difference between contract law and tort law. Whereas the former is aimed, in this view, at maximizing the welfare of contractual parties, the latter is preoccupied with minimizing the costs of accidents and the costs of their prevention. *Compare, e.g.*, Alan Schwartz & Robert E. Scott, *Contract Theory and the Limits of Contract Law*, 113 Yale L.J. 541

in order to allow people to promote their own goals by recruiting other people (or their resources) without immorally using these people.[29] By contrast, from an autonomy perspective, tort law focuses mainly on prescribing rules of action and of liability that reconcile the competing claims of liberty and security in fair ways.[30] Hence, whereas contract law consolidates expectations and expresses ideals regarding cooperative human interactions, tort law performs similar tasks with respect to conflicting human interactions.

Finally, the internal categorization of each field of private law also obeys this legal realist logic (i.e., normative distinctions between private law fields as the foundation of categorization). Property law, for example, is divided into different property institutions that parse the social world into distinct types of human interaction with respect to given categories of resources (this observation is the starting point of Chapter 8 below). Some property institutions govern arm's-length relationships between strangers (or market transactors), and are accordingly structured along the lines of the Blackstonian conception of property as "sole despotic dominion":[31] they are atomistic and competitive, and they vindicate people's negative liberty. Other property institutions, such as marital property, deal with intimate relationships and are therefore dominated by a much more communitarian view of property, in which ownership is a locus of sharing. Finally, many other property institutions governing relationships between people who are neither strangers nor intimates, such as landlords and tenants, neighbors, co-owners, and members of the same local community, lie somewhere along the spectrum between atomistic and communitarian norms. In all these cases, both autonomy and community are of the essence, and ownership thus implies both rights and responsibilities.[32]

(2003), with GUIDO CALABRESI, THE COSTS OF ACCIDENTS: A LEGAL AND ECONOMIC ANALYSIS (1970).

29. *See* CHARLES FRIED, CONTRACT AS PROMISE: A THEORY OF CONTRACTUAL OBLIGATION 7–17 (1981); Daniel Markovitz, *Contract and Collaboration*, 114 YALE. L.J. 1419 (2004); Joseph Raz, *Promises in Morality and Law*, 95 HARV. L. REV. 916, 933 (1982) (reviewing P.S. ATIYAH, PROMISES, MORALS, AND LAW (1981)).

30. *See* DAN B. DOBBS, TORTS AND COMPENSATION: PERSONAL ACCOUNTABILITY AND SOCIAL RESPONSIBILITY FOR INJURY 8–9 (2d ed. 1993); ARTHUR RIPSTEIN, EQUALITY, RESPONSIBILITY, AND THE LAW 6 (1999); Gregory Keating, *Rawlsian Fairness and Regime Choice in the Law of Accidents*, 72 FORDHAM L. REV. 1857, 1862–70 (2004). There are, to be sure, other accounts of the role of autonomy in torts. Thus, for example, Ernest Weinrib insists that corrective justice is the regulative principle of torts (and more generally of private law). *See* ERNEST J. WEINRIB, THE IDEA OF PRIVATE LAW (1995). But Weinrib too sees important distinctions between contracts and torts, with significant remedial consequences. *See* Ernest J. Weinrib, *Punishment and Disgorgement as Contract Remedies*, 78 CHI.-KENT L. REV. 55 (2003).

31. 2 WILLIAM BLACKSTONE, COMMENTARIES 2.

32. *See* DAGAN, *supra* note 22, at Pts. I & III.

III. Realist Taxonomies

Having recovered the value that realists place on legal taxonomy, my remaining task in this chapter is to consider the main attributes of the taxonomic enterprise in its realist rendition. As the following discussion demonstrates, three key features distinguish realist taxonomies from their doctrinalist counterparts.

Proponents of the doctrinalist taxonomic venture believe that legal taxonomy provides the best way of understanding law's "organizational claims" and, therefore, the law itself.[33] This view is deficient because, like the very project of doctrinal legal taxonomy, it assumes that taxonomy is exogenous to "law's self-understanding" and that legal classifiers merely describe, rather than affect, the legal landscape. This quietist assumption, that taxonomy is unrelated to the development of the law (i.e., the assumption that taxonomy merely reaffirms the status quo), is of course exactly what legal realism challenges as wrong and misleading.

The first and most fundamental distinctive feature of the realist taxonomy of law, therefore, is its relative dynamism. Karl Llewellyn, for example, invites lawyers to rethink law's received categories because, although legal classification cannot be eliminated, "to classify is to disturb" and hence "obscure some of the data under observation and give fictitious value to others." For this reason, classifications "can be excused only in so far as [they are] necessary to the accomplish[ment] of a purpose." And because purposes may change, "the available tradition of categories" should be periodically reexamined.[34] Rethinking legal categorization is important for a further reason: namely, because it may help expose otherwise hidden and sometimes unjustified legal choices of inclusion and exclusion.[35]

To avoid the pitfalls of essentializing the existing legal taxonomy, realists refuse to accept the existing legal categories as a given, and call instead for an ongoing (albeit properly cautious) process of identifying the human values underlying these categories and rethinking the legal rules that best promote them. The appeal to the prevailing legal taxonomy is never the end of the legal analysis, because invoking these categories always involves, at least potentially, some tinkering with their content as well as their boundaries. The realist approach takes the values underlying legal categories, not only the existing doctrinal content of these categories, as part and parcel of the legal analysis, and thus makes these values an object of ongoing critical and constructive

33. Smith, *supra* note 7, at 249–56.
34. KARL L. LLEWELLYN, *A Realistic Jurisprudence: The Next Step, in* JURISPRUDENCE: REALISM IN THEORY AND IN PRACTICE 3, 27 (1962).
35. *See* KARL N. LLEWELLYN, THE THEORY OF RULES 95, 97 (Frederick Schauer ed., 2011).

inquiry.[36] The realist taxonomic enterprise is thus both backward and forward looking, constantly challenging the continued validity and desirability of the normative underpinnings of existing legal categories, their responsiveness to the social context in which they are situated, and their effectiveness in promoting their contextually examined normative goals. (Here, we must rely on the vague notion of "promoting" to capture the complex ways in which law can facilitate human values. The normative analysis recommended by legal realism seeks to capture law's material effect on people's behavior, its expressive and constitutive impact, and the intricate interdependence of the two effects.[37])

At times, such an account helps to fill gaps in the law by prescribing new rules that bolster and vindicate these goals even further. At other times, it points out "blemishes" in the existing categories, rules that undermine the most illuminating and defensible account of such a legal category that should be reformed so that the law may live up to its own ideals.[38] This reformist potential may yield different types of legal reforms. In some cases, the reform is quite radical: the abolition of a legal category or an overall reconstruction of its content. In others, more moderate options are in order, such as restating the doctrine pertaining to a legal category in a way that brings its rules closer to its underlying commitments and, in the process, removing indefensible rules or adjusting one given category to the various social contexts in which it may be situated.[39]

The realist approach to taxonomy is thus an exercise in the kind of legal optimism so typical of the common law tradition. Rather than an attempt just to understand the existing legal terrain, it simultaneously aims to explain and develop legal categories in a way that accentuates their normative desirability while remaining attuned to their social context.

* * *

A second important characteristic of the realist taxonomic blueprint, which is again antithetical to the doctrinalist tenor,[40] is a strong preference for relatively narrow categories. Thus, Llewellyn finds wholesale legal categories (such as contracts or property) "too big to handle," as they encompass too "many heterogeneous items." He thus recommends "[t]he making of smaller categories— which may either be sub-groupings inside the received categories, or may cut

36. *Cf.* Jaffey, *supra* note 8, *passim* (although Jaffey mistakenly believes each "justificatory category" should necessarily have one "common underlying principle or justification"); Weinrib, *supra* note 3, at 37–38, 55 (although Weinrib is, of course, not a legal realist).

37. *See* DAGAN, *supra* note 22, at ch. 6.

38. *See* RONALD DWORKIN, TAKING RIGHTS SERIOUSLY 118–23 (1977).

39. For some examples for these different outcomes in the context of property law, see DAGAN, *supra* note 22, at 31.

40. *See* Peter Birks, *Definition and Division: A Mediation on* Institutes 3.13, *in* THE CLASSIFICATION OF OBLIGATIONS, *supra* note 3, at 1, 34–35; Weinrib, *supra* note 3, at 40.

across them."[41] By employing these narrow categories, lawyers can develop the law while "testing it against life-wisdom." Again, the claim is *not* that "the equities or sense of the particular case or the particular parties" should be determinative; rather, it is that decision making should benefit from "the sense and reason of some significantly seen *type* of life-situation."[42] Furthermore, I do not ignore the downside of categories that are too small: that there may be too many of them and that litigation will simply be about which of the multiple of small categories each case fits into. This short chapter does not offer any meta-theory of the optimal size of legal categories. My modest goal is to explain why realists argue for smaller categories than we currently employ based on a pragmatic (and somewhat impressionistic) judgment, which considers the balance of all these considerations.

The realist celebration of the traditional common law strategy of employing narrow legal categories, each covering only relatively few human situations, follows directly from the realist commitment to assure that law indeed serves life. As Herman Oliphant noted, this strategy "divide[s] and minutely subdivide[s] the transactions of life for legal treatment," with the desirable result of a significant "particularity and minuteness in the [legal] classification of human transactions." Narrow categories, Oliphant explained, help to produce "the discrimination necessary for intimacy of treatment," holding lawyers and judges close to "the [type of] transactions before them" and thus encouraging them to shape law "close and contemporary" to the human problems they deal with. Only where legal taxonomy adheres to the injunction of creating narrow categories does it facilitate one of the most distinct comparative advantages of lawyers (mostly judges) in producing legal norms—their "battered experiences of... brutal facts," namely their daily and unmediated access to actual human situations and problems in contemporary life. When law's categories are in tune with those of life so that an "alert sense of actuality checks our reveries in theory," lawyers uniquely enjoy "the illumination which only immediacy affords and the judiciousness which reality alone can induce."[43]

Indeed, our lives are divided into economically and socially differentiated segments (although, that is by no means to say that they are always

---

41. LLEWELLYN, *A Realistic Jurisprudence, supra* note 35, at 27–28, 32; LLEWELLYN, *Some Realism about Realism, in* JURISPRUDENCE, *supra* note 35, at 42, 70; *see also, e.g.,* William W. Fisher III, *The Development of American Legal Theory and the Judicial Interpretation of the Bill of Rights, in* A CULTURE OF RIGHTS 266, 275 (Michael J. Lacey & Knud Haakonssen eds., 1993).

42. LLEWELLYN, *The Current Recapture of the Grand Tradition, in* JURISPRUDENCE, *supra* note 35, at 215, 217, 219–20.

43. Herman Oliphant, *A Return to Stare Decisis,* 14 A.B.A.J. 71, 73–74, 159 (1928); *see also* Fisher, *supra* note 42, at 272–73, 275.

completely separate and distinct),[44] and each such "transaction of life" has some features that are of sufficient normative importance (that is, that gain significance from the perspective of some general principle or policy), which justify a distinct legal treatment.[45] If law is to serve life, it should tailor its categories narrowly and in accordance with these patterns of human conduct and interaction so that it can gradually capture and respond to the characteristics of each type of case.[46] Only in this way can law preserve the legitimacy of adjudication that partly relies, as may be recalled, on the fact that *legal* normative analyses are always situated in specific human contexts. (Chapter 8 adds an important normative dimension to this realist preference to narrow categories: the resulting multiplicity is importantly conducive to autonomy as self-authorship.)

* * *

Finally, the third important distinction between the doctrinalist and realist approaches to legal taxonomy relates to the possible relationships between different legal categories. Doctrinalists regard legal categories as necessarily autonomous and mutually exclusive, so that "the classified answer to a question must use categories which are perfectly distinct from one another."[47] Because the project of legal taxonomy for them is analogous to the project of classifying natural features of our world, they see the idea of some overlaps between categories as seriously misguided.[48] For the doctrinalist, the test of success for a legal taxonomy is precisely its success in generating a scheme where different categories, governed by differing principles,[49] "stand in splendid isolation from one another in legal discourse."[50] The ideal taxonomy for them is one that builds high walls of autonomy between legal categories,

---

44. *See* Peter Berger et al., The Homeless Mind: Modernization and Consciousness 63–82 (1973).

45. *See, e.g.,* Michael Walzer, Spheres of Justice: A Defense of Pluralism and Equality (1983); Elizabeth Anderson, Value in Ethics and Economics (1993); Elizabeth Anderson, *Pragmatism, Science, and Moral Inquiry, in* In the Face of Facts 10, 17 (Richard Wightman Fox & Robert B. Westbrook eds., 1998).

46. *See* Dagan, *supra* note 22, at Pts I. & III; Roy Kreitner, *Fear of Contract*, 2004 Wisc. L. Rev. 429, 461–78; Rakoff, *supra* note 19, at 219, 222, 225; Frederick Schauer, *Prediction and Particularity*, 78 B.U.L. Rev. 773 (1998); Alan Schwartz, *The Default Rule Paradigm and the Limits of Contract Law*, 3 S. Cal. Interdisc. L.J. 389, 415–19 (1994).

47. *See* Peter Birks, *Unjust Enrichment and Wrongful Enrichment*, 79 Tex. L. Rev. 1767, 1794 (2001)

48. *See id.* at 1781 ("It is no more possible for the selected causative event to be both an unjust enrichment and a tort than it is for an animal to be both an insect and a mammal.").

49. *See* Weinrib, *supra* note 3, at 39.

50. Bruce A. Ackerman, *The Structure of Subchapter C: An Anthropological Comment*, 87 Yale L.J. 436, 439 (1977).

defines one normative "core" per field, and jealously safeguards the boundaries between distinct legal fields.[51]

By contrast, realist taxonomies live comfortably with some degree of overlap between categories. Realists are not alarmed or embarrassed by overlaps because they are not impressed by the doctrinalist claim that overlaps are conceptually impossible. They highlight the confusion resulting from the presupposition of this claim, namely, that the endeavor of legal classifiers is exogenous to the object's character. They insist that, once this presupposition is set aside, complete autonomy becomes a rather extreme condition and should not, in any event, be the test of taxonomical success.[52] Quite the contrary, in most cases some overlaps are perfectly acceptable, even desirable. In justifying and framing principles for one area of the law, explains Bruce Ackerman, "lawyers often find that principles governing [another area] are relevant to their problem." Therefore, it should not be surprising to identify some relationships of dependence between legal categories, either through the subordination of one to the other or, as is probably more frequently the case, through mutual reciprocity, so that "either can be invoked as a source of argument in a lawyer's evaluation of the other."[53] This seems a straightforward proposition for realists, emanating from the mundane observation that life is messy, and that different contexts, while distinct in some senses, often raise overlapping normative concerns.[54]

Indeed, reciprocity, rather than autonomy, seems to be the name of the taxonomic game.[55] For example, there are important continuities between the underlying concerns and methodologies of contract law and those of torts. The influential tort law search for the cheapest cost avoider is frequently translated into an analysis that prescribes contractual defaults by attaching liability to the party who bears the least cost.[56] By the same token, at times, torts scholars helpfully use a contractarian approach—looking, to be sure, to a hypothetical contract behind some veil of ignorance—to justify an existing or suggested tort doctrine.[57] Correspondingly, some doctrines,

---

51. *See* Jacob Weinrib, *What Can Kant Teach Us about Legal Classification?*, 23 CAN. J. L. & JURIS. 203 (2010); *see also, e.g.*, Darryn Jensen, *The Problem of Taxonomy in Private Law*, 31 MELBOURNE U.L. REV. 516, 519 (2007).

52. *See* WADDAMS, *supra* note 12, at 226–27; Ackerman, *supra* note 51, at 439; Samuel, *supra* note 12, at 282–84.

53. Ackerman, *supra* note 51, at 439; *cf.* WADDAMS, *supra* note 12, at 110, 112, (confusing in this context governing principles and legal categories).

54. *See* Feinman, *supra* note 8, at 689.

55. *See also* WADDAMS, *supra* note 12, at 1–2, 7.

56. *See, e.g.*, ROBERT E. SCOTT & DOUGLAS L. LESLIE, CONTRACT LAW AND THEORY 19 (2d ed. 1993).

57. For two very different examples, see Alan Schwartz, *Proposals for Products Liability Reform: A Theoretical Synthesis*, 97 YALE L.J. 353 (1988) and Gregory C. Keating, *Rawlsian Fairness and Regime Choice in the Law of Accidents*, 72 FORDHAM L. REV. 1857 (2004).

such as product liability law, resist easy pigeonholing into either contracts or torts.[58] These overlaps imply neither the death of contract[59] nor of torts.[60] Rather, the lack of clear doctrinal boundaries separating these fields and the multiple overlaps in the system simply reflect the realist discount of the aesthetic appeal of doctrinal autonomy and the realist welcome of cross-boundary borrowings whenever they can facilitate the contextual normative analysis of law.[61]

Some may worry that overlaps destroy the point of taxonomy: once a legal category lacks the strong coherence of principle envisioned by the ideal of doctrinal autonomy, it is no longer helpful.[62] This worry, however, is exaggerated. To be sure, a degree of overlap that destroys any possibility of sensibly producing normative, and thus doctrinal, recommendations about any given legal category would indeed take the bite out of the taxonomical project. But the realist case for accommodating overlaps does not take this extreme position, and this chaotic predicament is definitely not the only alternative to strict doctrinal autonomy. Some overlaps between legal categories need not destroy the common denominators—the similarities holding together the rules of any given legal category.[63] As long as these common denominators are thick enough to yield sufficiently robust normative (and thus doctrinal) recommendations, holding on to the legal category is (realistically) justified.[64]

---

58. *See, e.g.,* 1 MARSHALL S. SHAPO, THE LAW OF PRODUCTS LIABILITY lxxvii (3d ed. 1994).

59. *See* GRANT GILMORE, THE DEATH OF CONTRACT (1974).

60. *See also* DAGAN, *supra* note 22, at 81 ("Like the unavoidable relationship of reciprocity between marital property law and other areas of both family law and property law, the law of creativity is rightly allied not only with fields of law that deal with speech, culture, and learning, but also with the more traditional areas of property law.").

61. *See* HANOCH DAGAN, THE LAW AND ETHICS OF RESTITUTION 34 (2004).

62. This is the claim of some unjust enrichment skeptics who argue that the failure of unjust (or unjustified) enrichment to serve as the guiding principle of the law of restitution implies that there is no good reason to retain (or revive) restitution as an important legal category. *See, e.g.,* Peter Jaffey, *Two Theories of Unjust Enrichment, in* UNDERSTANDING UNJUST ENRICHMENT 139 (Mitchell McInnes et al. eds., 2005). This claim frequently presents property, contract, and tort law as legal fields that provide the strong coherence of principle that restitution lacks, concluding that it is better to think of restitution as an element of one or more of these fields. *See, e.g.,* Steve Hedley, *Unjust Enrichment: A Middle Course?,* 2 OX. U. COMM. L.J. 181, 194–95 (2002).

63. *Cf.* Kit Barker, *Understanding the Unjust Enrichment Principle in Private Law: A Study of the Concept and Its Reasons, in* UNDERSTANDING UNJUST ENRICHMENT, *supra* note 63, at 79; Feinman, *supra* note 8, at 678, 699.

64. *Cf.* Todd S. Aagaard, *Environmental Law as a Legal Field: An Inquiry in Legal Taxonomy,* 95 CORNELL L. REV. 221, 225, 229, 236, 243, 245 (2010).

CONCLUDING REMARKS

Legal taxonomy is frequently portrayed as necessarily a formalist (or doctrinalist) endeavor, which realists are likely to dismiss.[65] This common wisdom is both mistaken and unfortunate. It is mistaken because realists should have a keen interest in the enterprise of legal categorization. Realists need not, to be sure, subscribe to the (doctrinalist) idea that the purpose of taxonomy is to organize the given terrain of legal rules. Rather, they can and indeed should reconstruct the role of taxonomy so as to incorporate their insights on the inherent dynamism of law and the important function of contextual normative analysis in the evolution of legal categories. This reconstruction implies that the main goals of legal categories are to consolidate people's expectations and to express law's ideals with respect to distinct types of human interaction.

Recasting legal categorization in these terms dramatically changes the nature of the taxonomic enterprise. Rather than aiming at the refinement of some eternal descriptive truths, legal taxonomy, in its realist rendition, is an ongoing enterprise constantly reinventing itself. Rather than seeking to transcend context, realist taxonomies are sensitive to context and seek to generate relatively narrow legal categories. Finally, rather than aspiring to produce a map of mutually exclusive legal categories, a realist legal taxonomy recognizes and accommodates substantial (although never overwhelming) overlaps among the various legal categories.

---

65. Or worse, legal taxonomy is portrayed as being subject to constant renegotiation between competing power-wielding lawyers. *See* Hugh Collins, *Legal Classifications as a Production of Knowledge System, in* THE CLASSIFICATION OF OBLIGATIONS, *supra* note 3, at 57, 68.

CHAPTER 7

༄

Remedies and Rights

OPENING REMARKS

Remedies are often understood, and sensibly so, as the last stage of legal analysis. Choosing the appropriate remedy and calibrating its magnitude is indeed the last task of litigation, an issue to be addressed only after resolution of the more fundamental questions pertaining to the parties' rights. Part of private law theory endorses this truism of legal practice, either by marginalizing the discussion of remedies or by studying remedies as exogenous to the analysis of the parties' rights. In this view, remedies are understood as means for enforcing rights. Choosing remedies and calibrating them properly is thus to be guided by concerns that have little to do with the content of these rights, such as the efficacy of effectuating such enforcement via the mechanism of a court order. This approach is reflected in, and may also be perpetuated by, the study of remedies as a separate subject in the curriculum.[1]

I have no quarrel with this perspective on remedies as such. But something significant is lost when we view remedies solely through these lenses, and the failure to integrate a theory of remedies into private law theory is thus unfortunate. Remedies serve not only as instruments of rights enforcement. They also participate, albeit in rather complex and imperfect ways, in the constitution of the rights they help enforce. This proposition does not collapse rights into remedies. Remedies fulfill an important enforcement function and, consequently, sometimes there are reasons (notably institutional ones) for certain

---

1. Incidentally, contract law theory is far less affected by this approach: contract theorists tend to address remedies and appreciate the significance of remedial choices to the understanding of contractual rights. The locus classicus for this is L.L. Fuller & William R. Perdue, Jr., *The Reliance Interest in Contract Damages*, 46 YALE L.J. 52 (1936). *See* Peter Benson, *Introduction, in* THE THEORY OF CONTRACT LAW: NEW ESSAYS 1 (2001).

gaps between the content of rights and the judicial response to their infringe-ment. Nonetheless, as I argue in Part I of this chapter, which relies on (and refines) some important (and forgotten?) contributions of Karl Llewellyn to legal theory, the constitutive role of remedies is quite significant.

Part II addresses one implication of this claim. Using a typology of the available measures of recovery following cases of profitable appropriation of rights (such as trespass, conversion, or the infringement of intellectual prop-erty rights), I show that remedies infuse subtlety into the rights domain. Thus, this rich and rather intricate repertoire of seemingly technical alterna-tives provides the law with important means for refining its doctrines. More specifically, choosing between monetary remedies is often a way for law to accommodate qualitative and normatively attractive distinctions between dif-ferent types of rights. If (and insofar as) the remedies afforded in private law cases are constitutive components of rights, the multiplicity of potential rem-edies is but the outer manifestation of the heterogeneity of rights we can have as private law actors.

By insisting that remedies law forces us to recognize the multiplicity of rights, I do not mean to agonize over the integrity of rights or undermine their role in facilitating freedom, quite the contrary. As will be shown, the diversity that remedies law introduces into the realm of rights is not bound-less. Multiplicity does not mean chaos but rather a more complex and nuanced structure that limits the number of distinct types of rights and standardizes their contents. Nor does multiplicity threaten freedom, but indeed the oppo-site: it enhances both freedom and individuality.

I. Rights and Remedies

I begin with the relationship between rights and remedies. Theorists fluctu-ate between a view of rights and remedies as interdependent or independ-ent, as well as between an approach that emphasizes rights and marginalizes remedies and its opposite. But a good case can be made for an intermediate position between interdependence and independence, which recognizes the importance of rights together with the significance of remedies. Gleaning some insights from prior contributions to this important topic will help to identify this position and appreciate its virtues.

A. From Hohfeld to Llewellyn, via Calabresi and Melamed

The starting point of almost every modern discussion of legal rights is (as it should be) Wesley Hohfeld's celebrated search for "the lowest common denominators of the law." Hohfeld maintained that not all legal relations may be reduced to rights and duties, and that in order to sufficiently cover the legal terrain and illuminate "common principles of justice and policy underlying the various jural problems involved" we need to enlarge the list of fundamental legal conceptions from two to eight: rights (or claims), duties, privileges, and no-rights (dealing with interpersonal substantive relations) as well as powers, liabilities, immunities, and disabilities (dealing with interpersonal procedural relations).[2] This Hohfeldian scheme has important implications for a rights discourse. One significant insight it generates is that it is helpful to think of legal rights as jural relations; in fact, Hohfeld's suggestion to express the eight fundamental legal conceptions in terms of their "opposites" and "correlatives" implies that defining them in a nonrelational fashion is impossible. The awareness that legal rights and privileges constitute juridical *relations* is indeed crucial. If rights (broadly defined) are advantages to their holders to the extent that they are disadvantages to those subject to their correlatives, we cannot merely look at the putative holder of such rights to determine how to allocate rights, privileges, powers, and immunities among the parties involved. We must also address the conflicting claims of those who would be vulnerable given the existence of such a right.[3]

This lesson will be the cornerstone of my celebration of the multiplicity of rights. Reaching that point, however, requires first considering another Hohfeldian assertion that, unlike this one, may confuse rather than clarify the understanding of legal rights. Hohfeld claims that rights should be carefully distinguished from, and not only be thought as dependent on, both "the character of the proceedings by which [they] may be vindicated" and the remedies arising from their violation.[4] For Hohfeld, the purpose of this proposition may have been rather limited and innocuous: to dissipate two "seriously erroneous notions" that follow from the view that there is a "rigid interdependence" between rights and remedies. Regarding both these specific concerns, Hohfeld was correct. Indeed, "the vindication proceedings" of *in rem* rights may be *in personam*. By the same token, not every case of *in rem* rights necessarily allows a dispossessed owner "the remedy of recovery of possession." In numerous cases, the owner of *in rem* rights may be divested "on various grounds of policy and convenience" so that he will in fact be unable to recover possession.[5]

Hohfeld's former claim may be premised on institutional reasons that, as shown below, explain and justify certain gaps between rights and remedies,

2. Wesley Newcomb Hohfeld, *Some Fundamental Legal Conceptions as Applied in Judicial Reasoning*, 23 YALE L.J. 16 (1913).

3. *See* Joseph William Singer, *The Legal Rights Debate in Analytical Jurisprudence from Bentham to Hohfeld*, 1982 WISC. L. REV. 975, 987, 994, 1022–23, 1050, 1056–59; *see also* DUNCAN KENNEDY, A CRITIQUE OF ADJUDICATION—*FIN DE SIECLE* 305, 319, 323 (1997); Andrei Marmor, *On the Limits of Rights*, 16 LAW & PHIL. 1, 10–14 (1996).

4. Wesley Newcomb Hohfeld, *Fundamental Legal Conceptions as Applied in Judicial Reasoning*, 26 YALE L.J. 710, 753 (1917).

5. *Id.* at 754–57, 763.

whereas his latter claim reveals some of the limitations of owners' dominion, which I address in Chapter 8. Both of these propositions vindicate Hohfeld's critique of the view that a rigid and necessary interdependence prevails between rights and remedies. But Hohfeld can be read as making a stronger argument: that remedies are in fact conceptually independent of rights.[6] This position, perhaps somewhat ambiguous in Hohfeld's account, is much clearer in Guido Calabresi and Douglas Melamed's influential theory of property rules versus liability rules.

For Calabresi and Melamed, resource allocation requires the law to make two distinct determinations: one for rights, another for remedies. First, the law must decide "which of the conflicting parties will be entitled to prevail." Having made this initial choice of entitlements, the state must also make "second order decisions" on the manner of protecting these entitlements. Insofar as these second-order decisions are concerned, the scheme of Calabresi and Melamed offers a choice between two rules: a property rule or a liability rule. A property rule compels "someone who wishes to remove the entitlement from its holder to buy it from him in a voluntary transaction in which the value of the entitlement is agreed upon the seller." No one can appropriate the entitlement without first securing its holder's consent; a court will issue an injunction in case anyone attempts to do so. By contrast, where a liability rule applies, "someone may destroy the initial entitlement if he is willing to pay an objectively determined value for it." Thus, liability rules are intended to facilitate the forced transfer of the entitlement from its holder. Where liability rules apply, injunctions are unavailable. Liability rules employ an external, objective standard of value for *ex post* compensatory damages.[7]

Like Calabresi and Melamed's own account, most of the voluminous literature their account evoked concentrates on the differential costs of property rules and liability rules as simply different means of entitlement protection, thus perpetuating the purported independence of remedies from rights. But such a radical disjunction is suspicious, because one way we understand the meaning and content of a right is by looking at how we protect it.[8] Remedies

---

6. For an account of tort law that accepts a similar disjunction between the trigger for the plaintiff's right of action and the available remedies, see Benjamin C. Zipursky, *Civil Recourse, Not Corrective Justice*, 91 GEO. L.J. 695, 710–13, 735, 748–52 (2003).

7. Guido Calabresi & A. Douglas Melamed, *Property Rules, Liability Rules, and Inalienability: One View of the Cathedral*, 85 HARV. L. REV. 1089 (1972).

8. Jules Coleman and Jody Kraus emphasize this point in their analysis of Calabresi and Melamed's framework, which resists the conventional treatment noted in the text. Coleman and Kraus argue that this framework makes little sense if we understand rights as "secured or protected liberties," demarcating "a realm of liberty or control." If the point of rights is "to secure a domain of control," rather than "to guarantee a particular level of welfare or utility," rights cannot be "reducible to or otherwise identifiable with a point on a right bearer's indifference curve...certainly not if one wants to maintain the distinction between autonomy and utility." Because "the most liability

should not be discussed independently of the rights they protect or vindicate, nor can rights be adequately analyzed and understood separately from the remedies their infringement may entail, because rights delineation is part of a deliberative process that ends with the application of law's coercive power. Because the remedies provided by private law to the plaintiff invoke such a power against the defendant, they must be justified along with the rights that they protect or vindicate.[9]

Situating remedies at the core of our understanding of rights, that is, perceiving remedies as constitutive components of rights, is one of the most important lessons of legal realism. Llewellyn's discussion of the historical transition from a discourse of remedies to a discourse of rights is particularly instructive.[10] Under the former, the pertinent question was: "On what facts could one man make use of any specific one of the specific ways of making the court bother another man?" This seems problematic to later writers. "Remedies seem to them to have a *purpose*, to be protections of something else. They could imagine these somethings and give them a name—*rights*, substantive rights." Rights have thus become the center of attention and remedies "relegated to the periphery" as "'adjective law' merely—devices more or less imperfect for giving effect to the important things, the substantive rights which make up the substance of the law." The substantive right, in this view, has a shape and scope independent of the accidents of remedies.

Llewellyn acknowledges the advantages of the shift from a remedies discourse to a rights discourse. This shift helped scholars realize that "procedure,

rules can secure is a level of welfare equal to the value of the right bearer's interest, including even his interest in his autonomy[,] . . . liability rules cannot, in this view, protect rights." But this conception of rights, Coleman and Kraus claim, is mistaken because it confuses one specific justification of rights with the meaning of rights, whereas "whether rights provide autonomy or are designed purely to guarantee a level of welfare is a contingent feature of them." And once we open up the possibility that rights can designate *either liberties or interests* "as warranting a privileged status," we realize that both property rules and liability rules are best understood not as different means of entitlement protection but rather "as devices for generating or specifying the *content* or *meaning* of such rights." Thus, Coleman and Kraus conclude, the choice between these types of rules depends on the purpose we want the right at issue to serve, which in turn is determined by the pertinent foundational or normative theory we adopt "*and* the facts of the world: that is, by a theory of what is desirable as constrained by what is feasible." *See* Jules L. Coleman & Jody Kraus, *Rethinking the Theory of Legal Rights*, 95 YALE L.J. 1335, 1339–40, 1342–43, 1345, 1369–71 (1986).

9. Taking this point to what may be perceived as its logical conclusion leads to a strong version of the interdependence thesis. *See, e.g.*, ERNEST J. WEINRIB, THE IDEA OF PRIVATE LAW 135 (1995); Avihay Dorfman, *What Is the Point of the Tort Remedy?*, 55 AM. J. JURIS. 105 (2010). But this point should not be taken to its logical conclusion because the justificatory burden regarding the content and structure of the remedial apparatus applied by private law is only part of the justificatory burden of our private law. *See supra* Chapter 5.

10. *See* KARL N. LLEWELLYN, *A Realistic Jurisprudence: The Next Step, in* JURISPRUDENCE: REALISM IN THEORY AND IN PRACTICE 3, 8–18, 21–23 (1962); LLEWELLYN, *Some Realism*

remedies, existed not merely because they existed, nor because they had value in themselves, but because they had a purpose.[11] From which follows immediate inquiry into what the purpose is, and criticism, if the means to its accomplishment be poor." However, Llewellyn insists that this advantage "should not obscure the price that was paid for the advance." One such setback is that the rights discourse tends to "double the tendency to disregard the limitations actually put on rules or rights by practice and by remedies." Coloring rules in terms of rights suppresses their relativity and the proper limitations of their propositions (which is, as may be recalled, an important lesson of understanding legal rights as jural relations). This simplification of legal doctrine artificially strengthens the apparent moral validity of the right-holder's claim, unjustifiably implying that no limitations, or at least as few as possible, should be recognized. In order to circumvent this trap, Llewellyn argues, we must understand that remedies are constitutive features of rights: rights should be understood as "convenient shorthand symbols for the remedies, the actions of the courts." Hence, for Llewellyn, not only "no remedy, no right," but "precisely as much right as remedy."

Indeed, in order to avoid the pitfalls of both a pure remedies discourse and a pure rights discourse we must: (1) realize that legal rights are neither necessarily absolute nor one-dimensional but are rather complex and variable, notably with respect to their normative roles;[12] (2) appreciate the diversity of possible remedies available respecting such rights in various contingencies as well as the constitutive role of remedies as per the content and meaning of rights; and (3) insist that although remedies indeed exist for a purpose that is captured in the language of rights, the scope and content of rights (and thus the availability of various types of remedies) are, or at least can and should be, carefully circumscribed according to their underlying rationales.[13]

---

about Realism, in JURISPRUDENCE, id., at 42, 63; KARL L. LLEWELLYN, THE BRAMBLE BUSH 93–94, 96–97 (1930).

11. Taking this important point seriously requires resisting views that conceptualize tort law around the remedial obligations following tortuous activities, thus obscuring the priority of discharging the primary obligations over remedying failures to do so. See Dorfman, supra note 9; Gregory C. Keating, Is Tort a Remedial Institution? (unpublished manuscript).

12. Cf. Leif Wenar, The Nature of Rights, 33 PHIL. & PUB. AFF. 223 (2005). Wenar develops "a several functions theory" of rights and defends it against both the monistic will and interest theories of rights and the "any-incident" theory of rights. Wenar argues that "there is no one thing that rights do for rightholders. Rights have no fundamental normative purpose in this sense. Rather, rights play a number of different roles in our lives. . . . [T]hey mark exemption, or discretion, or authorization, or entitle their holders to protection, provision, or performance." Id. at 248, 252.

13. See Richard Nolan, Remedies for Breach of Contract: Specific Enforcement and Restitution, in FAILURE OF CONTRACTS: CONTRACTUAL, RESTITUTIONARY AND PROPRIETARY CONSEQUENCES 35, 37–38 (Francis D. Rose ed., 1997).

B. A Cautionary Note: The Gaps

Notwithstanding this significant contribution of Llewellyn to the understanding of remedies as constitutive components of rights, realists are accused of conflating the distinction between right and remedy.[14] This charge, although somewhat overstated, is nonetheless justified and can help to refine the lessons of the previous section. Llewellyn, as noted, points to the different functions of rights and remedies: whereas the former stands for the purpose of legal rules, the latter serves as the means for calibrating their specific content. He does not, however, allow any space for gaps between rights and remedies ("precisely as much right as remedy"), which proves mistaken on two grounds: it obscures the fact that Hohfeld had highlighted, namely that right infringements may not always trigger a remedy that fully vindicates the right at stake, and it obscures the significance of the institutions that are responsible for right-enforcement.

Stephen Smith offers a critique of this understanding of the remedies provided by courts as if they always, and necessarily, "confirm or 'replicate' already-existing duties that defendants owe to plaintiffs."[15] This conception of the relationship between rights and remedies, which he dubs "the rubber-stamp view," obscures the distinction between "the question of how citizens should behave towards one another" and "the question of what courts should do on proof that a citizen has misbehaved." The realist focus on what courts do, Smith insists, is obviously significant as per the latter issue, but cannot be determinative as per the former: in order to know what legal rights we have, one also needs to take seriously "what courts say" and "consider why, and when, it might be reasonable for courts to refuse to make an order notwithstanding that the defendant had a legal duty to do the very thing the court was asked to order the defendant to do." Smith mentions three reasons for such possible gaps: (1) whereas "cost considerations [may be] irrelevant when asking what justice requires of citizens in their interactions with other citizens," they are "clearly relevant when considering how the state should go about delivering justice"; (2) because remedies invoke law's enforcement mechanisms more immediately than rights, "the question of when and how courts should make orders is closely tied to the question of when and how

14. *See, e.g.*, Coleman & Kraus, *supra* note 8, at 1347 & n.17. Coleman and Kraus also mention that legal realists fail to appreciate that "entitlements specify the conduct others must exhibit if they seek to conform to the relevant norms, not just the sanctions or liabilities they are likely to incur in the event their conduct fails to conform." As Part II of Chapter 2 argues, however, a charitable reading of the realist legacy suggests a much more subtle position regarding law's power and its normativity.

15. Stephen A Smith, *Rights and Remedies: A Complex Relationship, in* TAKING REMEDIES SERIOUSLY 31, 33, 39, 43–47, 49–52, 55, 57–60 (Kent Roach & Robert Sharpe eds., 2010); *see also* Daphna Lewinsohn-Zamir, *Can't Buy Me Love. Monetary Versus In-Kind Remedies*, 2013 U. ILL. L. REV. 151.

plaintiffs ought to be able to invoke the state's coercive powers"; and (3) remedies are "personalized directives, issued by a court, that command a specific individual to do a specific thing" and this specificity may mean that there may be things that remedies simply cannot do.

Smith concedes that "many, probably most, court orders" are "replicative." After all, "courts should ensure, so far as possible, that justice is done or achieved in society." Because they should also assume that the legal prescriptions should follow what justice requires, their "basic role, when they make orders, should be to ensure that the rights articulated in private law are affirmed in their orders." And yet, Smith argues that given the reasons mentioned above, there are also other ways in which rights and remedies are related: (1) At times, remedies transform rights into near substitutes as when, due to the "well-known institutional disadvantages associated with orders to [perform] non-monetary obligations," "courts refuse to order defendants to perform their private law duties, and instead order them to pay plaintiffs sums of money equal to the cost of engaging third parties to perform those duties."[16] (2) Another, more significant type of gap, occurs when courts "refuse entirely to order defendants ... to do what the private law requires them to do" due to the expiration of the limitation period governing that right: a limitation period is generally understood to be premised on considerations particular to the litigation and thus not to extinguish the plaintiff's private duty but only the defendant's right to a court order. (3) Finally, Smith alludes to cases in which courts issue orders that "create entirely new duties," focusing on orders to pay punitive damages, nominal damages, and damages for pain and suffering, which he analyzes as "symbolic orders."[17]

One may question whether Smith does not exaggerate the significance of these exceptions.[18] The first, transformative, type of remedy applies only where the substitute it provides is indeed close to the original: as Smith acknowledges "[t]hese institutional advantages of monetary orders would count for little if substituting a monetary obligation for a non-monetary obligation amounted

---

16. Smith uses this point in order to critique the efficient breach theory of contract. Insofar as the prevalence of expectation damages, as opposed to specific performance, indeed relies on such institutional concerns, it cannot serve as evidence for the content of promisees' rights. It is not clear, however, that these considerations can adequately account for the many types of cases in which specific performance is denied, and that there are no good reasons for conceptualizing this right in these cases as limited to the expectation interest. *See* Daniel Markovits & Alan Schwartz, *The Myth of Efficient Breach: New Defenses of the Expectation Interest*, 97 VA. L. REV. 1939 (2011).

17. Smith also mentions cases, notably in the context of family law, in which the court's wide discretion implies that remedies are given where plaintiffs have no rights.

18. Smith argues that remedies (or court orders in his terminology) are not part of private law, although they may be of evidential value to it. Rather, in his view, "[t]he law of court orders is fundamentally a branch of public law," as it determines our rights against courts (and not against one another).

to denying the plaintiff's rights or imposing an unfair burden on the defendant." The second type of cases, in which courts refuse to issue an order, is "rare." And the third category may be far narrower than Smith proclaims because at least some of the orders he typifies as symbolic may be conceptualized as vindicating plaintiffs' rights, as is the case where punitive damages are carefully addressed at the aggravated injury inflicted on the plaintiff by the defendant's malevolence, which injures her feelings of dignity and self-worth.[19]

Still, Smith's analysis correctly challenges Llewellyn's rubber-stamp account of remedies. But rather than supplant Llewellyn's account, his analysis can, and should, supplement it. (In fact, these claims should have been integrated into Llewellyn's own account because as a realist he should have considered the institutional contexts wherein rights are translated into remedies far more carefully.[20]) Smith's—and Hohfeld's—references to the possible gaps between rights and remedies can be so integrated because, as Smith acknowledges, the instances of remedies deviating from this account are the exception rather than the rule. This means that Llewellyn's excesses can be corrected and his account refined by looking into the possible gap between right and remedy and studying the types of cases where such a gap is likely to exist.

(Notice, however, that this proposition is limited to the gap between our private law rights and the remedies provided by courts in response to claims following their violations. The gap may unfortunately be much wider, with rights far less protected or vindicated, if we include cases where no such litigation is instigated or followed through for a variety of reasons, or where court orders are not properly enforced. This only means, however, that though we know injustice is rampant out there, we expect courts to refuse to give it their approval once they have a say.)

II. A Coherent Multiplicity

A. *Chaos and Order in Pecuniary Recovery*

These cautionary notes notwithstanding, the notion that remedies are not merely means to protect rights but rather constitutive features of these rights may seem troubling to private law theorists. If indeed different remedial responses constitute differing types of rights, the diversity of remedial apparatuses found in private law translates into a multiplicity of legal rights, which in turn appears to threaten the coherence of private law. This challenge

19. *See* Ernest J. Weinrib, *Punishment and Disgorgement as Contract Remedies*, 78 CHI.-KENT L. REV. 55, 91, 98 (2003); *cf.* Dorfman, *supra* note 9, at 156.

20. For a discussion highlighting the realist commitment to institutional analysis, see Roy Kreitner, *Biographing Legal Realism*, 35 L. & SOC. INQ. 765 (2010).

is further aggravated once we realize that, alongside the heterogeneity of remedies, our private law rights are also distinguished from each other by their applicable qualifications, limitations, and exceptions. (In fact, I discuss remedies in this chapter only as one, particularly important, example of a source of the potential complexity of our private law rights. Chapter 8 builds on the lessons of this chapter as per the multiplicity of legal rights in order to spell out the outline of a pluralistic account of property.)

On its face, the multiplicity of legal rights may indeed imply unbridled discretion for legal decision makers, which means that our private law is unprincipled and thus, unpredictable (maybe even unintelligible) and illegitimate. But before agonizing over the demise of private law, we should try to read the law more charitably and consider the possibility that such multiplicity can coexist with order and predictability and even more importantly, might be normatively attractive.[21]

I obviously cannot hope to adequately vindicate this optimistic proposition here, but I do hope that the following test case, which builds on my previous work,[22] is suggestive enough. My test case deals with rules governing monetary recovery following the profitable appropriation of different types of resources: land and chattels; copyright, trademarks, and patents; trade secrets, contractual relations and performance, and pre-contractual expectations; individual reputation and dignity, commercial attributes of personality, and even identity and physical integrity. This category of cases is deliberately simple in two ways. First, I focus only on claims for pecuniary remedies, thus making my example relatively less vulnerable to the institutional reasons, discussed earlier, for gaps between rights and (typically nonmonetary) remedies. Second, I do not discuss the entire terrain of rights infringements. Rather, I refer only to a subset of cases wherein the defendant *knowingly* appropriates an interest of the plaintiff in order to pursue a profitable activity that, in principle, is also *possible* without such an infringement. This paradigm is obviously much simpler than the typical accident case where the defendant engaged in an activity that *necessarily* but only *statistically* infringes others' rights.[23] (As I hint in the

21. This would also mean that although rights are rather multifaceted, they are not reducible to rules. *Cf.* Joseph Raz, *On the Nature of Rights*, 93 MIND 194 (1984).

22. *See* HANOCH DAGAN, UNJUST ENRICHMENT: A STUDY OF PRIVATE LAW AND PUBLIC VALUES chs. 2 & 4 (1997), on which the remainder of this section draws.

23. An additional important distinction that makes my test case easier is that, because I deal with cases of profitable invasions, the choice of applicable measure of recovery can credibly serve as evidence whether the law indeed sanctions a transfer subject to compensation or refuses to treat such compensation as a substitute to consent. By contrast, because in most accident cases the plaintiff's harm is greater than the defendant's profits, the fact that law's typical remedy in such cases is aimed at making the plaintiff whole cannot arbitrate between these rival interpretations. For a recent attempt to resolve this ambiguity, see Mark A. Geistfeld, *Tort Law and the Inherent Limitations of Monetary Exchange: Property Rules, Liability Rules, and the Negligence Rule*, 4(1) J. TORT L., art. 4 (2011).

next section, I hope that some of the lessons of the discussion below may be helpful in this type of case as well. But the two distinctions just noted add crucial dimensions that are missing in our test case, which suggest that it should not be read as simplistically applicable also in the context of accidents.)

Not all cases of appropriation of the various resources mentioned above lead to the same measure of recovery; rather, private law applies different measures of recovery to different resources.[24] Thus, concerning some resources, mere appropriation triggers a rather severe measure of recovery that allows the resource holder to choose between the fair market value of the resource or its unauthorized use and the net profit gained by the appropriator. In U.S. law, this is the case when appropriations infringe the plaintiff's rights to her identity, physical integrity, or land. On the other hand, the invasion of other types of resources triggers pecuniary recovery only if the defendant employed improper means.[25] Thus, the sheer appropriation of trade secrets or pre-contractual expectations triggers no liability. In between these two poles, there are several other interesting points. Thus, the infringement of copyright allows the plaintiff to choose between the fair market value of the copyright at issue and a proportional part of the defendant's profits. The infringement of patents, however, allows a plaintiff only the recovery of fair market value.

This diversity of recovery measures concerning the appropriation of different resources may seem perplexing at first sight. Indeed, if remedies are analyzed along the lines of the Calabresi–Melamed framework of examining the comparative efficiencies of different measures of recovery as different means of protecting entitlements, it is not easily explicable.[26] For anyone who appreciates the constitutive role of remedies but resists a pluralist conception of legal rights, this remedial diversity seems even more arbitrary.

This diversity, however, is by no means chaotic or unprincipled. The different pecuniary measures available to the injured party—from profits garnered by the appropriator at the resource-holder's expense, through various intermediate measures such as fair market value of the resource (or its use), and up to

24. This was first noted in Daniel Friedmann, *Restitution of Benefits Obtained through the Appropriation of Property or the Commission of a Wrong*, 80 COLUM. L. REV. 504, 512–13, 556–57 (1980).

25. Admittedly, this aspect relates to the exact scope of the right, rather than the type of remedy. It nonetheless serves my discussion here because, as noted, remedies' variability is only one example for the more general point of rights multiplicity.

26. A possible economic explanation for some remedial diversity may focus on the divergent subjective disutility people may experience from the appropriation of different types of resources. The difficulties of verifying these harms and the entailed risk of their under-compensation may suggest that, where transaction costs are not too high, the appropriation of constitutive resources triggers harsh measures of recovery. I am not familiar with any full-blown account of the appropriation paradigm along these lines and am somewhat skeptical that it may successfully account for this doctrine, given its need to carefully balance the different risks of under-compensation and the divergent levels of transaction costs.

mere compensation for the harm suffered—stand for different types of rights. The profits measure of recovery renders infringements pointless to potential invaders, thus implying that transfers can be made legitimate only by obtaining the resource-holder's consent prior to the transfer. By deterring nonconsensual invasions and insisting on consent as a prerequisite to any legitimate transfer, the profits remedy constitutes an entitlement that defines a domain of individual control over a resource. The remedy of fair market value, in contrast, does not deter appropriations—indeed, at times, it may even encourage them. Thus, where fair market value caps liability, the forced transfer of the relevant resource seems legitimate. Unless such a limitation can be attributed to some institutional reason along the lines discussed above, the *ex post* pecuniary recovery seems to serve here as a surrogate for *ex ante* consent. Fair market value as a remedy secures the economic value of the entitlement that, as no better proxy is available, measures its (objective) level of well-being or utility to its holder. Finally, recovery limited to compensation for the harm suffered sanctions the appropriator's claim to a share of the resource-holder's entitlement so long as the former does not actually diminish the latter's estate. Thus, the harm-based measure of recovery vindicates the value of sharing; it can be understood as a form of limited institutionalized altruism, a legal device that calls for other-regarding action and seeks to instill other-regarding motives.

This (skeleton of a) translation scheme of measures of recovery into types of entitlements[27] helps to expose the order that governs the diversity of measures of recovery dealing with cases of appropriation. Translating these remedies

---

27. The full translation scheme is captured in the following table (from DAGAN, *supra* note 22, at 22):

Measure of Recovery	Rationale	Vindication of...
Harm	*Sharing*	the invader's claim to share the entitlement with its holder without unduly harming her
Fair Market Value	*Well-Being*	the resource holder's well-being
Proportional Profits (where *Proportional Profits* exceeds *Fair Market Value*)	*Well-Being & Hypothetical Consent*	both the resource holder's well-being and her hypothetical consent
Profits	*Control*	the resource holder's control over the resources at her disposal
Max (*Fair Market Value, Profits*)	*Well-Being & Control*	both the resource holder's well-being and her control
Proceeds	*Control & Condemnation*	both the resource holder's control and society's condemnation

into types of entitlements, while remembering that the distribution of entitlements is organized by resource, is the key to understand and maybe even justify law's diversity.[28] Different resources are subject to different types of entitlements due to the qualitative distinctions between their respective social meanings.[29] More specifically, the qualitative distinctions between the various resources people hold, mirror (and arguably also shape) the intrinsic significance of those resources in their holders' lives, the degree to which they are perceived as constitutive of their holders' identities. The law vigorously vindicates people's control of their most precious, constitutive resources: their identities, physical integrity, reputations (as dignity), and land. Interests invested with a lesser degree of personhood—copyright and (to a smaller degree) the commercial attributes of one's personality and patents—are less protected. Finally, the mere appropriation of resources from the third group (which includes the least personal resources—contractual relations and performances, and information) does not trigger liability unless the invasion was conducted by improper means. It is mostly with regard to resources that are relatively remote from the crux of selfhood that a prescription of sharing applies.

B. Contingency, Normativity, and Critique

This understanding of the law of pecuniary remedies following appropriations may indeed bring order to a heterogeneous legal terrain, but this order seems to come at a price. The relative intrinsic value of resources is premised, after all, on socially contingent facts: the privileged resources mentioned above are resources to which people, here and now, are arguably attached because they are understood both by those people and by their society as reflecting their holders' identities. In other words, the social meaning of the resource in question—which is local rather than universal, contingent rather than necessary—determines its relative value.[30] But relying on such socially contingent

---

28. If one focuses on the availability of injunctions in these various contexts, one would admittedly find much more uniformity. But this uniformity seems to be misleading, because if indeed the general availability of injunctions would have stood for a uniform *Well-Being & Control* type of entitlement, it would have not made much sense for the law to limit the *ex post* pecuniary recovery to less than max (*Fair Market Value, Profits*) in any of the categories mentioned above. Therefore, it seems that the broad availability of injunctions must be analyzed in terms that deviate from the contours of the rights they vindicate. In other words, this is yet another gap between rights and remedies, which—as we have seen—makes translation exercises quite difficult and nuanced.

29. *See* Margaret J. Radin, *Property and Personhood*, 34 STAN. L. REV. 957, 992, 1013 (1982).

30. A similar characteristic applies regarding the way accident law makes qualitative distinctions between different types of activities based on their contingent social meanings. The claims that follow apply mutatis mutandis to this phenomenon, as the

facts seems problematic. Why should they matter to private law? What, in other words, is their moral significance? And is it possible to allow such facts of our existing social world to affect our legal prescriptions without collapsing into a legal regime that unreflectively entrenches our contingent reality?[31]

I believe that the contingency of the value that we, as a society, ascribe to certain resources does not undermine its moral significance. This proposition does not rely on the philosophically suspect metaethical positions of relativism, skepticism, or nihilism. These positions undermine any possibility of moral justification, evaluation, or criticism, thus undermining the idea of law itself.[32] Value pluralists, who reject these problematic positions, still insist that some significant degree of cross-cultural variability is morally acceptable. Following Isaiah Berlin, value pluralists maintain that human life is replete with competing values that cannot be reconciled, as well as with legitimate wishes that cannot be truly satisfied. Because some values intrinsically conflict, and because we cannot have everything we want, we must make choices. "The need to choose, to sacrifice some ultimate values to others, turns out to be a permanent characteristic of the human predicament."[33]

Many of our private law claims to resources (and activities) require the law to make such difficult accommodations. Every society is called upon to pick and choose certain resources (and activities) as more valuable and, given value pluralism, there is no single right choice. Frequently, the contingent social meanings of resources (and activities) will themselves determine the resources in which people invest their personalities (and the activities they perceive as indispensable to their lives). Usually, there is no reason to think that subjective valuations will be particularly idiosyncratic. Resources gain their significance as reflections of the self through *social* processes. People perceive certain resources as reflecting their personalities better than others, and thus attach subjective value to them because other people in society, to whom the self's external image is communicated, share with them the same symbolic understanding. Therefore, not only considerations of rule of law, but also the nature of the very phenomenon of constitutive property justifies law's reference to social (objective) meanings.

The contingency of the list of privileged resources does not render it morally insignificant.[34] The practice of personality reflection in resources is morally valuable because external identifications and registrations of the self in socially contingent resources impose consistency, permanency, and stability

text that follows implies. *See* Hanoch Dagan, *Qualitative Judgments and Social Meanings in Private Law: A Comment on Professor Keating*, 4 THEORETICAL INQ. L. 89 (2003).

31. *See* Stephen J. Schnably, *Property and Pragmatism: A Critique of Radin's Theory of Property and Personhood*, 45 STAN. L. REV. 347 (1993).

32. *See* STEVEN J. BURTON, JUDGING IN GOOD FAITH 19–21 (1992).

33. Isaiah Berlin, *Introduction*, *in* FOUR ESSAYS ON LIBERTY at l-li (1969).

34. *Cf.* MEIR DAN-COHEN, *Defending Dignity*, *in* HARMFUL THOUGHTS: ESSAYS ON LAW, SELF, AND MORALITY 150 (2002).

upon people's resolutions, plans, and projects; although the specific identity of these resources turns out to be a matter of contingent social fact, this practice requires responsibility, self-discipline, and maturity, and thus fosters people's moral development.[35] Indeed, many social practices that are absent from or insignificant in other social environments, places, and eras may well provide us with invaluable channels of self-expression or with means that expand our options and allow us to achieve objectives that would otherwise be unattainable.[36] Because these resources (and activities) are justifiably valuable, private law is justifiably deferential to these socially contingent facts.[37]

Yet, by no means does it follow that we must blindly accept the contingent content of our social world, either in general or in legal discourse. Quite the contrary: although private law theory needs to rely on contingent social practices, it can and should lead us to constantly reexamine our too-often implicit and even subconscious assumptions about the relative value of resources (and activities). By making these assumptions explicit, private law theory is potentially subversive because it helps us realize that in order to validate our current practices we need to justify the relative value we attribute to resources (and activities). The requirement of justification is always potentially challenging to some of our social practices because it requires a respectable universalistic façade at the very least—an idealized picture that can be, and often is, a fertile source of social criticism because it sets standards that our current practices do not necessarily live up to. The idealism of our social world, even if hypocritical, is the best source of any critical engagement.[38]

Take, for example, our understanding of land as constitutive property and the corresponding significance we attach to land ownership. Traditionally, land has been one of the most prominent objects of property rights in Western culture, accorded unique status as a symbol of the self and as a resource closely linked to personal freedom, rank, and power.[39] This social value invites a

---

35. *See* JEREMY WALDRON, THE RIGHT TO PRIVATE PROPERTY 353, 364–65, 369–70, 372–73, 378, 385 (1988); *see also* Peter G. Stillman, *Property, Freedom, and Individuality in Hegel's and Marx's Political Thought*, 22 NOMOS 130, 135 (1980).

36. *See generally* JOSEPH RAZ, *The Value of Practice*, *in* ENGAGING REASON: ON THE THEORY OF VALUE AND ACTION 202 (1999).

37. More precisely, the justification for resorting to the social meanings of resources and of activities is both (1) epistemic or pragmatic, namely: the ideals (on which the practices we have worked out over time are founded) are oftentimes helpful starting points to guide us to the right values; and (2) democratic, that is: at least some part of law's authority—especially the authority of the common law—rests on the way in which its evolution is a story of articulating in doctrine the values implicit in the community's practices facing normative challenges emerging out of real-life encounters.

38. *See* MICHAEL WALZER, INTERPRETATION AND SOCIAL CRITICISM 22, 30, 41, 43, 46–48, 61 (1987); *see also* Margaret Jane Radin, *Lacking a Transformative Social Theory: A Response*, 45 STAN. L. REV. 409 (1993).

39. *See* Clare Cooper, *The House as Symbol of the Self*, *in* ENVIRONMENTAL PSYCHOLOGY: PEOPLE AND THEIR PHYSICAL SETTINGS 435, 437–38 (Harold M. Proshansky et al. eds.,

certain degree of refinement: the distinction between "personal land" (such as the family home or farm) and "fungible land" (used solely for commercial purposes). If some of the legal privileges accorded to landowners are justified by reference to the nature of land as property of a constitutive nature, as they frequently are, then these privileges should arguably be limited to personal land only.[40] Indeed, thus used, the language of rights not only avoids the risk of reifying contingent choices that Llewellyn alluded to, but can also actively participate in reforming our nonideal social reality. Rights discourse can perform this task by helping us see the gaps between existing doctrinal rules and their justificatory premises, thus forcing us to rethink those cases in which the law does not live up to its latent ideals.[41]

CONCLUDING REMARKS

Private law theory tends to shy away from pluralistic accounts. But private law knows better. It tends to set up rather narrow categories corresponding to the differentiated segments of human conduct and interaction into which our lives are divided. The different types of available remedies and of possible qualifications, limitations, and even obligations, which some theorists may be tempted to treat as legalistic details, help private law to construct various types of rights. This variety and the contingent facts on which it partly relies should not be embarrassing. Quite the contrary, a truly liberal law must resist uniformity and endorse multiplicity, which is both freedom-enhancing and

---

2d ed. 1976); HERBERT MCCLOSKY & JOHN ZALLER, THE AMERICAN ETHOS: PUBLIC ATTITUDES TOWARD CAPITALISM AND DEMOCRACY 138 (1984); Russell W. Belk, *Possessions and the Extended Self*, 15 J. CONSUMER RES. 139, 153 (1988); Lynton K. Caldwell, *Land and the Law: Problems in Legal Philosophy*, 1986 U. ILL. L. REV. 319, 320; Donald W. Large, *This Land Is Whose Land? Changing Concepts of Land as Property*, 1973 WIS. L. REV. 1039, 1040; E. Doyle MaCarthy, *Toward a Sociology of the Physical World: George Herbert Mead on Physical Objects*, 5 STUD. SYMBOLIC INTERACTION 105, 116–17 (1984). *But see* Stephanie M. Stern, *Residential Protectionism and the Legal Mythology of the Home*, 107 MICH. L. REV. 1093 (2009).

40. First clues to such a distinction can be found in Hawkes Estate v. Silver Campsites, [1994] 7 W.W.R. 709, 721 (B.C.); Centex Homes Corp. v. Boag, 820 A.2d 194 (Sup. Ct. N.J. 1974); *see also* LORNA FOX, CONCEPTUALISING HOME: THEORIES, LAWS AND POLICIES (2007) (mapping the concept of home in other disciplines against existing legal frameworks and examining the possibilities for developing a coherent concept of home in law). More generally, if land or some other resource is important to the individual because only by owning and controlling it will property ensure a stability and maturity that would not otherwise be possible, meaning that, if, absent some constitutive ownership, people's moral development would be seriously at risk, then property (specifically, potentially constitutive property) must be available to all. *See* WALDRON, *supra* note 35, at 377–78, 385–86, 429, 444.

41. *Cf.* RONALD DWORKIN, TAKING RIGHTS SERIOUSLY 118–23 (1977).

individuality-enhancing. Furthermore, as I argue in more detail in Chapter 8, although there may be value in looking for a rather thin common denominator of the wide terrain of legal doctrine covered by wholesale legal categories such as contracts, torts, or property, it is remarkable to assume that such a common denominator can be robust enough to illuminate the existing doctrines or determinative enough to provide significant guidance as per their evaluation or development. Only by appreciating private law's multiplicity and understanding the normative value of the (at times contingent) choices on which it relies, as well as their potential critical bite, can private law theory provide a better understanding of the order embedded in this complex legal mosaic and, possibly, even fruitfully contribute to its improvement.

CHAPTER 8

✧

Pluralism and Perfectionism
in Private Law

OPENING REMARKS

Private law, more than any other part of law, structures our daily interactions. Justifiably then, many private law theories view its doctrines as encapsulating some fundamental normative commitments. To be sure, explicitly, or more frequently implicitly, private law theories do recognize the gap between values that should guide us as moral agents and values that should be entrenched in law. Given that law backs up its normative prescriptions with coercive power,[1] at least in a liberal legal system, its demands are typically more modest than those of morality. But even if we set aside the values that should be beyond the reach of the law (a category that theorists define in different ways), it is not surprising to find that values such as autonomy, utility, and community are the building blocks of private law theory.

Many private law scholars strive to formulate broad unified normative theories of property, contracts, torts, and restitution or, at times, even of private law as a whole. These monist accounts, as I call them, suggest that one value guides the various doctrines in these complex legal fields or that, even if more than one value shapes a given field, there is one particular balance of such values that guides the entire terrain, so that they are governed by one regulative principle. Thus, regarding property, my central example in this chapter, monist theorists typically argue—relying on either autonomy or utility or on an amalgam of the two—that exclusion is property's regulative principle. As Thomas Merrill and Henry Smith claim, "the core of property is the simple right of an

---

1. Even H.L.A. Hart, the most unwavering critic of theories of law that emphasize coercion, conceded the constitutive role of power in the nature of law. *See supra* Part I.A of Chapter 3.

owner to exclude the world from the resource," and other manifestations of property are situated at the periphery, being "refinements outside the core of property."[2] (According to a similarly monist account of contracts, contract law is by and large governed, or should be governed, by the will of the parties or by their mutual consent, irrespective of the type of contract at hand.[3])

The structural monism of these theories, such as the one examined in Part I, seems appealing. By conceptualizing an entire legal field such as property as revolving around one idea such as exclusion, monist theories tend to be parsimonious and elegant, thus satisfying an important demand of the practice of theorizing. They also avoid the seemingly intractable difficulties of pluralist theories in addressing contextual conflicts of values or contextual applications of values. Finally, the broad coherence monist theories celebrate means that the law talks to the people with one voice and is thus deserving of their obedience.

But monist theories can hardly account for the vast heterogeneity of our private law doctrines. Private law tends to set up rather narrow categories, each covering only relatively few human situations and governed by a distinct set of rules expressing differing underlying normative commitments. Thus, for example, property law includes, side by side, doctrines that by and large comply with a libertarian commitment to negative liberty (think fee simple absolute), alongside doctrines where ownership is mostly a locus of communitarian sharing (as in marital property) or the maximization and just distribution of the social pie of scientific knowledge and its products (as with patents), as well as many other doctrines vindicating various types of balance among these and other property values. A unifying theory of property that would be robust but would not turn into a straitjacket for such a diverse set of doctrines is hard to imagine.

Monist theorists seem to face rather unappealing choices. They can redefine their respective subjects (say, property law) so as to marginalize the considerable sections that are not really responsive to the regulative principle they advocate. Alternatively, they can discard any pretense to account for our existing law and present their theory as reformist, advocating a significant legal change that will indeed render that field monistically guided by their favorite regulative principle. Or, finally, they can come up with a sufficiently abstract and capacious regulative principle so as to encompass the heterogeneous legal

2. *See* Thomas W. Merrill & Henry E. Smith, *The Morality of Property*, 48 Wm. & Mary L. Rev. 1849, 1857, 1891 (2007).

3. For the will and consent theories of contract law, see, respectively, Charles Fried, Contract as Promise: A Theory of Contractual Obligation (1981), and Randy E. Barnett, *A Consent Theory of Contract*, 86 Colum. L. Rev. 269 (1986). One (although by no means the only) prominent monist torts theory finds the optimal deterrence of potential tortfeasors to be torts' regulative principle. *See, e.g.,* William M. Landes & Richard A. Posner, The Economic Structure of Tort Law 58 (1987).

materials they theorize about. Insofar as this last strategy leads to a victory, it tends to be a Pyrrhic one, at least for those who purport to develop a *legal* theory[4]: the common denominator of the wide terrain of legal doctrines covered by wholesale legal categories such as property, contracts, torts, or restitution is so thin that it can hardly illuminate the existing doctrines or be determinative enough to provide significant guidance as to their evaluation or development.

The lure of private law monism can and should be resisted.[5] Private law theory should take seriously the existing structural pluralism of private law and celebrate, rather than suppress (as variations on a common theme) or marginalize (as peripheral exceptions to a robust core) the multiple forms typifying private law. Part II considers four reasons for this position, and the two main ones should be briefly introduced here. One straightforward reason relies on value pluralism: as Isaiah Berlin famously observed, human life is replete with competing values that cannot be reconciled, as well as with legitimate wishes that cannot be truly satisfied.[6] Furthermore, even critics of value pluralism as a foundational position should follow suit. Many of these critics—notably: foundational monists who hold that the only ultimate value is autonomy, understood as the ability to be the author of one's life—should adopt the structural pluralist prescriptions due to their instrumental role in promoting this one foundational value.[7]

The pluralism of private law should not be confused with value neutrality. Although careful not to impose a specific conception of the good life on the citizenry, and happy to introduce and facilitate diverse forms of human interaction and human flourishing, private law is—as I argue in Part III—far from being value-neutral. Each one of its categories targets, in its own way and with respect to some intended realm of application, a set of human values that can be promoted by its constitutive rules. Although many of these rules function as defaults, the number of frameworks of social interaction and cooperation that private law facilitates is limited, and their content is relatively standardized. These features allow private law not only to consolidate people's expectations regarding these core types of human relationships but also to express law's normative ideals for these types of human interaction. Private law is not

4. *See supra* Chapter 4.

5. *Cf.* Yishai Blank, *The Reenchantment of Law*, 96 CORNELL L. REV. 633, 634 (2011).

6. ISAIAH BERLIN, FOUR ESSAYS ON LIBERTY, at l-li (1969).

7. Arguably, efficiency may also serve as the normative foundation of structural pluralism, but for this, it is not enough to show that efficiency considerations underlie many rules of various private law institutions. Rather, one must demonstrate that, like autonomy, efficiency also entails a robust commitment to pluralism. Furthermore, even if such a claim can be substantiated, there are likely to be differences between autonomy-based pluralism and efficiency-based pluralism. *See infra* text accompanying note 51.

shy of expressing the core perfectionist claim: that there are objective criteria of human good.

Accordingly, against the conception of property as exclusion, Part IV offers a pluralist conception of property. In this conception, which I defended at length in my book, *Property: Values and Institution*,[8] property is an umbrella for a set of institutions, serving a pluralistic set of liberal values: autonomy, utility, labor, personhood, community, and distributive justice. Property law, at its best, tailors different configurations of entitlements to different property institutions, with each such institution designed to match the specific balance between property values best suited to its characteristic social setting. Thus, what looks like a random mess from a monist viewpoint turns out to be a rich mosaic once the structural pluralist perspective is utilized. This mosaic is obviously important for foundational value pluralism. It is similarly valuable for people's autonomy[9]: whereas the fee simple absolute facilitates people's independence (and is thus indeed indispensible for liberal societies), law's support for other property institutions as well as the possibility of further tailoring a property institution to the interacting parties' preferences and conceptions of the good are crucial for facilitating people's ability to choose and revise their forms of interaction with other individuals respecting diverse types of resources.

I. One Monistic Failure

Property theory is a helpful case study of private law structural monism because it seems to be currently preoccupied with a search for a unified understanding of property. More specifically, one of the important recent developments in property theory is the intellectual rehabilitation of Blackstone's conception of property as "sole and despotic dominion."[10] After decades in which the bundle-of-sticks picture of property endorsed by the Restatement of Property[11] had been regarded as the conventional wisdom, several leading property scholars are again considering the right to exclude as the most

---

8. HANOCH DAGAN, PROPERTY: VALUES AND INSTITUTIONS (2011).

9. Property pluralism is necessary for promoting people's autonomy, but it is obviously not sufficient.

10. 2 William Blackstone, COMMENTARIES ON THE LAWS OF ENGLAND *2 (Univ. of Chi. ed. 1979) (1765–1769).

11. RESTATEMENT (FIRST) OF PROP. ch.1, intro note, § 5 (1936) (defining "property" as "legal relations between persons with respect to a thing" and "interest" as "varying aggregates of rights, privileges, powers, and immunities"). For the canonical statement of the bundle conception of property, see Wesley Newcomb Hohfeld, *Fundamental Legal Conceptions as Applied in Judicial Reasoning*, 26 YALE L.J. 710, 746–47 (1917) (conceptualizing property as "a complex aggregate" of rights (or claims), privileges, powers, and immunities).

defining feature of property. As Merrill and Smith argue, "the differentiating feature of a system of property [is] the right of the owner to act as the exclusive gatekeeper of the owned thing."[12]

These sophisticated accounts differ in their details, and addressing all of them exceeds the scope of this chapter,[13] but pointing out the common structure of the most appealing ones within this growing trend will suffice for my current purpose. To begin with, these accounts tend to be fiercely critical of the disaggregation of property into a bundle of sticks. By contrast, they celebrate what is perceived as the lay understanding of property as exclusion, highlighting the underappreciated wisdom in this conception, either in terms of autonomy or in terms of efficiency. The ensuing conclusion is that, although the penumbra of property may include shades and hues, its core is nicely captured by the owner's right to exclude.

Consider, for example, James Penner's influential account of property as exclusion.[14] In Penner's view, "property is what the average citizen, free of the entanglements of legal philosophy, thinks it is: the right to a thing," or, more precisely, the right to exclusively "determine how particular things will be used." The authority to exclusively determine the use of things, or the power to exclude others "from the determination of [their] use," he explains, is significant "because of the freedom it provides to shape our lives," which is an important part of "any fairly robust interest in autonomy." Penner argues that "property rights can be fully explained using the concepts of exclusion and use." Although use is more fundamental to autonomy than exclusion, the fact that "in the real world . . . the vast majority of the uses that a person will make of a thing are impossible if everyone tries to use the thing at the same time" entails the "obvious solution" of linking "rights of use with rights of exclusion." In other words, "the interest we have in purposefully dealing with things," either by way of "using in the narrow sense" or, more broadly, by "having some purpose in respect of the use to which the thing will be put," serves "a justificatory role" for the right to property, whereas the right to exclude others from such things is "the formal essence of the right."

For Penner, this "interest in exclusively using things" unifies property because it is "regarded as a justification which explains and dictates the contours of the right which protects it." Thus, understanding property as a bundle of sticks is misleading: all these sticks (or incidents), such as the right to

---

12. Merrill & Smith, *supra* note 2, at 1850; *see also, e.g.,* J.W. HARRIS, PROPERTY AND JUSTICE 29–30, 34, 65–66 (1996); Larissa Katz, *Exclusion and Exclusivity in Property Law,* 58 U. TORONTO L.J. 275 (2008).

13. I discuss these accounts in DAGAN, *supra* note 8, at chs. 2 & 3. This part draws on these chapters.

14. *See* J.E. PENNER, THE IDEA OF PROPERTY IN LAW 2, 5, 49–50, 69–71 (1997); J.E. Penner, *The "Bundle of Rights" Picture of Property,* 43 UCLA L. REV. 711, 745, 754, 765–66 (1996).

possess, use, manage, and so forth, are mere elaborations of what the right to exclude encompasses or entails.[15] Property is not "some bundled together aggregate or complex of norms, but a single, coherent right": "the right to exclusive use," which "correlate[s] with, or can be derived from, the duty of others to exclude themselves from the property." Penner endorses this idea of property not only because, as noted, it ensures independence that is in turn significant for autonomy, but also because—*pace* Blackstone's critics—it is *not* antisocial: "the ability to share one's things, or let others use them, *is* fundamental in the idea of property."[16] In property as exclusion, sharing comes about not as an external requirement but rather as a voluntary determination of the owner, so that permitting another to use one's property is tantamount to "adopting that use as one's own."

Although understanding property as a formless bundle of sticks open to ad hoc judicial adjustments indeed bears no resemblance to the law of property as lawyers know it or, even more important, as citizens experience it in everyday life, neither does the conception of property as a monistic institution revolve around the idea of exclusion.[17] To be sure, some parts of the property drama do indeed consist in governing the productive struggle between autonomous excluders, with each individual cloaked in the Blackstonian armor of sole and despotic dominion, and, as such, can reasonably be accounted for within the exclusion paradigm. And yet, the notion that property as an idea is about the owner's power to exclude is a great exaggeration (and a rather damaging one, as it tends to improperly bolster the cultural power of libertarian claims[18]).

Property can be understood as an exclusive right, and exclusion or exclusivity can exhaust the meaning of property and thus be properly described as its core, only if we set aside arbitrarily large parts of what constitutes property law, at least according to the conventional understanding found in the case law, the Restatements, and the academic commentary. Indeed, many property rules that prescribe the rights and obligations of members of local communities, neighbors, co-owners, partners, and family members, including rights regarding the governance of these property institutions, cannot be analyzed

---

15. For Penner, however, the right to sell or make other market transactions (as opposed to gifts) is, quite idiosyncratically, not part of the right to property. *See* PENNER, *supra* note 12, at 87–93. Thus, insofar as my critique of the unfortunate implications of exclusion-centrism deals with alienability, it does not necessarily apply to him.

16. This point is further emphasized in James Penner, *Ownership, Co-Ownership, and the Justification of Property Rights*, *in* PROPERTIES OF LAW 166, 166–67 (Timothy Benedict ed., 2006).

17. The source, or at least an important milestone in this notorious and misleading dichotomy, is BRUCE A. ACKERMAN, PRIVATE PROPERTY AND THE CONSTITUTION (1977).

18. *See* Stephen R. Munzer, *A Bundle Theorist Holds on to His Collection of Sticks*, 8 ECON. J. WATCH 265, 269 (2011).

fairly through terms of exclusion. Whereas exclusion is silent as to the internal life of property, these elaborate property governance doctrines provide structures for cooperative, rather than competitive or hierarchical, relationships.[19] Pace Penner, sharing and cooperation in these doctrines are not the choice of a person who already enjoys sole and despotic dominion but rather a constitutive feature of the property institution, which defines the content of that person's property right. Furthermore, in shaping the contours of these property institutions, concerns about insiders' governance may be as, or even more, informative than concerns about outsiders' exclusion.[20]

Limits on the right of individual or group property owners to exclude, whether by refusing to sell or lease or by insisting that nonowners do not physically enter their land, are also quite prevalent in property law.[21] In certain circumstances, the right of nonowners to be included and exercise a right to entry is even typical of property, as in, for example, the law of public accommodations, the copyright doctrine of fair use, and the law of fair housing, notably in the contexts of common-interest communities law and landlord–tenant law.[22] These rights of entry of nonowners are not an embarrassing aberration. Although inclusion is less characteristic of property than exclusion—in the limiting case of inclusion, namely, universal equal access, there is no owner—its manifestations are just as intrinsic to property and should not be perceived as external limitations or impositions. This is the case because, in a rather diverse set of circumstances, the limitations and qualifications of exclusion and the rights of nonowners to be included as buyers, lessees, or "physical entrants" are grounded in the very reasons— the very same property values—that justify the support of our legal system for the pertinent property institution.[23]

The claim that limitations on exclusion are internal to property seems rather obvious insofar as they are grounded in collectivist justifications for private property, such as the welfare or utility value of property.[24] But as we have seen

19. See generally DAGAN, supra note 8, at chs. 8–10; see also Gregory S. Alexander, Governance Property, 160 U. PA. L. REV. 1853, 1856–58 (2012).

20. Think, for example, of the frequently implicit reasons underlying doctrines dealing with the conditions under which legal conflicts between owners and third parties are resolved. See DAGAN, supra note 8, at ch. 1.

21. See, e.g., Kevin Gray & Susan Francis Gray, Civil Rights, Civil Wrongs and Quasi-Public Space, 1999 EUR. HUM. RTS. L. REV. 46, 78–79.

22. See DAGAN, supra note 8, at ch. 2; see also, e.g., JAMES GORDLEY, FOUNDATIONS OF PRIVATE LAW: PROPERTY, TORT, CONTRACT, UNJUST ENRICHMENT 130–39 (2006), discussing the doctrine of necessity.

23. Cf. Joseph W. Singer, No Right to Exclude: Public Accommodations and Private Property, 90 NW. U. L. REV. 1283, 1303 (1996).

24. In general, entitling the owner to determine the time and terms of a resource's use may well prove efficient. In certain types of cases, however, and not necessarily marginal ones, granting strict legal sanction to an owner's refusal to sell or lease, generally or to a certain subset of potential entrants, will prove detrimental to social

in Part IV of Chapter 5, this claim applies also to individualistic justifications, such as autonomy. As a general right-based justification of property,[25] the idea that personal autonomy requires individual property rights entails significant distributive implications because justifying law's enforcement of the rights of those who have property by reference to the role of property in serving people's autonomy (rather than to a specific event or attribute of property owners) necessarily implies that every human being is entitled to some property or, more precisely, to the property needed to sustain human dignity.[26] Such a claim by nonowners is surely relevant vis-à-vis the government, but may also be pertinent in private contexts. To see why, consider property's role in protecting people's negative liberty. Private property is often justified by reference to its function in protecting people's independence and security by spreading or decentralizing decision-making power.[27] This protective role, however, is not universally significant but rather particularly important to those who are part of the nonorganized public or of a marginal group with minor political clout.[28] The special significance of providing access to property to nonowners, together with the inverse relation between owners' wealth and power and the importance of safeguarding their right to exclude, point to categories of cases wherein our commitment to autonomy entails the nonowners' claim to entry rather than the owners' claim to exclude.[29]

welfare due to either market failures or the physical characteristics of the resources at stake. *See, e.g.*, Guido Calabresi & A. Douglas Melamed, *Property Rules, Liability Rules, and Inalienability: One View of the Cathedral*, 85 HARV. L. REV. 1089, 1106–10 (1972).

25. General right-based arguments for private property such as autonomy and personhood are distinct from two other types of arguments. As right-based arguments, they rely on an individual interest as opposed to a collective one; as general arguments, they rely on the importance of an individual interest as such rather than on a specific event, as do special right-based arguments. For an analysis of this distinction and its distributive implications, on which the text relies, see JEREMY WALDRON, THE RIGHT TO PRIVATE PROPERTY 115–17, 423, 425–27, 430–39, 444–45 (1988).

26. *See* JEREMY WALDRON, *Homelessness and the Issue of Freedom, in* LIBERAL RIGHTS 309 (1993); *see also* Thomas W. Merrill, *The Property Strategy*, 160 U. PA. L. REV. 2061, 2094 (2012).

27. *See, e.g.*, RANDY E. BARNETT, THE STRUCTURE OF LIBERTY: JUSTICE AND THE RULE OF LAW 139–42, 238 (1998); MILTON FRIEDMAN, CAPITALISM AND FREEDOM ch. 1 (1962); Cass R. Sunstein, *On Property and Constitutionalism*, 14 CARDOZO L. REV. 907, 914–15 (1993).

28. *See* Frank I. Michelman, *Possession vs. Distribution in the Constitutional Idea of Property*, 72 IOWA L. REV. 1319, 1319 (1987); Frank Michelman, *Tutelary Jurisprudence and Constitutional Property, in* LIBERTY, PROPERTY, AND THE FUTURE OF CONSTITUTIONAL DEVELOPMENT 127, 139 (Ellen Frankel Paul & Howard Dickman eds., 1990).

29. This conclusion is but one manifestation of the important insight that negative liberty must always be analyzed as only a means, however important, for people's autonomy. Hence, when it undermines rather than serves the more fundamental value of self-determination, it should be curtailed. *See* H.L.A. HART, *Between Utility*

Exclusion theorists need to choose among three alternatives, none of which seems particularly promising. One—probably the most prevalent—option is to redefine property law so as to set aside the rather capacious aspects of it where inclusion or governance looms large. Merrill and Smith argue in this vein that an owner's right to exclude is "the core of property," and that the "broad presumption" of the law is "that owners can dispose of property as they wish" so that "efforts to supplement exclusion with various devices governing proper use" are perceived as `peripheral "refinements to the core exclusionary regime of property law."[30] This strategy is doomed to fail because the doctrines that do not comply with the exclusion principle are in fact not marginal or peripheral to the life of property, but deal instead with some of our most commonplace human interactions regarding resources.[31]

Alternatively, exclusion theorists may discard any pretense to account for our existing legal landscape and present their theory as reformist, advocating a significant legal change that will use exclusion as property's sole regulative principle, thus making property law truly libertarian. This seems to be the (implicit) path of the recent revival of the Kantian conception of property,[32] which I cannot address in this chapter (but discuss and criticize elsewhere[33]). For my purposes here, stating the obvious price of this strategy should suffice: once a significant gap is shown to separate such a theory from the existing legal landscape, it can no longer purport to be a theory of property law as we know it.

Finally, exclusion theorists may follow Felix Cohen in claiming that every property right involves *some* power to exclude others from doing something.[34]

and Rights, in ESSAYS IN JURISPRUDENCE AND PHILOSOPHY 198, 206–07 (1983); WILL KYMLICKA, CONTEMPORARY POLITICAL PHILOSOPHY 120, 123–25 (1990).

30. Merrill & Smith, *supra* note 2, at 1851–52, 1891–92. Merrill and Smith argue that conceptualizing property around the owner's right to exclude is justified from a "range of possible sources" of "robust moral notions." *Id.* at 1855. But this commitment to value pluralism does not lead them to acknowledge the virtues of structural pluralism. Quite the contrary, their account of property as exclusion is one of the most influential accounts of structural monism.

31. See DAGAN, *supra* note 8, at chs. 2, 4, 8–10. Indeed, even Merrill's recent concession that property entails exclusion only vis-à-vis "strangers," as opposed to "potential transactors," "persons within the zone of privity," and "neighbors" does not go far enough. See Thomas W. Merrill, *The Property Prism*, 8 ECON. J. WATCH 247, 250 (2011).

32. Neo-Kantians advocate a legal architecture of a rather strict division between private and public law. Strong property rights and a viable welfare state, these authors claim, cluster as a matter of conceptual necessity. See ARTHUR RIPSTEIN, FORCE AND FREEDOM: KANT'S LEGAL AND POLITICAL PHILOSOPHY 2–3, 7–9 (2009); Ernest J. Weinrib, *Poverty and Property in Kant's System of Rights*, 78 NOTRE DAME L. REV. 795, 827–28 (2003).

33. See DAGAN, *supra* note 8, at ch. 3.

34. Dorfman's account of ownership, which centers on the normative status of owners vis-à-vis nonowners, nicely fits into this category. Dorfman avoids the difficulty of smuggling normatively disputed claims into the conceptual analysis by arguing that the only conceptual requirement of ownership is that owners have *some* measure of

But as Cohen further emphasized, this is a rather modest truism, which hardly yields any practical implications. Private property is also, as noted above, often subject to limitations and obligations, and "the real problems we have to deal with are problems of degree, problems too infinitely intricate for simple panacea solutions."[35] In other words, exclusion theorists adopting this strategy implicitly admit that their suggested conception of property can hardly arbitrate between different property configurations. And thus it offers (almost) no guidance as to the interpretation or development of property law. This does not imply that carefully delineated statements about the thin common denominator of the wide legal terrain covered by the wholesale category of property are meaningless or useless. As usual, the answer to the question concerning the correct level of abstraction is contingent on the purpose of the inquiry. Thus, thin propositions such as Cohen's may well be useful if, for example, they are invoked in the context of examining the proper boundaries of property law.

Although all three options are indeed disappointing, the failure of exclusion theory does not necessarily condemn other monistic accounts of property, let alone other parts of our private law. But given the prominence of exclusion as a characteristic feature of property and the way that at least some of its critique applies mutatis mutandis to other attempts to divine the conceptual core of property[36] (or of the other branches of private law[37]), it seems

---

authority. *See* Avihay Dorfman, *Private Ownership*, 16 LEGAL THEORY 1 (2010); *cf.* Merrill, *supra* note 26, at 2067–71, 2094–95 (arguing "what is often loosely described as the 'right to exclude' can be characterized with greater precision as twin rights of residual managerial authority and residual accessionary rights," and explaining both rights are "nearly always . . . constrained" and "qualified by obligations").

35. Felix S. Cohen, *Dialogue on Private Property*, 9 RUTGERS L. REV. 357, 362, 370–74, 379 (1954).

36. *See* DAGAN, *supra* note 8, at ch. 3 (describing and criticizing two other structurally monistic theories of property: the neo-Kantian and the neo-Aristotelian). For a comprehensive history of American property law that strongly supports the lack of constant, unified idea of property, see generally STUART BANNER, AMERICAN PROPERTY: A HISTORY OF HOW, WHY, AND WHAT WE OWN (2011).

37. Monist contract theorists resist structural pluralism by presenting (often implicitly) contract rules that apply only to specific transaction types as peripheral to contract law, and generic contract rules, which largely anticipate one contract institution, namely: one-shot arm's-length exchange transactions, as its core. *Cf.* Daniel Markovits, *Promise as an Arm's-Length Relation*, *in* PROMISES AND AGREEMENTS: PHILOSOPHICAL ESSAYS 295, 295 (Hanoch Sheinman ed., 2011). Just like with respect to property, marginalizing the former and essentializing the latter is unjustified because contract rules that target specific transaction types are no less important for realizing the values we attribute to contract law and are no less prevalent in our lives. *See* Hanoch Dagan, *Autonomy, Pluralism, and Contract Law Theory*, 76 LAW & COMTEMP. PROBS. Pt. V (forthcoming 2013). For a particularly provocative critique of treating symmetric discrete arm's-length exchange transactions as the core of contract law, see Clyde W. Summers, *Collective Agreements and the Law of Contracts*, 78 YALE L.J. 525, 526–27, 536–37, 564–68 (1969). For a critique of structural monism in restitution, see generally HANOCH DAGAN, THE LAW AND ETHICS OF RESTITUTION 11–36, 329–31 (2004).

advisable to pause in the quest for property's core and consider an altogether different way of thinking about property. This alternative conception of property takes to heart the reasons private law should follow the prescriptions of structural pluralism.

II. Reasons for Pluralism

The common (and implicit) presupposition of exclusion theories of property is that property law is, or should be, governed by one value or by one particular balance of values. But because structural monism is descriptively weak and, as I argue below, also normatively impoverished, it should be rejected. Rather than looking for the core unified normative foundation of property or, for that matter, of its sister private law doctrines, private law theory should offer pluralist accounts of its subject matters. The heterogeneity of private law in these accounts is not merely a result of differing applications of the same regulative principle as required by the different contexts covered by private law, a phenomenon many private law monists are happy to acknowledge.[38] Rather, structural pluralism insists that the heterogeneity of private law goes much deeper, that different parts of private law (or, better, its distinct branches) respond to and vindicate different values or different balances of values. The profound heterogeneity typical of existing law may be the result of compromises or sheer accident rather than of deliberate normative choices. Nevertheless, a pluralist turn in private law theory rests on good reasons and should therefore be welcomed and embraced.[39]

Structural pluralism can rely on a pluralist theory of value that, as Elizabeth Anderson claims, is appealing because "[o]ur evaluative experiences, and the judgments based on them, are deeply pluralistic." Worthwhile and potentially incompatible virtues and projects are many and diverse. Goods, more generally, are qualitatively different in the sense that they are governed and evaluated by specific norms, so that there are various "attitudes it makes sense to

For some initial demonstrations of the difficulties with structural monism in torts, see *infra* note 59.

38. One example of this (modest) type of pluralism is manifested in the account of private law as driven by concerns for communication costs, which Merrill and Smith have advanced in recent years regarding various property issues as well as other private law contexts. *See, e.g.,* Henry E. Smith, *Modularity and Morality in the Law of Tort,* 4(2) J. TORT L. art. 5, at 14–25 (2011); *see also, e.g.,* RICHARD A. POSNER, ECONOMIC ANALYSIS OF LAW 37–38 (7th ed. 2007) (demonstrating how physical characteristics of the resource at stake implicate efficient content of ownership).

39. One may query whether my concession that the heterogeneity embedded in existing law may be accidental can be reconciled with the moderate perfectionism I espouse. I think that it can: the former is a brute descriptive fact, whereas the latter is an aspirational command instructing players who may have influence on the law (notably legislators, judges, and academics) how they should address the legal materials with which

take up toward them and . . . distinct social relations and practices that embody and express these attitudes." Adopting a monistic theory of value, which "attempt[s] to reduce the plurality of standards to a single standard, ground, or good-constituting property," would do violence to "the self understandings in terms of which we make sense of and differentiate our emotions, attitudes, and concerns." Anderson admits the appeal of value monism, which provides a simple algorithm ("maximize value") for settling questions about what to choose, whereas pluralism has a hard time addressing these demands of practical reason given its claim of incommensurability.[40] But she still insists that pluralism allows comparative value judgments (and that when it does not, it is rational to rely on sheer preferences). Thus, and of particular importance for our purposes, goodness-of-a-kind judgments facilitate comparisons *within* practices given the "values internal to and constitutive of [these] practices." Such impersonal rankings are admittedly pointless in "more global judgments of overall value" given that no single ranking of a wide variety of competing ways of life is valid for everyone. And yet, choice among incommensurable states of affairs can be more or less rational based on contextual considerations, such as its meaning for the person choosing one. Likewise, because incommensurability is rarely lexical, it may permit "tradeoffs of higher for lower goods" while prohibiting other such tradeoffs "chosen for particular reasons or in such a way as to express an inappropriate regard to the higher good."[41]

Foundational pluralism is controversial.[42] But even its critics may find good reasons for normative and thus also structural pluralism, at least given certain foundational views.[43] Consider the ideal of personal autonomy stating that people should, to some degree, be the authors of their own lives, choosing among worthwhile life plans and being able to pursue their choice. As Joseph Raz explains, autonomy requires not only appropriate mental abilities and independence but also "an adequate range of options."[44] Although a wide

---

they work; the gap between description and prescription is (as usual) the unfortunate result of human fallibility and related imperfections.

40. Cass Sunstein, who relies heavily on Anderson, offers a definition of incommensurability that is particularly helpful in legal contexts: "Incommensurability occurs when the relevant goods cannot be aligned along a single metric without doing violence to our considered judgments about how these goods are best characterized." Cass Sunstein, *Incommensurability and Valuation in Law*, 92 MICH. L. REV. 779, 796 (1994).

41. ELIZABETH ANDERSON, VALUE IN ETHICS AND ECONOMICS 1, 5, 7, 12, 45, 49, 56–58, 63, 66–70 (1993).

42. For a strong critique, see RONALD DWORKIN, JUSTICE FOR HEDGEHOGS 88–122 (2011).

43. For the distinction between foundational and normative pluralism, see Elinor Mason, *Value Pluralism*, in THE STANFORD ENCYCLOPEDIA OF PHILOSOPHY, *available at* http://plato.stanford.edu/entries/value-pluralism/ (last visited Mar. 16, 2013).

44. The ideal of personal autonomy that I rely upon should be strictly distinguished from Kant's conception of personal independence. As Arthur Ripstein explains, Kantian independence is exhausted by the requirement that no one gets to tell anyone

range of valuable sets of social forms is available to societies pursuing the ideal of autonomy, autonomy "cannot be obtained within societies which support social forms which do not leave enough room for individual choice." For choice to be effective, for autonomy to be meaningful, there must be (other things being equal) "more valuable options than can be chosen, and they must be significantly different," so that choices involve "trade-offs, which require relinquishing one good for the sake of another." Thus, because autonomy admits and indeed emphasizes "the value of a large number of greatly differing pursuits among which individuals are free to choose," valuing autonomy inevitably "leads to the endorsement of moral pluralism."[45]

At the foundational, metaethical level, subscribing to a form of value pluralism based on a (monist) commitment to autonomy is clearly different from advocating value pluralism as a freestanding persuasion. Autonomy-based value pluralism recruits other values and supports the fracturing of our legal domain so as to properly promote them all as a means that is premised on, and should thus be guided by, the ultimate value of facilitating people's ability to be authors of their own lives. By contrast, foundational pluralism hesitates to grant a priori dominance to any value, including autonomy. Rather, it insists that, given the incommensurability of values, their relative importance is always and necessarily contextual. On its face, this difference may also suggest that prescriptions to law resting on an autonomy-based pluralism would be different from, and arguably more demanding than, those based on a foundational pluralism. But there are reasons to believe that the practical prescriptions that these positions will offer law will probably largely converge.[46] An autonomy-based pluralism must take seriously the state's obligation to provide a sufficiently diverse set of robust legal frameworks for people to organize their lives. And although structuring private law around the divergent values (and balances of values) underlying distinct legal doctrines is instrumental to autonomy, none of them is reducible to autonomy. Correspondingly, a foundational pluralism should neither dismiss nor downgrade the value of autonomy as a justification for respecting the diversity of human goods and responding

---

else what purposes to pursue. Therefore, unlike autonomy, Kantian independence is not a good to be promoted but a constraint on the conduct of others. *See* RIPSTEIN, *supra* note 32, at 14, 34, 45. By contrast, with Raz, this chapter discusses autonomy within teleological morality. For another teleological account of autonomy, see JAMES GRIFFIN, ON HUMAN RIGHTS 149–58 (2008).

45. *See* JOSEPH RAZ, THE MORALITY OF FREEDOM 372, 381, 395, 395, 398–99 (1986); *cf.* ROBERT NOZICK, ANARCHY, STATE, AND UTOPIA 309–12 (1974) (arguing a framework of utopia must offer different and divergent types of communities from which individuals can choose according to their own particular balance among competing values).

46. I do not mean to dismiss a priori the possibility of meaningful divergences too. It is an interesting contingency that I do not discuss here.

to their distinct constitutive values (even if not as the regulative principle of every given legal doctrine).

Either way, because many of these plural values cannot be realistically actualized without the active support of viable legal institutions, law should facilitate (within limits) the coexistence of various social spheres embodying different modes of valuation. Indeed, despite the appeal of monism's global coherence, value pluralism makes it reasonable and even desirable for law to adopt more than one set of principles and, therefore, more than one set of coherent doctrines.[47] The commitment to facilitate a plurality of reasonable but conflicting ideals and conceptions of the good provides lawgivers some latitude and imposes on them a distinct obligation. Latitude is given for making choices, where such choices are necessary, among morally acceptable possibilities: if value pluralism is correct, any such good faith choice is legitimate.[48] The obligation, however, is to make these choices for people only when necessary, and thus to create and maintain a structurally pluralist legal regime, which includes alternative facilitative institutions and provides for relatively broad scope of freedom for individuals to adjust the rules of these institutions so that they are better attuned to the individuals' purposes. Furthermore, the boundaries between these private law institutions should in principle be open, enabling people to freely enter and exit institutions, thus choosing their own ends, principles, forms of life, and associations by navigating their way among them. (This mobility, to be sure, should be curtailed where it becomes a source of abuse, as in cases of opportunistic exit.[49])

A structurally pluralist private law includes different and sufficiently diverse types of institutions, each incorporating a different value or different balance of values. Indeed, what makes a legal doctrine a legal institution is the fact that it is internally monist: namely, it is governed by one regulative principle—a given value or balance of values.[50] (This also means that legal

---

47. As Raz argues, in a world of incommensurable human values a monistic legal voice is repressive. The plurality of normative voices may thus be conducive to our collective coexistence. Raz therefore rejects coherence as an independent value while acknowledging the virtue of normative *local* coherence if, but only if, it derives from the normative injunction to found a given area of the law on one certain value or on a given balance among pertinent values. Joseph Raz, *The Relevance of Coherence*, in Ethics in the Public Domain: Essays in the Morality of Law and Politics 261, 281–82, 291–304 (1994).

48. This point, interestingly enough, is one of the most important insights of the natural law tradition. *See* Neil MacCormick, *Natural Law and the Separation of Law and Morals*, in Natural Law Theory 105, 125–29 (Robert P. George ed., 1992).

49. *See* Dagan, *supra* note 8, at 164, 183–84, 204.

50. In other words, in a structurally pluralist private law—that is: a private law that is sufficiently subdivided—there is room for both *value* monist and *value* pluralist private law institutions. On the emerging understanding of private law taxonomy, see *supra* Chapter 6. (Notice that the monism of discrete private law institutions does not negate overlaps among their underlying normative commitments, because many of

institutions and social spheres do not overlap: whereas the former reflect, and to some extent shape the latter, legal institutions are likely to be narrower than social spheres, allowing people real choice regarding each major type of human activity and interaction.) Although at a certain point the marginal value from adding another distinct institution is likely to be nominal in terms of autonomy, pluralism implies that law's supply of these multiple institutions should not be guided only by demand. Demand for certain institutions generally justifies their legal facilitation, but absence of significant demand should not necessarily foreclose it insofar as these institutions add valuable options of human flourishing that significantly broaden people's choices. This effect is likely to be particularly noteworthy regarding institutions that are relatively different from existing institutions, especially from the more popular ones; indeed, private law pluralism should embrace and support institutions that rely on minority views or on utopian theories. Only in this way can law recognize and promote the autonomy-enhancing function of pluralism and the individuality-enhancing role of multiplicity.[51]

These conclusions are further strengthened in the context of the current discussion on the desirability of structural pluralism in private law. Consider first the prudential significance of the fact that at stake is law, as opposed to other less coercive domains of practical reasoning. Any discussion about the law must, as noted in Part II of Chapter 2, pay attention to its coercive power. The concern with coercion is justified not only by the obvious fact that judgments prescribed by law's carriers can recruit the monopolized power of the state to back up their enforcement, but is also premised on the institutional and discursive means that tend to downplay at least some of the dimensions of legal power. The institutional division of labor between "interpretation specialists" and the actual executors of their judgments, and our tendency as lawyers and even as citizens to "thingify" legal constructs and accord them an aura of obviousness and acceptability, are built-in features of law that make the danger of obscuring its coerciveness particularly troubling. We should consequently beware of assigning too much power to lawmakers who, as fallible human beings, may make mistakes, and at times even prefer their self-interest to the public good.[52]

---

these institutions resort to the same inventory of private law values, albeit in different balances. *See infra* text accompanying notes 114–115.)

51. *Cf.* RAZ, *supra* note 45, at 417–18 (arguing "the autonomy principle permits and even requires governments to create morally valuable opportunities" so as "to create an environment providing individuals with an adequate range of options.").

52. A similar consideration underlies one of the strongest instrumental arguments for freedom of speech, relying on "a distrust of the ability of government to make the necessary distinctions, a distrust of governmental determinations of truth and falsity, an appreciation of the fallibility of political leaders, and a somewhat deeper distrust of

A commitment to structural pluralism can limit the coercive effects of private law. At pathological moments of breakups followed by litigation, the power over the litigants that a pluralist regime assigns decision makers may be no different than that allocated by a monist system. But the dramas at the endgame of interpersonal relationships and legal institutions should not obscure the significance of the *ex ante* choices available to people entering and shaping these relationships. From this perspective, a structurally pluralist private law along the lines noted seems superior to its monist counterpart because it opens up options for choice rather than channeling[53] everyone to the one possibility privileged by law.[54] (Consider, for example, the choice offered by law among various forms of commercial incorporation.) A pluralist private law regime thus allows individuals to navigate their course so that they bypass certain legal prescriptions, avoiding their potential implications and hence the power of the people who have issued them. This effect of structural pluralism is distinctly acute with respect to private law because caution regarding legal decision making is particularly required with respect to this area, given that the risk of blurring the coerciveness of private law, which tends to blend into our natural environment, is uniquely high.[55] Beyond its intrinsic appeal, therefore, structural pluralism in private law can be read as a prudential response to these significant institutional concerns.

(On its face, this effect may not always apply because increasing the repertoire of legal categories or private law institutions, each backed by such monopoly power, may at times limit the parties' legal imagination, thus impairing their ability to contractually regulate their economic and interpersonal relations. But, as I argue below,[56] the claim that forcing parties to explicitly contract about their relationship is autonomy enhancing is a dubious one. Moreover, even if—or to the extent that—it is true, this effect seems to be offset by the greater choice of options provided by institutions that would cease to exist or become available only in rather circumscribed types of cases were it not for the support of the law (such as relationships placing individuals in vulnerable positions), as well as by a greater choice-making capability within legally facilitated institutions.)

In some categories of private law only one decision is called for, and there is no possibility of *ex ante* election, so lawmakers must make choices. Generally, only one set of rules can govern activities such as driving. Therefore, though

governmental power in a more general sense." FREDERICK SCHAUER, FREE SPEECH: A PHILOSOPHICAL ENQUIRY 86 (1983).

53. I use the word "channeling" as standing for something much stronger than (and different in kind from) "encouraging." *See infra* Part III.

54. *Cf.* Richard A. Epstein, *Bundle-of-Rights Theory as a Bulwark against Statist Conceptions of Private Property*, 8 ECON. J. WATCH 223, 233 (2011) (arguing "it is the unitary conception of property rights that is in fact vulnerable to creeping statism").

55. *See* Robert W. Gordon, *Unfreezing Legal Reality: Critical Approaches to Law*, 15 FLA. ST. U. L. REV. 195, 212–14 (1987).

56. *See infra* text accompanying notes 66 and 72–73.

some views may hold that value pluralism is relevant in transportation law, road accidents law cannot follow the prescription of structural pluralism at the core of this chapter. In a broad range of private law categories, however, this is not the case, as revealed by the crucial facilitative function of private law. Like other parts of law, private law plays a role in all legal functions: resolving disputes, channeling and coordinating people's conduct, distributing entitlements and obligations, and expressing values. But the channeling and coordinating function, and especially the facilitative or enabling role, is particularly significant in private law. Much of private law functions in our lives as a significant source of stable default frameworks of interpersonal interactions. Indeed, private law seems to be law's main instrument for providing reliable facilities for voluntary arrangements, thus allowing people to pursue (valuable) projects and (worthy) ends of their choice.[57]

This emphasis on the empowering potential of private law explains and justifies its relatively wide scope of freedom of contract. Mutability obviously typifies much of contract law, but is also broadly present in property matters, where the traditionally immutable areas of servitudes and marital property have tended recently to shift from mandatory to default rules.[58] Even tort law recognizes, albeit to a limited degree, people's freedom of contract by allowing certain types of interacting parties to set for themselves the trade-off of risks and benefits—hence the doctrines of informed consent and express assumption of risk. Moreover, in both contract and property—as well as in segments of tort law and of the law of restitution that prescribe (again, default) "rules of the game" for activities in which people can but need not engage, or for social roles they can, but do not have to undertake[59]—private law should also facilitate people's autonomy by adding options, as it indeed does. Given the endemic difficulties of asymmetric information and collective action,

57. *See* Joseph Raz, *The Functions of Law, in* The Authority of Law: Essays on Law and Morality 163, 169–70 (1979); Steven D. Smith, *Reductionism in Legal Thought*, 91 Colum. L. Rev. 68, 72–73 (1991); *cf.* Scott J. Shapiro, Legality 171 (2011) (arguing "legal systems are institutions of social planning" whose "fundamental aim" is "to enable communities to overcome the complexity, contentiousness, and arbitrariness of social life"). The reason from law's functions is not independent of the reason from autonomy discussed above. But it is still helpful to think about the autonomy-enhancing effect of private law's pluralism as a manifestation of law's facilitative function.

58. *See* Restatement (Third) of Prop.: Servitudes §§ 2.1, 2.4, 2.6, 3.2 (2000); Principles of the Law of Family Dissolution: Analysis and Recommendations 1053, 1060–61 (2002) [hereinafter "ALI Principles"].

59. *See* Hanoch Dagan, *Restitution and Relationships*, 92 B.U. L. Rev. 1035, 1038–48 (2012) (discussing various doctrines covering voluntary relationships in which restitutionary rules either reinforce relationships from within or safeguard them from without); *cf.* Gregory C. Keating, *Irreparable Injury and Extraordinary Precaution: The Safety and Feasibility Norms in American Accident Law*, 4 Theoretical Inquiries L. 1, 70 (2003) (explaining that because heightened risks associated with motorcycles are intrinsic to an activity that we find distinctively valuable, law deems "infeasible" any

facilitation is rarely exhausted by a hands-off policy and a corresponding hospitable attitude to freedom of contract. Rather, facilitation requires the law's active empowerment in providing institutional arrangements, including reliable guarantees against opportunistic behavior. As I argue below, private law should add only options that are conducive to human flourishing and should be ready to eliminate options undermining it;[60] and in some contexts, it should also refrain from adding too many options.[61] And yet, at least for this (again, rather significant) part of private law, the guidance of structural monism seems particularly inapt.

III. Moderate Perfectionism

Rejecting monism in private law is not an invitation to subscribe to neutrality. Rather, private law pluralism can, should, and does coexist with some degree of perfectionism. Some of this perfectionism results from the difficulties inherent in the notion of private law neutrality, which render it either (almost) impossible or (quite) unintelligible. Other reasons, more important for my present purpose, derive from the fact that some measure of perfectionism is inherent in the very commitment to pluralism, especially insofar as it is perceived as autonomy enhancing and when embedded in a justificatory practice such as law. In both cases, private law is driven to pursue a moderate measure of perfectionism. Although private law, loyal to its pluralism, is careful not to impose one-size-fits-all prescriptions, it is still a profoundly normative—indeed perfectionist—practice.

The notion of private law neutrality in the sense of a refusal to embrace any controversial moral claim is problematic, at least from a teleological perspective, because every position that private law may take implies the promotion of one substantive moral view, occasionally at the expense of others. Every choice of a set of legal rules governing a particular type of interpersonal relationship facilitates and entrenches one ideal vision of the good in that particular institution. Because private law must allocate rights and entitlements on the basis of *some* vision of the relationship at hand, no substantively neutral way of allocating them is possible.[62] Even when contract law or any other part

---

precaution that "transforms the activity of motorcycling" by "killing the joy of [this] activity"). A similar locus of structural pluralism in torts and restitution may revolve around types of involuntary interactions that are governed by different rules for different types of actors (say, individuals versus corporate entities). *See* DAGAN, *supra* note 37, at 35–63 (analyzing emerging divergence between rules governing mistaken payments in private settings and those applicable in institutional settings).

60. *See infra* text accompanying note 69.
61. *See infra* text accompanying note 78.
62. *See, e.g.,* DON HERZOG, HAPPY SLAVES: A CRITIQUE OF CONSENT THEORY 151 (1989); Sunstein, *supra* note 40, at 818–19.

of private law adopts majoritarian default rules explicitly aimed at replicating the preferences of most contracting parties, it must take notice of possible systemic problems of asymmetric information and of the parties' bounded rationality,[63] and in any event it may entrench the choices its rules reflect.[64] Furthermore, even such a majoritarian scheme is inevitably premised on certain normative foundations such as the commitment to personal autonomy or the maximization of aggregate social welfare and, therefore, is, by definition, guided by these ideals of contract.

Finally, consider the most extreme instrument the law may use in order to remain neutral: a regime that would allow parties to engage in an activity or enterprise only if they actively choose their own terms.[65] Even such a scheme, which forces parties to explicitly contract about their relationship, would hardly be neutral. Such a forced contracting system would be quite burdensome, rendering certain types of interpersonal relationships but not others too costly to enter into, at least for some. It would also, at least in many contexts, still miss the "authentic" substantively neutral position, because all contracting schemes ratify whatever background expectations and power imbalances presently exist between the parties.[66]

And yet, private law perfectionism is not only the inevitable consequence of the failure of private law neutrality but is actually compatible with, indeed closely related to, structural pluralism. Pluralism and perfectionism can happily coexist for three reasons. First and most obviously, value pluralism, even of the foundational stripe, is different from the philosophically suspect metaethical positions of value relativism, skepticism, or nihilism, which undermine any possibility of moral justification, evaluation, or for that matter criticism, thus undermining the idea of law itself.[67] Rather, alongside its recognition of a broad menu of incommensurable human alternatives, value pluralism acknowledges a minimal core of moral truths: "Forms of life differ.

---

63. *See, e.g.,* Ian Ayres & Robert Gertner, *Filling Gaps in Incomplete Contracts: An Economic Theory of Default Rules,* 99 YALE L.J. 87, 97–100 (1989); Russell B. Korobkin & Thomas S. Ulen, *Law and Behavioral Science: Removing the Rationality Assumption from Law and Economics,* 88 CALIF. L. REV. 1051, 1076–84 (2000). Needless to say, such majoritarian schemes should also make sure they do not validate practices that systemically externalize costs.

64. *See* Russell Korobkin, *Inertia and Preference in Contract Negotiation: The Psychological Power of Default Rules and Form Terms,* 51 VAND. L. REV. 1583, 1602 (1998); Russell Korobkin, *The Status Quo Bias and Contract Default Rules,* 83 CORNELL L. REV. 608, 675 (1998).

65. *Cf.* Jeffery Evans Stake, *Mandatory Planning for Divorce,* 45 VAND. L. REV. 397, 400 (1992); Barbara Stark, *Marriage Proposals: From One-Size-Fits-All to Postmodern Marriage Law,* 89 CAL. L. REV. 1479, 1520–21 (2001).

66. *See* Frances E. Olsen, *The Family and the Market: A Study of Ideology and Legal Reform,* 96 HARV. L. REV. 1497, 1504–507, 1509–13 (1983).

67. *See, e.g.,* STEVEN J. BURTON, JUDGING IN GOOD FAITH 19–21 (1992).

Ends, moral principles, are many. But not infinitely many: they must be within the human horizon."[68] Thus, value pluralism not only allows but also requires the invalidation of such interpersonal practices as the racially restrictive covenants discussed in *Shelley v. Kraemer*,[69] which threaten to undermine this core by infringing the most fundamental humanistic prescriptions. Although identifying the specific content of this minimal core is obviously a significant task that cannot be undertaken here, both autonomy-based pluralism and freestanding pluralism imply that this core must be located around the maxim of treating every person as a human being whose dignity—or normative agency—fundamentally matters.[70]

Moreover, when pluralism is autonomy-based as in Raz's view, perfectionism does not merely signal the limits of pluralism but also explains its grounding and thus guides the state in its implementation. Raz's pluralistic state is emphatically not blind to the truth or falsity of moral ideals; rather, its "goal" is "to enable individuals to pursue valid conceptions of the good and to discourage evil or empty ones." The liberal state should therefore provide "a multiplicity of valuable options," a mission Raz correctly insists is bound to be frustrated by a hands-off attitude of the law that "would undermine the chances of survival of many cherished aspects of our culture."[71] Furthermore, if the role of private law is to offer a rich repertoire of forms of human interaction, law need not just worry about preserving the valuable existing forms but also may, and at times should, provide innovative alternatives.[72]

68. Isaiah Berlin, *The Pursuit of the Ideal*, in The Crooked Timber of Humanity: Chapters in the History of Ideas 1, 11 (Henry Hardy ed., 1991); *see also, e.g.*, John Kekes, The Morality of Pluralism 32–34, 137–38 (1993); Michael Walzer, Thick and Thin: Moral Argument at Home and Abroad 1–19 (1994).

69. 344 U.S. 1 (1948). *Shelley* held that judicial enforcement of racially restrictive covenants is an exercise of state action that violates the Fourteenth Amendment. As I argue elsewhere, the best justifications for *Shelley*'s rule—and for the Fair Housing Act, 42 U.S.C. § 3601 (2006)—come from within, rather than without, private law. *See* Dagan, *supra* note 8, at 52–54; *see also* Carol Rose, *Shelley v. Kraemer*, in Property Stories 169, 182–84, 200 (Gerald Korngold & Andrew P. Morriss eds., 2004) (arguing *Shelley* is best explained based on welfarist commitment of property law to minimize negative externalities on third parties who may not share preferences of existing transactors).

70. *See* Dworkin, *supra* note 42, at 315; Griffin, *supra* note 44, at 44–48.

71. Raz, *supra* note 45, at 133, 162, 265.

72. On its face, this proposition also means that the state is obliged to support this rich repertoire so as to ensure *equal* opportunity in the realization of each and every such form, but this conclusion is both overly demanding and democratically questionable. It is too demanding because pluralism implies that society has an obligation to help provide only "a fairly rich array of options." Thus, if a person cannot realize one conception of a worthwhile life—and every conception "has its own degree of difficulty of realization" both generally and regarding each of us individually—there are others "that one can also value and that can become fully worthwhile lives for one to live." Griffin, *supra* note 44, at 162. The state's obligation must be limited to a minimum level of facilitation rather than to a standard of equal support, also because a

This point seems particularly valid insofar as private law's more cooperative frameworks are concerned, in a spectrum running from one-shot arm's-length transactions up to long-term intimate relationships. The reason is that, at least in a liberal environment where exit is always legally available, the more cooperative an interpersonal relationship, the more vulnerable its participants are to one another. Thus, private law institutions, which are relatively cooperative, are particularly dependent upon law's supply of anti-opportunistic devices in order to remain viable alternatives for human interaction and flourishing. In certain contexts and for some parties, social norms and other extralegal reasons for action, or the possibility of *ex ante* explicit contracting, may be sufficient to overcome these obstacles. But in many other categories of cases, law's active support by way of creating robust default institutions—the empowering role of private law—is likely to be the sine qua non of the viability of these challenging though still promising types of interpersonal relationships.[73]

Finally, law's support of multiple forms also tends to be perfectionist due to the characteristic features of law. The institutions that law supports are often not inventions but are typically grounded in social reality and correspond to the social sense of the good of the institution.[74] In supporting such institutions, however, law does not simply duplicate prevalent social perceptions. At least at its best, it does not blindly accept the contingent content of our social world. Legal discourse, as Part II of Chapter 2 emphasizes, is an exercise in reason giving. And reason giving—for our purposes, the type of arguments that inform the development of our private law institutions—is always potentially challenging to our social practices. It requires, at the very least, a respectable universalistic façade, an idealized picture that may be hypocritical but can be, and often is, a fertile source of critical engagement because it sets standards that our current practices do not necessarily live up to.[75] Thus, although the pluralist account of private law relies on existing law, it also provides important critical resources. In other words, the inspirational role of our private law doctrines serves as a bridge between the descriptive and the normative aspects of the pluralist account of private law.

requirement of equality would mean that society cannot rank different forms. Such an outcome would contradict the ideal of perfectionist pluralism, unduly limiting the ability of society's members, this time as a collectivity, to be authors of their particular (and potentially unique) collective lives.

73. *See generally* DAGAN, *supra* note 8, at chs. 2, 8–10. Private law's facilitative or empowering role also seems crucial in enabling individuals to pursue altruistic purposes using private and public donative trusts.

74. For a discussion of the justification for resorting to these social meanings, see *supra* Part II.B of Chapter 7.

75. *See* MICHAEL WALZER, INTERPRETATION AND SOCIAL CRITICISM 22, 30, 41, 43, 46–48, 61 (1987); *see also* Margaret Jane Radin, *Lacking a Transformative Social Theory: A Response*, 45 STAN. L. REV. 409, 421 (1993).

This feature of private law discourse is surely compatible with autonomy-based pluralism insofar as the ideals embedded in our social institutions indeed serve its meta-commitment to autonomy. But reliance on such ideals is also amenable to Anderson's claim that one of pluralism's main means for overcoming the difficulty of addressing conflicts of values is by judgments that are internal and constitutive of our diverse practices.[76] Furthermore, the onus of justifying recourse to any given normative foundation for any given institution is far less burdensome for structural pluralism than for structural monism, for two reasons. The first is that what counts in structural pluralism is the big picture of multiple legal institutions rather than any given one, and that picture is either autonomy-based or founded on freestanding pluralism. The second, related reason is that structural pluralism is committed to offer, in appropriate contexts, new institutions that may rely either on minority views or on utopian theories.

The moderate perfectionism of private law follows these guidelines of structural pluralism. Each of its categories (or subcategories) targets a specific set of human values to be promoted by its constitutive rules in one subset of social life. Both the existing categories and their underlying values are always subject to debate and reform, so that some institutions may fade away while new ones emerge and yet others change their character or split. But at any given moment, each such category consolidates people's expectations regarding core types of human relationships so that they can anticipate developments when entering, for instance, a common interest community, or indeed invading other people's rights. Thus, a set of fairly precise rules alongside informative standards founded on the regulative principles of these property institutions governs each of these types of legal categories, enabling people to predict the consequences of future contingencies and to plan and structure their lives accordingly.[77] Furthermore, the categories of private law also serve as means for expressing normative ideals of law for these types of human interaction. Both roles—consolidating expectations and expressing law's ideals—require some measure of stability. To form effective frameworks of social interaction and cooperation, law can recognize a necessarily limited and relatively stable number of categories, whose content must be relatively standardized. The standardization prescription is particularly stringent regarding the expressive role, which mandates limiting the number of legal categories because law can effectively express only a given number of ideal types of interpersonal relationships.[78]

---

76. *See supra* text accompanying note 40.

77. *See also infra* note 114 and accompanying text.

78. In addition to the reasons discussed in the text, law may justifiably resist adding another legally facilitated institution when such an addition is likely to undermine the good of an existing valuable one by, for example, diluting people's participation in it via a process of adverse selection.

Sheer multiplicity of private law institutions would certainly not have served pluralism, or at least not a type of pluralism founded on autonomy or sufficiently respectful of people's autonomy, had individuals been unable to choose the institution they wished to be part of when forming the relevant interpersonal relationship. Therefore, private law's scheme of thoroughly normative institutions keeps open the boundaries between them, making (nonabusive) navigation within this diversity a matter of individual choice. In many contexts, this choice suffices to preserve autonomy, notwithstanding the perfectionism of private law.[79] Private law, then, should strive to open up alternative legal schemes for closely related types of activities. One prominent example is the important differences among the various types of potentially profit-making institutions, such as co-ownerships, partnerships, close corporations, and publicly held corporations.[80] Another is the conception of cohabitation as a regime that is different from regular contracts as well as from marriage and offers an intermediate level of commitment, thus discharging "society's responsibility to provide a diversity of spousal institutions."[81]

This last example, however, also shows both the tension between private law's pluralism and its perfectionism and the limits of an external type of choice (choice among institutions). The unique symbolic status of marriage in society and the various tax and other benefits unique to marriage make a couple's choice between marriage and nonmarriage not a neutral one.[82] The reason for this is probably that law's perfectionism in the sphere of intimacy is rather thick, at least thicker than it is in the sphere of business, where law provides more external choice. And yet, even regarding the former sphere—let alone in other parts of private law—a liberal law committed to pluralism allows us, as it should, to choose not only among its various institutions but also within each one of them. Subject to the limits of private law's pluralism and to other (by no means insignificant) provisos noted briefly above, as well as to opt-outs that run counter to the core social meaning of a given institution (such as a prenuptial agreement providing that a given marriage would last for a week or a month),[83] private law neither should nor does set immutable rules but only

---

79. In other words, as long as there is sufficient competition among the various private law institutions, even immutable institutions would do. *See* Randy E. Barnett, *The Sounds of Silence: Default Rules and Contractual Consent*, 78 VA. L. REV. 821, 902–05 (1992).

80. *See generally* DAGAN, *supra* note 8, at ch. 10.

81. Shahar Lifshitz, *Married against Their Will? Toward a Pluralist Regulation of Spousal Relationship*, 66 WASH. & LEE L. REV. 1565, 1569 (2009).

82. *See* Carolyn J. Frantz, *Should the Rules of Marital Property Be Normative?*, 2004 U. CHI. LEGAL F. 265, 272.

83. Implicitly, the pluralist account offered here also sets limits on opt-ins, an issue that raises important questions as to the core meaning of the legal institutions at hand. Thus, although the case for allowing same-sex couples to participate in the institution of marriage seems to me obvious, the cases of polygamy and of other types of intimate relations (say, between adult siblings) are more complicated.

defaults. In certain contexts, law may legitimately regulate and at times even strictly scrutinize such opt-outs in order to guarantee procedural and substantive fairness.[84] Nonetheless, even when there are good reasons for making its prescriptions somewhat "sticky," private law tends to use defaults. To allow for meaningful social pluralism, parties should be allowed, within the constraints mentioned, to enter into private agreements that alter the rules of the pertinent institution if they so choose, tailoring their arrangements in accordance with how they prefer to cast their interpersonal relationships. (Such diversity *within* existing categories may at times trigger a bifurcation of one legal category into two—or more—once a sufficiently frequent atypical use calls for an independent status.[85])

Allowing people to opt out does not usually undermine law's functions of consolidating expectations and expressing ideals for core types of human interaction. People may legitimately wish to accommodate arrangements to their particular needs and circumstances. Because the goods of these institutions can and often are realized in various forms, law should affirm this plurality.[86] Moreover, choice is often a precondition for the meaningful realization of the more associational or communitarian values promoted by certain private law institutions.[87] The goods of these institutions—for instance, marriage as a locus of intimacy, care, commitment, and self-identification—are dependent on choice and thus cannot be legally coerced.[88] Finally, and most crucially from a pluralist point of view in both of its renditions, citizens in a liberal society should be free to reject messages sent by the law and to repudiate the values recommended by the state for (almost) any legal institution. Thus, it is not only inevitable but also desirable that law's lessons are not inescapable commands.

IV. Property as Institutions

The idea that our private law is structurally pluralistic is not at all radical. Contract law, for example, used to be arranged according to "typical contractual relationships" and, notwithstanding (or is it due to?) the great unifying force

---

84. *Cf.* Ian Ayres, *Regulating Opt Out: An Economic Theory of Altering Rules*, 121 YALE L.J. 2032, 2036, 2061–62, 2073 (2012).

85. The gradual legal recognition of the home as a category, which is distinct from land, may be a case in point. *See generally* LORNA FOX, CONCEPTUALISING HOME: THEORIES, LAWS AND POLICIES (2007).

86. This is true even regarding marriage. *See* Iris Marion Young, *Mothers, Citizenship, and Independence: A Critique of Pure Family Values*, 105 ETHICS 535, 536, 552–53 (1995).

87. *See* Kenneth L. Karst, *The Freedom of Intimate Association*, 89 YALE L.J. 624, 637 (1980).

88. *See* DAGAN, *supra* note 8, at 202–03.

of the classical contract theory that followed, we have witnessed a constant development of specialized fields of contract. As Roy Kreitner maintains, this "grouping... of fact situations by contract type" is a salutary strategy because it supplies "some guidance regarding the relative weight of conflicting contract principles."[89] In line with the claims of this chapter, Kreitner argues that only such focus on contract types can properly provide "an understanding of contract that respects the multiplicity of... purposes inherent in contract law" and the way in which different purposes "take on varying levels of importance with regard to the different types of contract," thus appropriately linking contract theory "with the practices of contracting parties and the courts."[90] Elsewhere I claim that this understanding of contract—rather than the one in which contract rules monistically piggyback on people's expressions of their will[91]—is also entailed by autonomy (as self-authorship), because only this pluralist conception is sufficiently committed to offering people a diverse set of robust frameworks to form collaborative (and risky) contractual arrangements, both discrete and impersonal, as well as long-term and relational.[92] As this part demonstrates, the situation is not that different in regard to property law. And yet, although Kreitner has recently observed that "[p]luralism is on the agenda of contract theory,"[93] property theory has recently veered in the opposite direction, as shown in Part I. In the last part of this chapter, therefore, I return to property in order to demonstrate the viability, indeed the desirability, of a pluralist turn in property theory.

The conception of property as exclusion, which is the most conspicuous genre of structural monist accounts in recent property theory, implies that rejecting the notion that property is a monist institution revolving around this core idea of exclusion necessarily means that we are left with the understanding of property as a formless bundle of sticks open to ad hoc judicial adjustments. This bundle conception of property has a grain of truth: as Hohfeld rightly observed, property has no canonical composition and, therefore, a reference

89. Roy Kreitner, *Multiplicity in Contract Remedies*, in COMPARATIVE REMEDIES FOR BREACH OF CONTRACTS 19, 38 (Nili Cohen & Ewan McKendrick eds., 2005).
90. *Id.* at 19–20.
91. *See supra* text accompanying note 3.
92. *See* Dagan, *supra* note 37.
93. Roy Kreitner, *On the New Pluralism in Contract Theory*, 45 SUFFOLK U. L. REV. 915, 915, 923–24 (2012). Kreitner identifies three recent variants of pluralism in contract theory and offers a "pluralist statement" of the conception of contract as "an encompassing and multi-faceted institution" that has no core: "[T]here is no one idea that encapsulates the *sine qua non* of contract, no nodal point from which all the instantiations of the institution of contract flow." Contract, in this view, is "a framework for cooperation among societal agents," which "serves as an infrastructure that provides a means to carry out a range of collaborative projects." This infrastructure, Kreitner adds, "provides benefits even to those who are not using it at any given moment, because it structures in productive ways the interactions (actual and potential) among past, present, and future participants."

to the concept of property cannot, or at least should not, entail an inevitable package of incidents.[94] But property is not, as the bundle metaphor might suggest, a mere laundry list of rights with limitless permutations. Instead, as the *numerus clausus* principle prescribes, property law offers only a limited number of standardized forms of property at any given time and place.[95] Not only do ordinary people not buy into the idea of open-ended bundles of rights, but property law itself has never applied it either.

Although (or maybe because) the binary choice offered by exclusion theorists is natural for anyone who looks for a monistic understanding of property,[96] it is wrong and misleading. Whereas both the exclusion and the bundle conceptions of property betray our experience, a third possibility is more in line with property's real-life manifestations and, furthermore, is also normatively appealing. Rather than a uniform bulwark of exclusion or a formless bundle of rights, I offer a structurally pluralist and moderately perfectionist understanding of property, in which property is an umbrella for a set of institutions. Each such property institution entails a specific composition of entitlements that constitute the contents of an owner's rights vis-à-vis others, or a certain type of others, with respect to a given resource.[97]

The particular configuration of these entitlements is by no means arbitrary or random. Rather, it is, or at least should be, determined by its character, namely, by the unique balance of property values characterizing the institution at issue. At least ideally, these values both construct and reflect the ideal ways in which people interact in a given category of social contexts—such as market, community, and family—and with respect to a given category of resources—such as land, chattels, copyright, and patents. The ongoing process of reshaping property as institutions is oftentimes rule-based and usually addressed with an appropriate degree of caution. And yet, the possibility of repackaging, highlighted by Hohfeld, makes it (at least potentially) an exercise in legal optimism, with lawyers and judges attempting to explicate and develop existing property forms by accentuating their normative desirability while remaining attuned to their social context.

Some property institutions are structured along the lines of the Blackstonian view of property as sole despotic dominion. These institutions are atomistic and competitive, and vindicate people's negative liberty. Liberal societies justifiably facilitate such property institutions, which serve both as a

94. *See* Hohfeld, *supra* note 11, at 747.
95. *See* Thomas W. Merrill & Henry E. Smith, *Optimal Standardization in the Law of Property: The Numerus Clausus Principle*, 110 YALE L.J. 1, 9–24 (2000).
96. For a recent reliance on this false binarism as a springboard for celebrating the exclusionist conception of property, see Henry E. Smith, *Property as the Law of Things*, 125 HARV. L. REV. 1691, 1705–706 (2012).
97. Indeed, Henry Smith is wrong both in arguing that my conception of property collapses into "ad hockery" and in claiming that it pays little attention "toward the

source of personal well-being and as a domain of individual freedom and inde-pendence.[98] In other property institutions, such as marital property, a more communitarian view of property may dominate, with property as a locus of sharing. In yet many others along the strangers–spouses spectrum, shades and hues will be found. In these various categories of cooperative property institutions, both liberty and community are of the essence, and the applicable property configuration includes rights as well as responsibilities. This variety is rich, both between and within contexts: it provides more than one option for people who want, for example, to become homeowners, engage in business, or enter into intimate relationships.[99]

Indeed, property law supports a wide range of institutions that facilitate the economic and social gains possible from cooperation. Some of these institutions, such as a close corporation, are mostly about economic gains, including securing efficiencies of economies of scale and risk spreading, with social benefits merely a (sometimes pleasant) side effect. Other institutions, such as marriage, are more about the intrinsic good of being part of a plural subject, where the raison d'être of the property institution refers more to one's identity and interpersonal relationships, whereas the attendant economic benefits are perceived as helpful by-products rather than the primary motive for cooperation. The underlying characters of the divergent relationships prove to be the key to explaining the particular property configuration that serves as the default for the property institution at hand.[100]

Thus, property law appropriately facilitates the "sphere of freedom from personal ties and obligations"[101] constituted by the impersonal norms of the more market-oriented property institutions. It does not, however, allow these norms to override those of the other spheres of society. Property relations mediate some of our most cooperative human interactions as spouses, partners, members of local communities, and so forth, and imposing the impersonal norms of the market governing the fee simple absolute on these divergent spheres might have effectively erased or marginalized these spheres of human interaction and human flourishing. On its face, these types of interactions can be facilitated by contractual arrangements between despotic

possible specialization of the parts [of the system] in achieving the goals of the whole." Henry E. Smith, *Property Is Not Just a Bundle of Rights*, 8 ECON. J. WATCH 279, 287 (2011); *see also* Part II of Chapter 9.

98. *See* JOHN RAWLS, POLITICAL LIBERALISM 298 (1993).

99. *See generally* DAGAN, *supra* note 8, at chs. 1, 3–4, 8, 10; *see also, e.g.*, Daniel B. Kelly, The Right to Include (unpublished manuscript) (carefully distinguishing three primary forms by which law facilitates owners' right to include others in use or possession of their property: leases, licenses, and easements).

100. *See* DAGAN, *supra* note 8, at ch. 10.

101. ANDERSON, *supra* note 41, at 145.

owners.[102] However, as is the case more generally in private law, lack of legal support might have undermined these more cooperative types of interpersonal relationships[103] Thus, for example, had life tenants and remaindermen been required to negotiate so as to set up their relationship by contract, the situation would have been "one of bilateral monopoly and transaction costs might [have been too] high," even if setting aside the possibility that "the remaindermen might be children (born or even unborn)."[104] In numerous other cases property law creates sophisticated governance mechanisms, serving property institutions such as trusts, common-interest communities, or marital property, which both help overcome the endemic vulnerabilities of participants in such cooperative interpersonal relationships, and play an important role in the consolidation of expectations and the expression of normative ideals regarding these core categories of interpersonal relationships.[105] Contractual freedom, significant as it is, cannot replace the robust governance mechanisms of property law.

Property institutions vary not only according to the social context but also according to the nature of the resource at stake.[106] The resource is significant because its physical characteristics crucially affect its productive use.[107] Thus, for example, the fact that information consumption is generally non-rivalrous implies that, when the resource at hand is information, use may not always necessitate exclusion.[108] The nature of the resource is also significant in that society approaches different resources as variously constitutive of their possessors' identity.[109] Accordingly, resources are subject to different property configurations: whereas the law vigorously vindicates people's control of their constitutive resources, the more fungible an interest, the less emphasis property law will need to place on its owner's control.[110]

---

102. *See* Thomas W. Merrill, *Property as Modularity*, 125 HARV. L. REV. F. 151, 157–58 (2012).

103. *See supra* text accompanying note 73.

104. Richard A. Posner, *Comment on Merrill on the Law of Waste*, 94 MARQ. L. REV. 1095, 1096 (2011).

105. *See* Hanoch Dagan, *Inside Property*, 63 U. TORONTO L.J. 1, 3–10 (2013).

106. *See* STEPHEN R. MUNZER, A THEORY OF PROPERTY 303 (1990).

107. *See* Richard A. Epstein, *On the Optimal Mix of Private and Common Property*, *in* PROPERTY RIGHTS 17, 19–20 (Ellen F. Paul et al. eds., 1994).

108. *See* Mark A. Lemley, Ex Ante *versus* Ex Post *Justifications for Intellectual Property*, 71 U. CHI. L. REV. 129, 143 (2004).

109. *See* Margaret Jane Radin, *Property and Personhood*, 34 STAN. L. REV. 957, 992, 1013 (1982). For conflicting accounts as to the empirical validity of this observation regarding homes, compare Stephanie M. Stern, *Residential Protectionism and the Legal Mythology of the Home*, 107 MICH. L. REV. 1093, 1144 (2009), with Janice Nadler & Shari Seidman Diamond, *Eminent Domain and the Psychology of Property Rights: Proposed Use, Subjective Attachment, and Taker Identity*, 5 J. EMPIRICAL LEGAL STUD. 713, 746 (2008).

110. *See generally* HANOCH DAGAN, UNJUST ENRICHMENT: A STUDY OF PRIVATE LAW AND PUBLIC VALUES 40–49, 63–108 (1997).

One may ostensibly wonder whether any real choice is provided in this dimension given that only one form applies to any given resource. But this challenge does not undermine private law's pluralism. At times, private law develops, or at least acknowledges, competing property institutions governing the same resource, as in the cases of common-interest communities alongside the fee simple absolute and the creative commons alongside copyright.[111] Moreover, even absent such intra-resource legal variety, choice is not necessarily absent: because the social meaning of resources is conventional, law's commitment to multiplicity is manifested here in providing people with choices to be owners of more or less constitutive resources, where ownership of constitutive resources has different implications than ownership of fungible ones.

Given that the meaning of property is not homogeneous but varies with its social settings and with the categories of resources subject to property rights, searching for property's core is futile and misleading, at least if this core is supposed to be robust enough to have a meaningful role in the development of property law. Trying to impose a uniform understanding of property on these diverse property institutions, which enable diverse forms of association and therefore diverse forms of good to flourish, would be unfortunate. As Part II claims, it would undermine private law's core commitments to autonomy-enhancing pluralism and individuality-enhancing multiplicity. Furthermore, Penner's claim—which is typical to most exclusion theorists—that a uniform Blackstonian conception of property reflects the lay understanding of property is not only condescending but also probably mistaken. No technical competence is needed to see the basic thrust of the distinctions between the institutions of property. Leaving specifics aside, nothing is mysterious or confusing about the different meanings of holding a traditional fee simple estate, owning a unit in a common-interest community, or having a share in a publicly held corporation.[112] Thus, we have no reason for thinking that these differences are not widely known as well as easily understood and internalized.[113] In fact, as I argued in Part III, the law is justified in limiting the number of these property institutions and standardizing their incidents by

---

111. *See* DAGAN, *supra* note 8, at ch. 4.

112. *Cf.* Gregory S. Alexander, *The Concept of Property in Private and Constitutional Law: The Ideology of the Scientific Turn in Legal Analysis*, 82 COLUM. L. REV. 1545, 1560–70 (1982).

113. The fact that people's understanding of property follows the rough contours of its legal structure should not be surprising. Property, like many other important social institutions, is a legal concept and thus necessarily artificial. Therefore, although the constitutive power of law is undoubtedly limited, the appeal of exclusion theorists to the everyday understanding of property, which implies that the concept is independent of law, is highly problematic. *See generally* Roy Kreitner, *On the Use and Abuse of Blackstone*, 10 THEORETICAL INQUIRIES L. FORUM (2009), *available at* http://services.bepress.com/tilforum/vol10/iss1/art1.

constructing them as either precise rules or informative standards[114] precisely because of their role as default frameworks of interpersonal interaction that serve to consolidate expectations and express the law's normative ideals for core types of human relationships.

Indeed, the conception of property as institutions not only resists subscribing to one normative commitment as the sole regulative principle that guides property law, but also rejects the notion that one particular balance of property values should guide the entire property terrain. Instead, it insists that we take the heterogeneity of our existing property doctrines seriously and endorse the understanding of property as an umbrella of property institutions, where each institution stands for a distinct balance of property values. In other words, although different property institutions are (or should be) guided by and large by distinct regulative principles, these principles reflect different balances among the various property values. This means that although specific property institutions are (by and large) normatively coherent, their coherence reflects a specific balance among the values that are present (albeit in a different mix) in other institutions as well.

Thus, the conception of property as institutions follows the prescriptions of private law's structural pluralism in promoting rather than undermining, as does property monism, the autonomy-enhancing function of pluralism and the individuality-enhancing role of multiplicity. Property as institutions complies with the injunction to facilitate, within limits, the coexistence of a variety of social institutions embodying different underlying, reasonable (albeit at times conflicting) modes of valuation. As long as the boundaries between the multiple property institutions are open and the (nonabusive) navigation within this variety is a matter of individual choice, the commitment to personal autonomy that drives Penner and probably most other exclusion theorists does not necessitate the hegemony of the fee simple absolute,[115] nor does it undermine the value of other, more communitarian or utilitarian property institutions.[116] The eradication or marginalization of the fee simple absolute could indeed have threatened liberal ideals about property. Insofar as this property institution remains a viable alternative, however, the availability of several different but equally valuable and obtainable proprietary frameworks of interpersonal interaction makes autonomy more, rather than less, meaningful.[117] This is especially the case given that the conception of property as

114. *See infra* Chapter 9.
115. Indeed, notwithstanding the familiar qualifications of the right to exclude even as per the fee simple absolute, exclusion can helpfully serve as the regulative principle of this particular property institution.
116. The same conclusion applies regarding the utilitarian case for property as exclusion. *See* DAGAN, *supra* note 8, at 44, 47.
117. The text explains why Smith's recent claim that exclusion is "at the core" of the architecture of property because it is a "default, a convenient starting point," Smith,

institutions not only facilitates choice among the various property institutions but is also, for the reasons mentioned in Part III, particularly hospitable to the internal type of choice, namely, the choice within each one of these institutions. Understanding the institutions of property as unifying normative ideals for core categories of interpersonal relationships comfortably coexists with a rather broad realm of freedom of contract regarding property rules. Therefore, the pluralist conception of property propounded in this chapter endorses the recent shift in property law, most significantly manifest in the traditionally immutable areas of marital property and of servitudes, away from mandatory rules and toward default rules.[118]

In and of itself, choice among multiple property institutions does not yet satisfy the prescriptions of the kind of structurally pluralist and moderately perfectionist private law this chapter advocates. Indeed, as described, the various property institutions constituted by law do not supply a mere assortment of disconnected choices but offer instead a repertoire that responds to various forms of valuable human interaction. Admittedly, regarding many property institutions, law often falls short of the human ideals it represents. But these gaps, as noted in Part III, only validate the normative teeth of a pluralist account of property. These imperfections of property law imply that, rather than searching for a unifying normative account of property law in its entirety, the main task of property theory is to distill the distinct human ideals of the various property institutions, to elucidate the ways each of them contributes to human flourishing, and to offer, if needed, a reform that would force these property institutions to live up to their own implicit promises (or would require the marginalization—or maybe even elimination—of normatively indefensible property institutions).[119] In other words, the practical

---

supra note 96, at 1705, still does not assign to exclusion its proper role. On the one hand, in designing a liberal property law regime, exclusionary property institutions are more than defaults—they are necessary components. And yet, on the other hand, a private law system that is properly committed to autonomy should resist privileging any particular property institution by treating its characteristics as fundamental features of property as a whole.

118. *See supra* note 58 and accompanying text. This liberal approach to freedom of contracts must, of course, be subject to the legitimate verification interest of third parties insofar as they are affected by such opt-outs. *See* Henry Hansmann & Reinier Kraakman, *Property, Contract, and Verification: The Numerus Clausus Problem and the Divisibility of Rights*, 31 J. LEGAL STUD. 373 (2002); *see also* DAGAN, *supra* note 8, at 32–33. Interestingly, the commitment to freedom of contract is one of the conspicuous differences between my conception of property and one of the most prominent conceptions of property advanced by exclusion theorists: Merrill and Smith's account, which is premised on communication costs. *See* Hanoch Dagan, *Judges and Property*, in INTELLECTUAL PROPERTY AND THE COMMON LAW (Shyam Balganesh ed. forthcoming 2013).

119. This renders the pluralist conception of property inherently dynamic. *See* Dagan, *supra* note 105, at 15–16. To be sure, this dynamism does not necessarily fully protect against the contingency of exacerbating an evil system. This is, however, always the risk

payoff of discarding property monism in favor of structural pluralism lies in the fact that the latter approach situates the normative inquiries regarding property law at the correct level. Thus, on the one hand, it resists smuggling normatively disputed claims by way of purportedly conceptual presumptions, and on the other, it structures these normative inquiries so that they properly address both the social context and the nature of the resource.

CONCLUDING REMARKS

Private law in general and property law more particularly play a significant, though at times implicit, role in the drama of modern liberal societies. They form diverse sets of institutions, allowing people to be the authors of their lives' narratives by making choices to engage in various types of interpersonal relationships in a variety of social spheres that embody different modes of valuation. This facilitative role of our private law neither renders it neutral nor implies the exclusion of ideals from this broad and diverse domain. Rather, this fundamental feature of liberal private law relies on a subtle combination of pluralism and perfectionism, which "asserts the existence of a multitude of incompatible but morally valuable forms of life . . . coupled with an advocacy of autonomy."[120] Because this profound characteristic eludes the broad strokes of monist theories of private law, these theories neither properly elucidate the existing legal terrain nor do they address some of the most promising ways in which private law theory can contribute to the evaluation, interpretation, and development of private law. The appeal of private law monism is obvious. But for private law theory to better account for the law it seeks to illuminate and to helpfully participate in the law's unfolding development, it should resist this temptation, transcend monism, and follow the spirit of our private law by embracing both its complexity and its multiplicity.

with interpretive theories, and we should not also overstate this risk. On the one hand, the evil of normatively corrupt private law systems is likely to derive not only from this risk, but also from other sources external to private law (e.g., a morally despicable constitutional regime). On the other hand, an articulation of the ongoing reconstructive account of private law necessarily sets limits on the types of normative claims that are eligible for serving as the normative infrastructure of a private law institution.

120. RAZ, *supra* note 45, at 133.

CHAPTER 9

✿

Private Law Pluralism and the Rule of Law

OPENING REMARKS

In the previous chapters, I have characterized private law as structurally pluralist and moderately perfectionist. Its pluralism implies that property, contracts, torts, and unjust enrichment are merely broad umbrellas for narrower private law institutions sharing some thin common denominators. Property law, for example, my central example in this chapter, is composed of a set of diverse doctrines that cannot be reasonably described as being governed by one coherent regulative principle, at least if that principle is to be robust enough to play a meaningful role in the development of this heterogeneous body of law. Thus the search for property's core is futile. But a careful study of various property institutions (such as fee simple absolute, co-ownership, common-interest communities, marital property, copyrights, patents, and the like) is valuable and important because the regulative principles of *these* institutions—and here comes the perfectionist nature of private law—express our society's ideals for core categories of interpersonal relationships regarding various resources and consolidate people's expectations in their regards.

I hold that this structural pluralist account of private law (and of property law more particularly) fits our private law better than its monist counterparts and is also normatively superior to these alternative understandings, such as the exclusion conception of property. By facilitating and possibly enabling a diverse set of interpersonal relationships, a pluralist conception of private law participates in the state's obligation to empower people to make real choices among viable alternatives, and thus be the authors of their own lives. One implication of the perfectionist nature of private law is that its institutions are subject to ongoing normative and contextual reevaluation and possible, even if properly cautious, reconfiguration. They are thereby forced to live up to their promise as valuable options of human flourishing, thus making a significant contribution to worthwhile life plans.

In this chapter I assume that this understanding of private law, which is summarized in Part I, is appealing both in terms of its fit to our legal practice and in terms of its normative desirability. My current mission is to examine whether this understanding, despite its multiplicity, dynamism, and disavowal of neutrality, complies with the rule of law. There are, or at least so I argue, two key aspects to the rule of law—the requirement that the law be capable of guiding its subjects' behavior and the prescription that law may not confer on officials the right to exercise unconstrained power[1]—and they are both importantly connected to people's autonomy. On its face, a pluralist and perfectionist understanding of private law is vulnerable on both fronts. If this first impression is correct, defending this conception of private law would require a choice between downplaying the significance of the rule of law for private law, and showing that the rule of law deficit generated by a pluralist and perfectionist private law is dwarfed by its normative virtues.

Fortunately, as I hope to show, there is no real friction between private law pluralism and the guidance and constraint strands of the rule of law. Private law pluralism neither requires nor should it imply adopting the dubious nominalistic approach of case-by-case adjudication, which indeed undermines guidance. Rather, because private law institutions are supposed to consolidate expectations and express ideals of interpersonal relationships, private law pluralism supports, even requires, relatively stable and internally coherent—albeit properly narrow—doctrinal categories.[2] Each such private law institution is governed by fairly precise rules alongside informative standards founded on the regulative principles of these institutions, enabling people to predict the consequences of future contingencies and to plan and structure their lives accordingly. These private law institutions are shaped and developed through both legislation and adjudication. Courts are appropriately involved in many of these processes because (at least insofar as private law is concerned) they typically enjoy no less legitimacy, from either a participation or accountability perspective, than legislatures. Likewise, although the plurality of values involved in the molding of our private law institutions' regulative principles makes this a challenging endeavor, we have no grounds for assuming that the requirement of normative contextual inquiry typifying common law adjudication does not reliably constrain this judicial power.

---

1. By identifying guidance and constraint as the two aspects of the rule of law, I join Martin Krygier's meta-claim whereby, in order to understand the rule of law, we must begin with its telos. *See* Martin Krygier, *Four Puzzles about the Rule of Law: Why, What, Where? and Who Cares?, in* NOMOS L: GETTING TO THE RULE OF LAW 64, 67–73 (2011).

2. *See supra* Chapters 6 and 8.

Consequently, no comparison is now required between the virtues of the rule of law and those of my account of private law. To be sure, it is not my claim that no private law system would have scored better than private law pluralism in terms of guidance or constraint. But if the claims just mentioned (which are elaborated in Parts II and III) are correct, private law pluralism seems to score quite high on both fronts. Thus, if one supports a threshold conception of the rule of law, private law pluralism would probably pass it. Even barring such a threshold—meaning a situation wherein the rule of law and substantive virtues must always be balanced—my conclusions imply (assuming that private law pluralism is indeed worth endorsing substantively) that adding the concerns of the rule of law to the picture is unlikely to lead to its abandonment, at least when compared with alternative (that is: monist) approaches to private law.[3]

Reconciling private law pluralism and the rule of law does not vindicate the conventional perception that the rule of law is only marginally interesting to private lawyers—quite the contrary. Much of the resistance of private law theorists to embracing pluralism and perfectionism, despite their saliency in the practice of our private law, rests implicitly on rule of law concerns. Explicitly articulating these worries in the language of the rule of law and demonstrating why a pluralist and perfectionist private law neither fails to guide people's behavior properly nor sanctions unconstrained judicial power may thus allow private law theorists to celebrate these core features of private law instead of marginalizing or suppressing them. Moreover, this exercise is useful not only to private law theory but also to our understanding of the rule of law. Tracing how a pluralist and perfectionist private law complies with the rule of law may enrich our perspective on both the guidance and the constraint aspects of the rule of law.

I. Structural Pluralism in Private Law

Private law is canonically divided into property, contracts, torts, and unjust enrichment, and nothing in what follows will necessarily challenge this division. Yet, legal actors—judges, practicing lawyers, academics, lobbyists, and

---

3. Although conformity with the rule of law is an inherent value of law, my understanding of the rule of law implies that Joseph Raz is correct when insisting that (1) it is a matter of degree, and (2) it may conflict with other values, so that less conformity may at times be preferable because it helps to realize these values. *See* JOSEPH RAZ, *The Rule of Law and Its Virtues, in* THE AUTHORITY OF LAW: ESSAYS ON LAW AND MORALITY 210, 222, 225, 228–29 (1979). *See also, e.g.,* JOHN GARDNER, LAW AS A LEAP OF FAITH: ESSAYS ON LAW IN GENERAL 33, 192, 195–96 (2012). *Contra* Ernest J. Weinrib, *The Intelligibility of the Rule of Law, in* THE RULE OF LAW: IDEAL OR IDEOLOGY 59 (Allan Hutchinson & Patrick Monahan eds., 1987).

the like—sometimes assume that this division carries some important justificatory burden. To take one example, consider the analysis that many lawyers apply to the question of whether copyright is property. Notwithstanding the vigorous debate between advocates of the information industry and champions of the public domain, many players on both sides seem to assume that classifying copyright as a species of property is bound to bolster the claims of the former at the expense of the latter. The (usually implicit) presupposition of both sides to this debate is that property is a more or less monist concept that, at its core, is the owner's right to exclude. Thus they imply that this exclusion principle is significant to the point of affecting real-life consequences concerning the scope of authors' rights. Rather than the innocuous cohabitation of various property doctrines under the broad category of property, it is these presuppositions that are the target of my critique because I consider them both wrong and misleading.[4] Just like its sister categories of contracts, torts, and unjust enrichment, property is far too heterogeneous a field to be guided by one regulative principle (such as exclusion), at least when defined as one that generates significant doctrinal prescriptions. Therefore, classifying copyright as property does not necessarily imply an expansion of the scope of authors' rights.[5]

The starting point of structural pluralism in private law, which is part of the (lost) legacy of American legal realism, is that broad legal categories such as property, contracts, torts, or unjust enrichment are merely convenient "umbrellas" for a more diversified landscape. Along these lines, Herman Oliphant celebrated the traditional common law strategy of employing narrow legal categories, each covering only relatively few human situations. This strategy, described in Chapter 6, will have the benefit of capturing the details and particularity of actual human transactions. Thus it holds legal actors accountable to the realities of human life and encourages them to continue shaping the law to meet these contemporary realities. The traditional common law strategy thereby facilitates one comparative advantage of lawyers (notably judges) in producing legal norms: their daily access to actual human situations and problems in contemporary life.[6] Similar convictions led Karl Llewellyn to insist that wholesale legal categories, such as property, contracts, or torts, are too large to deal with because they contain too many heterogeneous situations, making it nearly impossible to incorporate life-wisdom into the practice of law. To preempt certain responses, let me clarify that the claim (at least

---

4. For similar expressions of these presuppositions in the context of the so-called new property and in regard to body parts, which are thus subject to the very same line of criticism, see, respectively, J.W. HARRIS, PROPERTY & JUSTICE 151, 304 (1996), and ALAN HYDE, BODIES OF LAW 73 (1997).

5. *See* HANOCH DAGAN, PROPERTY: VALUES AND INSTITUTIONS ch. 4 (2011).

6. Herman Oliphant, *A Return to Stare Decisis*, 14 A.B.A. J. 71, 73–74, 159 (1928).

Llewellyn's claim—and mine) is *not* that decisions should be made on an ad hoc basis according to the particularities of the parties or case. Rather, it is that decisions should reflect and benefit from the realities and life-situations commonly seen.[7]

Property law follows the prescriptions of structural pluralism by setting up a number of distinct property institutions. Each governs a specific social context or a given resource and is typified by a particular configuration of property owners' entitlement corresponding to a particular property value or balance of such values serving as its regulative principle. There are two (representative) polar opposite property institutions. The first, as recognized by the Blackstonian view of fee simple absolute, is structured to value complete and sole dominion. The second, such as marital property, values a more communitarian view of property. There are, of course, many other property institutions between these polar opposites; thus there is a spectrum of property institutions to be found. This variety of institutions allows individuals choice, offering multiple forms for home ownership, business endeavors, or intimate relationships.[8]

To be sure, the similarities among the various property institutions (or the various types of torts, contracts, or unjust enrichments) justify studying them together and treating them as the subject matter of unified scholarly analysis. Often, however, these similarities merely mean that studying the various institutions of property law requires us to ask similar questions, such as: What is the appropriate scope of an owner's exclusion? Or: What is the optimal governance regime for this property institution? At times, these similarities imply some overlap in the pertinent values that affect the regulative principles of these diverse institutions. For example, personhood concerns inform a certain subset of property institutions, whereas utility is significant in another subset. These similarities ensure that reflecting on the variety of property institutions (or the diverse families of contracts, torts, or unjust enrichments) is likely to yield some useful cross-fertilization. They do

---

7. *See* KARL L. LLEWELLYN, A *Realistic Jurisprudence: The Next Step, in* JURISPRUDENCE: REALISM IN THEORY AND IN PRACTICE 3, 27–28, 32 (1962); KARL L. LLEWELLYN, *Some Realism about Realism, in* JURISPRUDENCE, *supra*, at 42, 59–60; KARL L. LLEWELLYN, *The Current Recapture of the Grand Tradition, in* JURISPRUDENCE, *supra*, at 215, 217, 219–20. Frederick Schauer has argued that the concrete examples faced by judges distort their judgment rather than illuminating it because they systematically trigger certain cognitive biases. *See* Frederick Schauer, *Do Cases Make Bad Law?*, 73 U. CHI. L. REV. 883 (2006); *see also* LARRY ALEXANDER & EMILY SHERWIN, DEMYSTIFYING LEGAL REASONING 111–14 (2008). But as Jeff Rachlinski shows, alongside the cognitive weaknesses of adjudication, courts also have several cognitive advantages over legislatures, which might facilitate superior lawmaking. *See* Jeffrey J. Rachlinski, *Bottom-Up versus Top-Down Lawmaking*, 73 U. CHI. L. REV. 933, 950–61 (2006).

8. *See generally* DAGAN, *supra* note 5, at chs. 1, 3–4, 8, 10. For a structural pluralist account of contract law, see Hanoch Dagan, *Autonomy, Pluralism, and Contract Law Theory*, 76 LAW & CONTEMP. PROBS. (forthcoming 2013).

not imply, however, the type of normative coherence needed to justify making membership in one of these wide areas of law a reason for any concrete prescriptive consequence.[9]

Accordingly, the pluralist conception of property as institutions takes the heterogeneity of our existing property doctrines seriously. It understands property as an umbrella for a limited and standardized set of property institutions, which serve as important default frameworks of interpersonal interaction. All these institutions mediate the relationship between owners and nonowners regarding a resource, and in all property institutions owners have some rights to exclude others. This common denominator derives from the role of property in vindicating people's independence. Alongside this important property value, however, other values also play crucial roles in shaping property institutions. As briefly indicated in Part IV of Chapter 8, property can and does serve our commitments to personhood, desert, aggregate welfare, social responsibility, and distributive justice.[10] Different property institutions offer differing configurations of the entitlements constituting the contents of an owner's rights vis-à-vis others, or a certain type of others, with respect to a given resource. At least at its best, this plurality allows property law to vindicate differing balances among these property values according to their characteristic settings, namely, the type of social relationship in which they are situated and the nature of the resource at stake. Although the cohabitation of different property values and divergent property institutions within property is always contentious, property law—again, at its best—offers principled ways of accommodating this happy plurality.

Of course from a monist viewpoint the heterogeneous landscape of property law may seem chaotic and disorderly, but it turns out to be valuable once a perspective of structural pluralism is applied. Indeed it is indispensable for people's autonomy.[11] The fee simple absolute is essential for liberal societies, but law's support for other property institutions is just as crucial for autonomy, which is precisely why the conception of property as institutions resists the way exclusion theory privileges this one property institution—the fee simple absolute—and suppresses the others as variations on a common theme, or marginalizes them as peripheral exceptions to a robust core. As Joseph Raz explains, autonomy understood as the ideal that people should, to some degree, be the authors of their own lives, requires not only appropriate mental capabilities and independence but also an ability to choose from a range of options. This requires both valuable and varying options so that a choice implies a trade-off: choosing one good over another. Autonomy

---

9. *See supra* note 4 and accompanying text.
10. *See* GREGORY S. ALEXANDER & HANOCH DAGAN, PROPERTIES OF PROPERTY pt. I (2012).
11. *See supra* Chapter 8.

requires "a large number of greatly differing pursuits," and thus, inevitably endorses moral pluralism.[12]

Given the diversity of acceptable human goods from which autonomous people should be able to choose as well as their distinct constitutive values, the state must recognize a sufficiently diverse set of robust frameworks for people to organize their life. And because many of these plural values cannot be realistically actualized without the active support of viable legal institutions,[13] law should, within limits, facilitate the coexistence of various social spheres embodying different modes of valuation. Hence, although the global coherence in monistic conceptions of broad private law fields such as property is appealing, it is reasonable and even desirable for law to adopt more than one set of principles and, consequently, more than one set of coherent doctrines.[14] Accordingly, a structurally pluralist property law includes sufficiently diverse types of institutions, each incorporating a different value or different balance of values. Boundaries between these institutions are open, enabling people to freely choose their goals, principles, forms of life, and associations by navigating their way among them. Only in this way can law recognize and promote the individuality-enhancing role of multiplicity.[15]

Implicit in this account is the twofold role of property institutions and their private law counterparts. These institutions consolidate people's expectations when, for example, entering a joint tenancy or a common-interest community, or, for that matter, using another person's copyrighted work. They may also perform an expressive and cultural function, affecting people's ideals and consequently their preferences regarding these categories of relationships. Both roles require some measure of stability. To form effective frameworks of social interaction and cooperation, property law can recognize a necessarily limited number of categories of relationships and resources. This prescription of standardization, enshrined in property law as the *numerus clausus* principle, is particularly acute with regard to the expressive role. This role mandates limiting the number of property institutions because law can effectively express only so many ideal categories of interpersonal relationships.[16]

Sheer multiplicity is obviously not sufficient. The legal conventions encapsulated in private law (our private law institutions) do not supply merely an assortment of disconnected choices. Rather, they offer a repertoire that

---

12. *See* JOSEPH RAZ, THE MORALITY OF FREEDOM 372, 381, 395, 398–99 (1986); *cf.* ROBERT NOZICK, ANARCHY, STATE, AND UTOPIA 309–12 (1974). The ideal of personal autonomy should be strictly distinguished from Kant's conception of personal independence. *See* ARTHUR RIPSTEIN, FORCE AND FREEDOM: KANT'S LEGAL AND POLITICAL PHILOSOPHY 14, 34, 45 (2009).

13. *See* Hanoch Dagan, *Inside Property*, 63 U. TORONTO L.J. 1, 8–10 (2013).

14. *See* JOSEPH RAZ, *The Relevance of Coherence, in* ETHICS IN THE PUBLIC DOMAIN: ESSAYS IN THE MORALITY OF LAW AND POLITICS 261, 281–82, 291–304 (1994).

15. *Cf.* RAZ, *supra* note 12, at 417–18, 425.

16. *See* DAGAN, *supra* note 5, at 31–35.

responds to various forms of valuable human interaction. Admittedly, regarding many private law institutions, law often falls short of the human ideals they represent. But these gaps mean only that, rather than searching for unifying normative accounts of property, contracts, torts, or unjust enrichment in their entirety, the main task of private law and theory is twofold: first, to distill the distinct human ideals of the various private law institutions in order to elucidate the ways each of them contributes to human flourishing, and second, to offer reform, if needed, that would force these private law institutions to live up to their own implicit promises. (To be sure, if these promises themselves turn out to be disappointing or, worse, unjust, or if the repertoire of private law institutions is not sufficiently diverse, private law theory should call, respectively, for amending these promises or adding institutions that can enrich its inventory.)

The pluralist understanding of private law is thus inherently dynamic. Although existing private law institutions are and should be the starting point of any analysis of private law questions, they are never frozen. Rather, as institutions structuring and channeling people's relationships, they are subject to ongoing—albeit properly cautious—normative and contextual reevaluation and possible reconfiguration. The conservative baseline of this approach derives not only from the pragmatic reality that existing rules cannot be abandoned completely, but also from the recognition that existing law represents a cumulative judicial and legislative experience that deserves respect. In turn, the forward-looking perspective of this endeavor is premised on an understanding of law as a dynamic enterprise. Its content unfolds through challenges to the desirability of normative underpinnings in private law institutions; their responsiveness to their social context; their effectiveness in promoting their contextually examined, normative goals; and the sufficiency of the repertoire private law offers for any given type of activity. In this way, this understanding of private law follows the common law method described by Llewellyn as "a functioning harmonization of vision with tradition, of continuity with growth, of machinery with purpose, of measure with need," mediating between "the seeming commands of the authorities and the felt demands of justice."[17]

At times, this process helps to fill gaps in the law by prescribing new rules that further bolster and vindicate these goals. At other times, it points out "blemishes" in the existing doctrine, rules that undermine the most illuminating and defensible account of such a private law institution, which should be reformed so that an institution lives up to its own ideals.[18] This reformist potential has actually yielded different types of legal reforms throughout the history of property. In some cases, the reform is relatively radical—the

---

17. Karl N. Llewellyn, The Common Law Tradition 37–38 (1960).
18. *See* Ronald Dworkin, Taking Rights Seriously 118–23 (1977).

abolition of a property form (as was the case, for all practical purposes, with the fee tail form[19]) or an overall reconstruction of its content (as with lease-holds[20]). Sometimes more moderate options are in order, such as restating the doctrine pertaining to a property form in a way that brings its rules closer to its underlying commitments and, in the process, removing indefensible rules. The best recent example for such moderate reform is probably the transforma-tion of the property form of servitudes, discussed in some detail below.[21]

II. The Rule of Law as Guidance

Henry Smith has recently argued that this pluralist conception of property can hardly be distinguished from the bundle understanding of property. Accordingly, he has claimed, this conception irreparably undermines stabil-ity. Referring to my book *Property: Values and Institutions*, where I developed this conception of property, Smith argues that stability is not "yet another detachable feature or lever to be dialed up or down" or "a factor to be balanced whenever we are deciding on the supposedly separable sticks in the bundle," but is rather "a feature that can only be evaluated as an aspect of the system." And although it may be important for the system to serve "values like com-munity, autonomy, efficiency, personhood, labor, and distributive justice," we must reject "[t]he idea that doctrines are part of an issue-by-issue balancing of [these values]." Smith's claims rely on the view that the only alternative to the exclusion school of property is "to invoke a plethora of general principles to be balanced as specific situations present themselves." And given that "ad hocery itself is not a feature that can easily be dialed down," Smith concludes that nothing separates my account of property from the understanding of property as "an ad hoc, unstructured bundle."[22]

To understand Smith's critique of ad hocery, consider his defense of con-cepts in property. Concepts "pick out categories" and thus serve as "mental shortcuts," which are essential given "people's cognitive limitations" "for pre-diction, communication, and abstract thought." Conceptualism, which he claims is rightly associated with formalism, is thus helpful precisely because of its "relative indifference to context": "To be useful, the concept has to pick out enough facts to serve the purpose in question but not so many that it entails too much complexity." Smith argues that the objection of legal realists

19. *See* DUKEMINIER ET AL., PROPERTY 200–201 (7th ed. 2010).

20. *See generally* Edward H. Rabin, *The Revolution in Residential Landlord–Tenant Law: Causes and Consequences*, 69 CORNELL L. REV. 517 (1984).

21. *See infra* text accompanying notes 32–59 and 103–10.

22. Henry E. Smith, *Property Is Not Just a Bundle of Rights*, 8 ECON. J. WATCH 279, 287 (2011); Henry E. Smith, *Property as the Law of Things*, 125 HARV. L. REV. 1691, 1705–706 (2012).

(such as me) to defining exclusion "as any baseline or starting point," which is reminiscent (in his view) of the realists' "nominalistic impulse," is misguided because it downplays and may undermine the important function of concepts "in reducing information costs and building the overall architecture of property." Thus, rejecting the exclusionary conception of property might substitute rigidity with "near-chaos." Exclusion is "the baseline for delineation purposes," not because it is "the moral 'core' of property" but rather because "it is the general case, and governance is special." Only the presumption of exclusion, Smith insists, can assure that we keep the bundles "lumpy" and "opaque," allow property to function as "something more that high transaction costs prevent us from fully achieving by contract," and avoid "hard-to-predict ripple effects through the entire system."[23]

This critique of property pluralism, and hence of private law pluralism more generally, must be taken seriously. The conception of property as a formless bundle of sticks open to ad hoc judicial adjustments bears no resemblance to the law of property as lawyers know it or as citizens experience it in everyday life. More generally, and more significantly for my purposes, if—as Smith contends—property (or private law) pluralism necessarily collapses into such unstable nominalism, it necessarily undermines the rule of law.

In order to fully appreciate its power, Smith's critique can be recast in terms of one of the most prominent understandings of the rule of law. In this view, associated mostly with Raz, the rule of law is organized around the idea that "the law should be such that people will be able to be guided by it"; that law should "provide effective guidance."[24] Although seemingly thin, the guidance conception of the rule of law, which is often broken up into lists of formal requirements,[25] is intimately connected with people's autonomy, understood as self-authorship. By requiring that "government in all its actions [be] bound by rules fixed and announced beforehand," the rule of law enables people "to foresee with fair certainty how the authority will use its coercive power in given circumstances, and to plan [their] affairs on the basis of this knowledge."[26] Only a relatively stable and predictable law can serve as a "safe basis for individual

---

23. Henry E. Smith, *On the Economy of Concepts in Property*, 160 U. PENN. L. REV. 2097, 2100–02, 2105–06, 2113, 2116–17, 2123, 2128 (2012).

24. RAZ, *supra* note 3, at 213, 218. As the following text clarifies, the requirement of law's guidance is important because of law's coercive power. But unlike the conception of the rule of law as constraint, the emphasis here is not on limiting this power and thus its potential abuse, but rather on circumscribing its detrimental effects on people's self-authorship. This is also why the desirability of predictability to autonomy may be disputed in more benevolent authority settings, such as parenthood.

25. *See, e.g.*, LON L. FULLER, THE MORALITY OF LAW 39 (rev'd ed. 1964).

26. F.A. HAYEK, THE ROAD TO SERFDOM 54 (1944). To be sure, in general, Hayek's account of the rule of law is more amenable to the constraint conception. *See* Trevor Allan, *The Rule of Law as Private Law*, in PRIVATE LAW AND THE RULE OF LAW (Lisa Austin & Dennis Klimchuk eds., forthcoming 2014). Furthermore, relying on Hayek for the conception that founds the rule of law on our commitment to self-authorship

planning," which is a prerequisite to people's ability to "form definite expectations" and plan for the future. Law's participation in creating and securing stable "frameworks for one's life and action" increases "[p]redictability in one's environment," and therefore "one's power of action," thus facilitating people's "ability to choose styles and forms of life, to fix long-term goals and effectively direct one's life towards them."[27]

The guidance conception of the rule of law is often associated with the idea coined by Justice Antonin Scalia[28] that the rule of law is the law of rules. According to this view, in order to "provide maximally effective guides to behavior," the preferred form of the law must be that of "a 'rule,' conceived as a clear prescription that exists prior to its application and that determines appropriate conduct or legal outcomes."[29] Open-ended standards that allow (let alone require) judges to consult law's underlying commitments in each case they must settle jeopardize, so the argument goes, this virtue of "the rule of rules": rules "are designed to translate the implications of normative values into concrete prescriptions" and must therefore be "sufficiently determinate" so as to be followed by their appliers "without first resolving the very normative questions [they] are designed to settle" or "considering whether the local outcome of the rule conforms to the values [they are] supposed to advance."[30]

On its face, the "normative dynamism" of the pluralist conception of private law poses a serious threat to the rule of law as guidance. In line with the common law tradition, private law pluralism conceptualizes adjudication as "a process that allows judges to remake the existing doctrinal propositions in the process of applying them." But if rules "are defeasible when direct application of their background rationales would generate a different result" then "the constraint of the rule *qua* rule seems to disappear." If normative commitments can always upset existing doctrinal propositions and require that they be discarded or modified, then these propositions seem to be no more than rules of thumb. As Frederick Schauer argues in criticizing the common law tradition, "[r]ules of this sort, capable of modification at the time of application

---

is somewhat ironic. Hayek gives no significance to nongovernment factors, which can deprive people of control over their life in ways as debilitating as those implemented by governments; his views are also alien to the Razian notion that government is responsible for actively ensuring a range of choices.

27. RAZ, *supra* note 3, at 220, 222; *cf.* David Dyzenhaus, *Liberty and Legal Form,* PRIVATE LAW AND THE RULE OF LAW, *supra* note 26 ("[C]ompliance with legality is liberty producing.").

28. *See* Antonin Scalia, *The Rule of Law as a Law of Rules,* 56 U. CHI. L. REV. 1175 (1989).

29. Richard H. Fallon, Jr., *"The Rule of Law" as a Concept in Constitutional Discourse,* 97 COLUM. L. REV. 1, 14–15 (1997).

30. Emily Sherwin, *Rule-Oriented Realism,* 103 MICH. L. REV. 1578, 1589, 1590, 1591 (2005) (reviewing HANOCH DAGAN, THE LAW AND ETHICS OF RESTITUTION (2004)). *See generally* LARRY ALEXANDER & EMILY SHERWIN, THE RULE OF RULES (2001).

and thus incapable of constraining that application, differ so much from our ordinary conception of rules as guides and constraints that it hardly pays to speak of them as rules at all."[31]

* * *

I claim that, properly interpreted, private law pluralism conforms to the prescriptions of the guidance conception of the rule of law and also fits this conception's emphasis on rule-based decision making insofar as this emphasis is indeed justified (which, as will be shown, it not always is). An example demonstrating many of the characteristics I find in private law pluralism will be helpful.

Neponsit Property Owners' Ass'n v. Emigrant Industrial Savings Bank[32] is the first major decision on the enforceability of the assessment covenant, whose validity at that time (1938) was very much in doubt.[33] This makes *Neponsit* a significant milestone in one of the most important developments of American land law in the last century: the emergence of common-interest communities, a property institution that by now is a major form of land ownership. My choice of this property institution and of this particular case are not fortuitous: no one can hope to provide a reasonable account of common-interest communities without considering governance, which is obscured in the exclusionary conception of property with its excessive focus on property's foreign affairs.[34] *Neponsit* is the landmark decision that enlisted servitudes law into facilitating the governance of this property institution.

As Justice Lehman noted when delivering the decision of the New York Court of Appeals, Neponsit had unquestionably intended that the covenant should run with the land. The difficulties posed by this case were elsewhere, in the "age-old essentials of a real covenant" set by "ancient rules and precedents," according to which "a covenant will run with the land and will be enforceable against a subsequent purchaser" only if it "is one 'touching' or 'concerning' the land with which it runs," and if "there is 'privity of estate' between the promisee or party claiming the benefit of the covenant and the right to enforce it, and the promisor or party who rests under the burden of the covenant."[35]

---

31. Frederick Schauer, *Is the Common Law Law?*, 77 Calif. L. Rev. 455, 455–56, 464, 467 (1989); *see also, e.g.*, Pierre Legrand, *European Legal Systems Are Not Converging*, 45 Int'l & Comp. L.Q. 52, 68–70 (1996). To be sure, Schauer admits that "rules of thumb are useful guides for prediction and useful to consult when time is short," but he insists that because rules of thumb can only indicate "the result likely to be reached by the rationales or justifications lying behind the rule...they are intrinsically unweighty." Schauer, *supra*, at 467.
32. 15 N.E.2d 793 (N.Y. 1938).
33. *See* Dukeminier et al., *supra* note 19, at 872.
34. *See generally* Dagan, *supra* note 13, at 6–7.
35. *Neponsit*, 15 N.E.2d at 795.

Does "an affirmative covenant to pay money for use in connection with, but not upon, the land which it is said is subject to the burden of the covenant" indeed touch or concern the land? The "touch and concern" test developed by old English cases is, says the court, "too vague to be of much assistance" and, as such, leaves the enforceability question "'for the court to determine in the exercise of its best judgment upon the facts of each case.'" The court mentioned that some prior cases may imply that only negative covenants "which compel the covenanter to submit to some *restriction on the use* of his property, touch or concern the land" and, therefore, affirmative covenants do not run with the land. It also noted, however, the cases that, notwithstanding this seemingly bright-line distinction, enforce "promises to pay money...as covenants running with the land, against subsequent holders of the land who took with notice of the covenant." Acknowledging the difficulty of classifying these exceptions or formulating "a rigid test or definition which will be entirely satisfactory or which can be applied mechanically in all cases," the court moves on to state "a reasonable method of approach" to such cases, namely: "that a covenant which runs with the land must affect the legal relations—the advantages and the burdens—of the parties to the covenant as owners of particular parcels of land and not merely as members of the community in general, such as taxpayers or owners of other land." Although the results of this test may still be "a matter of degree," it is—the court insists—superior to the negative/affirmative distinction because it does not "exalt technical form over substance," and because it also accounts well for quite a few prior cases.[36]

Applying this test to the question at hand allows the court to conclude with a rather bright-line rule regarding the specific issue of assessment covenants. While the payments at hand serve "public purposes" upon land other than the land conveyed to a grantee's predecessors in title, through that conveyance grantees obtain "not only title to particular lots, but an easement or right of common enjoyment with other property owners in roads, beaches, public parks or spaces and improvements in the same tract." In order for the "property owners of these easements or rights" to fully enjoy them in common, these public improvements "must be maintained." This happy outcome can be achieved only if the burden of paying this cost is "inseparably attached to the land which enjoys the benefit."[37]

The court had to pass yet another hurdle. Although "[v]arious definitions have been formulated of 'privity of estate' in connection with covenants that run with the land...none of such definitions seems to cover the relationship" between a property owners' association, which "has been organized to receive the sums payable by the property owners and to expend them for the benefit of such owners," and a subsequent purchaser. The *Neponsit* court alluded to

36. *Id.* at 795–97.
37. *Id.* at 797.

the rather tortuous privity doctrine, but refused to have its analysis obscured by its technical details:

> Only blind adherence to an ancient formula devised to meet entirely different conditions could constrain the court to hold that a corporation formed as a medium for the enjoyment of common rights of property owners owns no property which would benefit by enforcement of common rights and has no cause of action in equity to enforce the covenant upon which such common rights depend.

Thus, the court held that a corporate plaintiff such as Neponsit, which "has been formed as a convenient instrument by which the property owners may advance their common interests," should be able to enforce the covenants at hand.[38]

* * *

Neponsit set bright-line rules on the standing of property owners' associations and the validity of the assessment covenant. It also prescribed the standard articulating the regulative principle underlying the property form of covenants, thereby serving as the springboard for the development of common-interest communities, which are the fastest-growing property institution in America. On both fronts, *Neponsit* demonstrates the happy cohabitation of private law pluralism and the guidance conception of the rule of law.

The first and most obvious aspect of *Neponsit* worth mentioning is its bright-line rules establishing the validity of assessment covenants and the standing of homeowners associations,[39] which were (almost literally) necessary preconditions for the subsequent flowering of common-interest communities. This simple observation attests that, notwithstanding Smith's assertion to the contrary, a pluralist conception of property or of private law can, and indeed should, distance itself from the dubious nominalist approach of case-by-case adjudication. Private law pluralism neither requires nor should it indeed imply focusing on the equities of the particular case or the particular parties. By the same token, private law pluralism should not imply rule-sensitive particularism allowing judges to depart from rules whenever the outcome of a particular case so requires, while taking into account both substantive values and the value of preserving the rule's integrity.[40] Private law pluralism does not suggest substituting clear rules with open-ended discretionary decision making. Instead, it stands for the proposition that reasoning about private law rules should involve reasoning about the normatively appropriate character of

---

38. *Id.* at 797–98.
39. Later cases indeed show that *Neponsit* is standing for such rules. *See, e.g.*, Riverton Cmty. Ass'n v. Myers, 142 A.D.2d 984, 985 (N.Y. App. Div. 1992); Lincolnshire Civic Ass'n v. Beach, 64 N.Y.S.2d 248 (N.Y. App. Div. 1975).
40. *See* Sherwin, *supra* note 30, at 1591–94.

the private law institution at hand—given the social context of the relevant property institution's and the nature of the resource at hand—and not about property (or contracts, torts, or unjust enrichment) writ large. Given that the number of property institutions is limited and the role of the property values in their regard is confined to a few deliberative moments, we need not assume that private law pluralism cannot, to a significant extent, be rule-based.[41] More importantly, given the significance of stability and predictability in the institutions of property and of private law more generally to function in con-solidating expectations and expressing ideals of interpersonal relationships,[42] private law pluralism is not only capable of setting bright-line rules, but is in fact, if properly executed, inclined to do so.

Indeed, the identification of legal realism with nominalism, although prevalent,[43] is mistaken. Although a small minority among realists does endorse the dubious ad hoc approach of case-by-case adjudication,[44] most realists take a very different position.[45] They realize that law's use of cate-gories, concepts, and rules is unavoidable, even desirable,[46] and that many legal reasoners should in most cases simply follow rules, which is why realists indeed take pains to improve legal rules.[47] Thus, for example, the property values of autonomy, personhood, utility, labor, community, and distributive justice neither are nor should be invoked as reasons for particular outcomes of specific property cases, but rather as reasons for property rules or standards.

41. *Cf.* Michael Lobban, *Legal Theory and Judge Made Law in England, 1850–1920*, 40 QUADERNI FIORENTINI 553 (2011); Jeremy Waldron, *Stare Decisis and the Rule of Law: A Layered Approach* (2011), *available at* http://papers.ssrn.com/abstract=1942557. Lobban's survey of the codification debate concludes that common law rules were shown to be different from legislated ones—"[t]hey were more flexible and had to be interpreted not according to a verbal formula, but according to the broader case law context from which they had emerged." But Lobban also shows that advocates of codification had successfully demonstrated that "the common law was not a mass of undigested chaos but that it contained rules which could be identified and articulated." Lobban, *supra*, at 580. Waldron claims that this approach to precedent, as opposed to one that conceptualizes precedent as an exercise of analogical or case-by-case reason-ing, follows (among others) our commitment to the rule of law. *See also* Larry Alexander & Emily Sherwin, *Judges as Rule Makers, in* COMMON LAW THEORY 27 (Douglas E. Adlin ed., 2007).

42. *See supra* text accompanying note 16.

43. *See, e.g.*, RONALD DWORKIN, TAKING RIGHTS SERIOUSLY 15–16 (1977); MORTON HORWITZ, THE TRANSFORMATION OF AMERICAN LAW, 1870–1960, at 202 (1992).

44. *See, e.g.*, FRED RODELL, WOE UNTO YOU, LAWYERS! 169–74, 201–02 (1940).

45. *See, e.g.*, Andrew Altman, *The Legacy of Legal Realism*, 10 LEGAL STUD. FORUM 167, 171–72 (1986); Todd D. Rakoff, *The Implied Terms of Contract: Of "Default Rules" and "Situation Sense," in* GOOD FAITH AND FAULT IN CONTRACT LAW 191, 216 (Jack Beatson & Daniel Friedmann eds., 1995).

46. *See, e.g.*, LLEWELLYN, A *Realistic Jurisprudence, supra* note 7, at 27; *see also, e.g.*, Walter Wheeler Cook, *Scientific Method and the Law, in* AMERICAN LEGAL REALISM 242, 246 (William W. Fisher III et al. eds., 1993); *supra* Chapter 6.

47. Karl Llewellyn, the most important legal realist, was of course the principal draftsman of article 2 of the Uniform Commercial Code.

Recognizing these values as the normative infrastructure of property law should advise *some* legal actors—notably, judges of appellate courts—to *occasionally* use new cases as triggers for an ongoing refinement of the doctrine and as opportunities for both revisiting the normative viability of existing rules qua rules and reexamining the adequacy of the legal categorization that organizes these rules. In fact, much of *Property: Values and Institutions* is similarly devoted to the identification of property rules that best promote the property values underlying the property institutions to which they belong.

* * *

Besides prescribing rules regarding the validity of assessment covenants and the standing of homeowners associations, *Neponsit* significantly transformed the doctrinal analysis of covenants more generally. Although not formally overruling the complex requirements of touch and concern and of privity, *Neponsit* explicitly criticized the technical niceties of these doctrines. It pointed out that, even where they took the form of a rule (as in the affirmative/negative covenants distinction), courts have tended to use such a rule merely as a rule of thumb, arguably because of its undue detachment from any reasonable understanding of the regulative principle that should guide this area of the law. Thereby, *Neponsit* also paved the way for the substitution of the old (vague) tests of touch and concern and of privity with more substantive elements focusing on the role of covenants in the landowners' endeavor to pre-regulate their relationships qua landowners—or, more precisely, in their capacity[48] as participants in the property institution of common-interest communities—so as to facilitate their common enjoyment of certain public improvements and advance their common interests.[49] Both the critical and the reconstructive sides of this part of *Neponsit* are relevant for my purposes.

In criticizing the preexisting doctrinal rules, the court reminds us that, at times, a complex set of rules may fail to adequately serve as a guide for action. Regulating a wide range of conduct is complex, and technical nonintuitive complexity may undermine the guidance value of rules.[50] In such circumstances (and *Neponsit*'s reconstructive side comes into play here), less precise norms—vague standards—may be needed, such as *Neponsit*'s focus on the role of covenants in facilitating landowners' ability to enjoy the potential

---

48. *See* Christopher Essert, *The Office of Ownership*, 63 U. TORONTO L.J. (forthcoming 2013).

49. This process culminated in the Restatement of Servitudes, which replaces the touch and concern requirement with a list of "public policy" issues that justify invalidating servitudes, and substitutes the privity test with rules that properly accommodate the verification interest of third parties. *See* RESTATEMENT (THIRD) OF SERVITUDES §§ 3, 5 (2000).

50. *See* RICHARD A. POSNER, THE PROBLEMS OF JURISPRUDENCE 48 (1990); Timothy Endicott, *The Value of Vagueness*, *in* PHILOSOPHICAL FOUNDATIONS OF LANGUAGE IN THE LAW 14, 23, 28, 30 (Andrei Marmor & Scott Soames eds., 2011).

benefits of common-interest communities. Even though such standards do not provide bright-line instructions, they may still guide people's actions. As Jeremy Waldron claims, although complying with such a vague standard "may be more onerous than" complying with a bright-line rule, a standard can still be action-guiding, channeling and directing people's behavior. People aware of this kind of vague standard (or their lawyers who are actually the active players at the relevant moments of common-interest community formation) can "[t]ake it on board," make for themselves "the evaluative judgment that the norm requires," and thus monitor and modify their behavior accordingly.[51]

This conceptualization of standards as appeals to people's practical reasoning also sheds light on the types of issues wherein standards can be particularly guidance-friendly, as well as on the kind of legal reasoning that can accentuate the guidance potential of standards. It explains the truism that, given normative consensus on the pertinent issue, one may expect broad agreement regarding the application of a standard, and thus expect it to be particularly helpful as a guide.[52] Furthermore, in cases lacking such social agreement, the guidance capacity of standards as appeals to people's practical reasoning can rely on the significance of judicial reasoning in the common law tradition. Because "the justification of a common law rule is as important as the norm itself,"[53] refining the justification of a norm (or, for my purposes, explaining the role of a regulative principle in promoting the social ideal underlying its private law institution) helps its addressees figure out its intended content and realm of application. Finally, in addition to the benefits these vague standards can provide "as is," this type of "mud" can, and usually does, create further "crystals" over time, namely, more bright-line rules to implement its prescriptions.[54]

Both of these aspects seem to be at work regarding property institutions generally and the *Neponsit* doctrine more particularly. To see why, recall that by structuring property as a limited number of identifiable and standardized forms and dividing the other fields of private law along similar lines,[55] private law facilitates stable categories of human interaction.[56] Unlike the broad and heterogeneous private law fields to which they belong, each of these private

51. *See* Jeremy Waldron, *Vagueness and the Guidance of Action*, *in* LANGUAGE IN THE LAW, *supra* note 50, at 58, 65–66, 69.

52. *See* FULLER, *supra* note 25, at 50, 92; Fallon, *supra* note 29, at 49–50; John Gardner, *Rationality and the Rule of Law in Offences against the Person*, 53 CAMBRIDGE L.J. 502, 513, 515–17 (1994).

53. Douglas E. Adlin, *Introduction*, *in* COMMON LAW THEORY 1, 3 (Douglas E. Adlin ed., 2007).

54. *See* Carol M. Rose, *Crystals and Mud in Property Law*, 40 STAN. L. REV. 577 (1988).

55. *See, e.g.,* Roy Kreitner, *Multiplicity in Contract Remedies*, *in* COMPARATIVE REMEDIES FOR BREACH OF CONTRACTS 19, 19–20, 38 (Nili Cohen & Ewan McKendrick eds., 2005).

56. *See supra* text accompanying note 16.

law institutions is internally coherent, meaning it is more or less guided by one regulative principle, one value, or balance of values. Thus, given social consensus as to this regulative principle, or even without it but with the law clarifying (in constitutive cases such as *Neponsit*) what this regulative principle is and making it sufficiently stable (meaning it is not revisited so frequently as to make law incapable of guiding behavior), legal subjects or their lawyers are likely to be aware of the "character" of an institution and form their expectations accordingly.[57] (Recall that "the rule of law does not require that law's guidance never change. It requires that the prospect of change should not make it impossible to use the existing law as a guide."[58]) Therefore, insofar as property law or private law more generally cannot use only bright-line rules but must also rely on vague standards, using the various property (or private law) institutions as its building blocks seems optimal from a guidance perspective, at least by comparison to the alternative of using the broad private law fields of property, contracts, torts, and unjust enrichment.[59]

* * *

My claims regarding the guidance potential of private law pluralism that, as I mentioned in Part I, are inspired by legal realism, are ostensibly threatened by the legal realist critique of doctrinal determinacy.[60] Legal realists argued that the irreducible choice among the many potentially applicable doctrinal sources competing to control any given case, all of which can be expanded, contracted, or variously interpreted or elaborated, means that legal doctrine is always open to multiple readings.[61] Unlike their image in some caricatures of legal realism, however, most realists did not challenge the predictability of legal doctrine. While persuasively insisting that legal doctrine qua doctrine can never constrain decision makers, they recognized that the convergence

---

57. This does not mean, of course, that such guidance is always effective. Thus, even the New York Court of Appeals failed at times to rely on and properly apply *Neponsit's* reformulation of the regulative principle of covenant law. *See, e.g.*, Eagle Enters. v. Gross, 349 N.E.2d 816 (N.Y. 1976).

58. TIMOTHY A.O. ENDICOTT, *The Impossibility of the Rule of Law, in* VAGUENESS IN LAW 185, 193 (2000); *see also, e.g.*, GARDNER, *supra* note 3, at 41; MATTHEW H. KRAMER, OBJECTIVITY AND THE RULE OF LAW 114 (2007).

59. Smith acknowledges that "[o]ptimal concepts [] have a medium level of generality"—Smith, *supra* note 23, at 2105—but nothing in his critique supports the assertion that the correct level of abstraction in private law is that of such broad and heterogeneous legal fields.

60. *See* Lisa Austin, *Pluralism, Context and the Internal Life of Property: A Response to Hanoch Dagan*, 63 U. TORONTO L.J. 22 (2013).

61. *See supra* section I.B.1.b of Chapter 2. This radical claim has often been domesticated. Thus, even Frederick Schauer, who recently elaborated on the consequences of taking seriously the realist distinction between real rules and paper rules—but does not consider the effects of multiplicity—ends up with the conclusion that the significance of the realist critique of doctrinal determinacy can only be evaluated empirically. *See* Frederick Schauer, *Legal Realism Untamed* 20, 28, 32–34 (Va. Pub. Law & Legal Theory Research Paper No. 2012-38, 2012), *available at* http://ssrn.com/abstract=2064837.

of lawyers' background understandings at a given time and place generates a significant measure of stability.[62] Thus, rather than threatening the compatibility of private law pluralism with the guidance conception of the rule of law, legal realism merely insists that such guidance does not inhere in the doctrine as such and rests instead on the broader social practice of law.[63] In the present case, guidance rests on the prevalent understanding of the private law institution's character, which reflects the regulative principle governing its constitutive rules.

Llewellyn thus argued that, although adjudication is necessarily creative, it is invariably constrained by legal tradition. Cases are decided with "a desire to move in accordance with the material as well as within it...to reveal the latent rather than to impose new form, much less to obtrude an outside will." The case law *system* imposes "a demand for moderate consistency, for reasonable regularity, for on-going conscientious effort at integration." The instant outcome and rule must "fit the flavor of the whole"; it must, as we have seen in *Neponsit*, "think with the feel of the body of our law" and "go with the grain rather than across or against it." Legal realists begin with the existing doctrinal landscape because it may and often does incorporate valuable normative choices, even if implicit and sometimes imperfectly executed. They nonetheless recognize that the existing legal environment always leaves interpretive leeway. Furthermore, they believe that law's potential dynamism, as long as properly cautious and not too frequent, is laudable because it represents our perennial quest "for better and best law" and, therefore, our judges' "duty to justice and adjustment," thus implying an "on-going production and improvement of rules."[64]

III. The Rule of Law as Constraint

However fortunate this conclusion may appear to be in terms of guidance, it seems to be alarming in terms of another understanding of the rule of law. The conception of the rule of law discussed so far has focused on the subjects of law and their guidance, whereas henceforth it will focus on the government.[65]

---

62. *See supra* section III.B.2.a of Chapter 2; *see also, e.g.,* ALEXANDER & SHERWIN, *supra* note 30, at 32–34.

63. *See* Frederick Schauer, *Editor's Introduction, in* KARL N. LLEWELLYN, THE THEORY OF RULES 1, 5, 7–8, 18, 20–24 (Frederick Schauer ed., 2011); *see also* Fallon, *supra* note 29, at 16–17; Margaret Jane Radin, *Reconsidering the Rule of Law*, 69 B.U. L. REV. 781, 803 (1989).

64. LLEWELLYN, THE COMMON LAW TRADITION, *supra* note 17, at 36, 38, 190–91, 217, 222–23; K.N. Llewellyn, *The Normative, the Legal, and the Law-Jobs: The Problem of Juristic Method*, 49 YALE L.J. 1355, 1385 (1940).

65. This focus on the government, to be sure, is important because it affects people.

Consider the notion that the rule of law is the flip side of the rule of man. Although its literal interpretation, as Albert Ven Dicey put it, is "absurd" because "[p]olitical institutions … are made what they are by human voluntary agency," a more substantive understanding of this contrast implies that the rule of law stands for "the absence of arbitrary power on part of the government."[66] This characterization explains E.P. Thompson's spirited claim that the rule of law is "an unqualified human good" as it represents "the imposing of effective inhibitions upon power and the defense of the citizen from power's all-intrusive claims."[67] Unrestrained power is frightening because of its potential devastating impositions; even more fundamentally, unrestrained power renders us mere objects, dominated by the power-wielder.[68] The conception of the rule of law as constraint seeks to address these grave concerns.

Waldron traced the main contours of the idea that the rule of law stands for the absence of unconstrained power. The rule of law in this conception, he explains, corresponds to an "aspirational idea," wherein law must purport to be guided by "justice and the common good that transcend the self-interest of the powerful." Its main mission, therefore, is "to correct abuses of power,"[69] and to "take the edge off human political power, making it less objectionable, less dangerous, more benign and more respectful."[70] Accordingly, the core requirement of the rule of law as constraint is to insist on "a particular mode of the exercise of political power: governance through law." It thus maintains that "people in positions of authority should exercise their power within a constraining framework of public norms, rather than on the basis of their own preferences, their own ideology, or their own individual sense of right and wrong."[71]

In a sense, insofar as private law pluralism follows the guidance conception of the rule of law, it also addresses the concerns of unconstrained judicial

66. A.V. DICEY, INTRODUCTION TO THE STUDY OF THE LAW OF THE CONSTITUTION 188, 196 (10th ed. 1959); *see also, e.g.*, RONALD A. CASS, THE RULE OF LAW IN AMERICA 3, 17–18 (2001).

67. E.P. THOMPSON, WHIGS AND HUNTERS: THE ORIGIN OF THE BLACK ACT 266 (1975); *see also* DAVID DUDLEY FIELD, *Magnitude and Importance of Legal Science* (address at the opening of the Law School of the University of Chicago, Sept. 21, 1859), *reprinted in* 1 SPEECHES, ARGUMENTS, AND MISCELLANEOUS PAPERS OF DAVID DUDLEY FIELD, at 530 (A. Sprague ed., 1884); GARDNER, *supra* note 3, at 213. *But cf.* RAZ, *supra* note 3, at 219 ("Many forms of arbitrary power are compatible with the rule of law.").

68. *See* Krygier, *supra* note 1, at 79–80. Parenthetically, note that the conception of the rule of law as constraint is thicker than that of the rule of law as guidance, but serves a thinner understanding of individual autonomy.

69. Jeremy Waldron, *The Concept and the Rule of Law*, 43 GA. L. REV. 1, 11, 32 (2008).

70. Jeremy Waldron, *Is the Rule of Law an Essentially Contested Concept (in Florida)?*, 21 L. & PHIL. 137, 159 (2002).

71. Waldron, *supra* note 69, at 6, 31; *see also, e.g.*, Krygier, *supra* note 1, at 75–76, 78, 82, 88; *cf.* David Dyzenhaus, *Recrafting the Rule of Law*, in RECRAFTING THE RULE OF LAW: THE LIMITS OF LEGAL ORDER 1, 7, 9 (David Dyzenhaus ed., 1999).

power, because the requirement to identify and articulate a general norm imparts *some* element of impersonality.[72] But is this an adequate answer to the challenge at hand? Consider the possibility of allowing property doctrines (or their contracts, torts, and unjust enrichment counterparts) to rest on the pertinent property values (liberty, personhood, labor, well-being, community, and distributive justice) without a predetermined formula for measuring and balancing these values.[73] Would not such an option entail unbridled judicial discretion, inviting these unaccountable officials to apply their subjective (or self-serving) normative preferences?[74]

To appreciate this challenge, consider Duncan Kennedy's account of "the experience of legal reasoning as an activity pursued in a medium that is at once plastic and resistant." Somewhat along the lines of my claim regarding the conventional rather than purely doctrinal underpinnings of the guidance function of private law pluralism,[75] Kennedy argues that an interpreter of legal materials "works to create or to undo determinacy, rather than simply registering or experiencing it as a given." Rather than being "'qualities' or 'attributes' inherent in the norm," this argument continues, determinacy or indeterminacy are effects "produced contingently by the interaction of the interpreter's time, energy, and skill with an...'essential' nature of the rule [at hand]." And therefore, Kennedy concludes, "we predict a result *because we anticipate that no work will be done to destabilize the initial apprehension.*"[76]

Some may find this account an affront to the rule of law, posing "the specter of the usurpation of power by an unaccountable elite," misrepresenting political decisions "as if they were matters of law," and thus making "the rule of law ideal...a fraud."[77] Kennedy's response to this worry is that "juristic work intended to inflect the law in the judge's (or jurist's) preferred ideological direction" is legitimate.[78] But this defense seems far from comforting. We need not object to such "judicial activism," Kennedy argues, because we

72. *See* Waldron, *supra* note 41, at §3; *cf.* William Lucy, *Abstraction and the Rule of Law*, 29 OXFORD J. LEGAL STUD. 481 (2009).

73. Notice that in these (not too many) deliberative moments in which judges rethink the regulative principles of a private law institution, they do not (and should not) solely rely on conventional morality, and thus cannot (solely) rely on prevalent social conventions.

74. *See* Austin, *supra* note 60.

75. *See supra* text accompanying notes 61–63.

76. DUNCAN KENNEDY, LEGAL REASONING: COLLECTED ESSAYS 3, 159–61, 167 (2007).

77. BRIAN Z. TAMAHANA, ON THE RULE OF LAW: HISTORY, POLITICS, THEORY 125 (2004); Brian Z. Tamahana, *How an Instrumental View of Law Corrodes the Rule of Law*, 56 DEPAUL L. REV. 469, 493 (2006); *see also, e.g.*, ROBERT H. BORK, THE TEMPTING OF AMERICA 4–5 (1990) (criticizing "the politicization of law" and its reduction "to a tame instrument of particular political thrust"); Martti Konskenniemi, *Constitutionalism as Mindset: Reflections on Kantian Themes about International Law and Globalization*, 81 THEORETICAL INQUIRIES L. 9, 25 (2007).

78. KENNEDY, *supra* note 76, at 163.

should not expect that the notion of obedience or fidelity to law might help jurists to decide whether to employ "ideologically oriented work strategies" to transform, or at least destabilize, "initial apprehensions of what the materials require." To think otherwise is to adhere to a "fetishized or reified belief in the rule of law," rather than to maturely realize that the jurist's "role constraint is no more than 'do your best under all the circumstances to do something politically good.'"[79]

* * *

The anxieties that friends of the rule of law as constraint experience in light of statements that collapse law into politics inform many critiques of judge-made law in general and of the common law more particularly.[80] These concerns cannot be easily dismissed even by those (such as myself) who agree with Kennedy that law, like politics, cannot avoid addressing normative commitments, and furthermore do not deny that politics, like law, must rely on the aspiration to constrain decision-makers' power. The reason for this is that the appropriate modes of constraining power in these two realms are different: "participatory politics is . . . situated between the realm of the market (that focuses on preferences) and that of the law (that must always strive for public-regarding justification)," so that in politics—even in its ideal form—"neither convictions nor preferences should be excluded."[81]

Taking the critical legal studies' critique of the rule of law seriously,[82] Ernest Weinrib, who is a friend of common law, proposes a radical but seemingly attractive understanding of private law purporting to be an adequate response to the challenge of preserving the distinction between law and politics.[83] Weinrib's account builds on a particularly demanding reading of the rule of law as constraint: Aristotle's claim that the rule of law is "differentiated from the rule of men" by being "the embodiment of intelligence without appetite." In order to "sustain the possibility" of this injunction, Weinrib argues, law must not be "subservient to external ideals"; it must, in other words, be "conceptually sealed off from the interplay of extrinsic purposes." Rather than promoting purposes such as the plural values that inform private law pluralism, the rule of law rests on the view that law "constitutes, as it were, its own ideal, intelligible from within and capable of serving as [a] constraint upon the radical idealisms which postulate its depreciation."

---

79. *Id.* at 6–8, 165, 168.

80. *See respectively* Waldron, *supra* note 70, at 142–43; Frederick Schauer, *The Failure of the Common Law*, 36 ARIZ. ST. L.J. 765, 781–82 (2004); *see also, e.g.*, Angelo Piero Sereni, *The Code and Case Law*, *in* THE CODE NAPOLEON AND COMMON LAW WORLD 57–58, 74–76 (Bernard Schwartz ed., 1956); Robert S. Summers, *A Formal Theory of the Rule of Law*, 6 RATIO JURIS 127, 134, 137–38 (1993).

81. Hanoch Dagan, *Political Money*, 8 ELECTION L.J. 349, 356 (2009).

82. Ernest J. Weinrib, *Legal Formalism: On the Immanent Rationality of Law*, 97 YALE L.J. 949, 1015–16 (1988).

83. Weinrib, *supra* note 3, at 60, 63, 70–71, 78, 80–81, 83.

Private law, Weinrib claims, especially in the common law tradition, "makes a show of [such] a self-contained rationality." This is the case because the "adjudicator in a private law dispute [must] follow through and give specificity to the order implicit in the nature of the transactions, and his reasons for judgment are the public announcement of the intimations of this order in the context of a particular occurrence." This is the case because, by being "presented with two parties only, a plaintiff and a defendant," the court is "structurally cut off from consideration of overall welfare" and is strictly confined to "the litigants' assertions of right[s] arising out of particular courses of dealings." In this way, "[t]he structural features of the form of corrective justice place it conceptually beyond the reach of political determination," thereby rendering "law intelligible as its own end," and justifying "the common law's self-understanding of the adjudicative process which regards the judge's decision not as the exercise of political choice but as an act of cognition."

Weinrib's claim that the rule of law requires private law to adhere to corrective justice and exclude any collective or public values from our understanding of property (or of its sister private law doctrines) is, if successful, devastating to private law pluralism.[84] Fortunately, it is not. The main reason for its lack of success,[85] which I have discussed at some length elsewhere[86] and can only address briefly here, is anticipated by Weinrib himself when he notes that the integrity of this position "depends upon whether [corrective justice is indeed] immune to the projection on to [it] of extrinsic purposes."[87]

Weinrib significantly illuminates the unique justificatory burden generated by the bipolar structure of private law litigation: private law is structured as a drama between plaintiff and defendant and must therefore require correlativity between the defendant's liability and the plaintiff's entitlement. But Weinrib's more ambitious claim (and the one that is relevant here) concerning private law's airtight insulation from collective values does not stand. Although private law is not just one of many strategies of regulation, it neither is nor can be dissociated from our social values. Quite the contrary, in order for the correlativity inquiry to even begin, and indeed be intelligible, we need to determine what exactly is the content of the parties' rights, a

84. Weinrib's thesis threatens, of course, not only private law pluralism, but also most (if not all) of the competing monistic conceptions of private law.
85. Another significant shortfall of Weinrib's conception of the rule of law is that it does not properly address the significance of the prospective effects of every significant legal pronouncement, which must imply that judges should be able to justify their decisions to those who will be subject to them even if they are not participating in the judicial drama at hand. *See* Hanoch Dagan, Law as an Academic Discipline, *available at* http://ssrn.com/abstract=2228433.
86. Hanoch Dagan, *The Distributive Foundation of Corrective Justice*, 98 MICH. L. REV. 138 (1999); DAGAN, *supra* note 5, at 58–60, 63–66; *supra* Chapter 5. The next two paragraphs draw on these sources.
87. Weinrib, *supra* note 3, at 75.

determination that necessarily invokes our public values. To be sure, not every value can qualify for the task. By and large, only values that participate in the regulative principle that underlies the private law institution at issue, meaning only values that inform our ideal vision of the interpersonal relationship at hand, can legitimately be taken into account. The implication is that the values underlying private law are not identical to those guiding public law, that not only one set of values underlies private law (or any one of its broad fields) in its entirety, and that in most cases these values are not to be directly engaged by judges deciding specific cases. At the same time, the implication is also that private law is deeply affected by our public values, so that corrective justice cannot render private law intelligible from within, sealed off from our social ideals.

Indeed, the pivotal role of private law in defining our mutual legitimate claims and expectations in our daily interactions undermines the legitimacy of a private law regime that ignores these values. The parties' *ex ante* entitlements, from which correlativity must be measured, are best analyzed by reference to our social values. Rather than being divorced or abstracted from our social values, private law both reflects these values and at times even participates in their formation.

* * *

The fact that Weinrib's strategy is not a panacea able to set aside the concerns of the rule of law as constraint is insufficient to redeem private law pluralism, as it merely reinstates the challenge of constraint. There seem to be two aspects to this challenge: one from legitimacy and the other from determinacy.[88]

The sheer fact that judges, unlike legislators, are often unelected ostensibly suffices to condemn their significant impact on our private law as illegitimate application of power. But the question of legitimacy should be examined in much more nuanced and comparative terms.[89] To determine the proper domain of judicial creation and modification of private law institutions, if any, we need to examine potential bases for the legitimacy of judicial rulemaking in private law matters. Though I could not possibly hope to provide an adequate account of legitimacy in a liberal democracy here, the following remarks should suffice to support the claim that the legitimate scope of judicial rulemaking in private law is in fact rather broad.[90]

---

88. Both aspects are raised by Austin, *supra* note 60.

89. My discussion of legitimacy draws on Hanoch Dagan, *Judges and Property*, in INTELLECTUAL PROPERTY AND THE COMMON LAW (Shyam Balganesh ed., forthcoming 2013); *cf.* GARDNER, *supra* note 3, at 200–01; SCOTT J. SHAPIRO, LEGALITY 331, 358 (2011).

90. Note that I do not make a claim for judicial supremacy, as in judicial review. My sole focus is on the legitimacy of judicial rulemaking where legislatures are silent.

Consider first the notion that state power can be legitimate only if it is a product of its citizens' coauthorship. To be meaningful, the ideal of coauthoring the normative commitments that (necessarily) serve as the foundation of our private law entitlements must not be axiomatically attached solely to the legislative process.[91] Rather, a commitment to coauthorship requires a more careful comparative account of meaningful participation and deliberation in legislation and in adjudication. This account can look at the participation of the citizens (directly or via elected representatives) or focus on the participation of the subset of citizens who are likely to be affected by the private law development at hand.

In general, participation and deliberation will more likely be found in legislation than in adjudication because lawmaking is legislation's only task, whereas in adjudication it emerges as part of the resolution of discrete disputes.[92] But the broad or representative participation that might significantly foster collective coauthorship does not seem typical of legislation on many private law matters. Take (again) property: some property doctrines, such as the law of common-interest communities that serves as my main example in this chapter, may seem too mundane as a subject for robust public deliberation.[93] By contrast, when the creation or modification of property institutions provides significant opportunities for rent seeking, as in the repeated extensions of the term and scope of copyright, the legislative process tends to be dominated by interest groups promoting narrow distributive goals,[94] and thus cannot meaningfully count as collective coauthorship.

The ideal of participation by parties affected by the proposed development of private law is a more realistic expectation. But insofar as this participatory ideal is concerned, adjudication fares quite well and, in some contexts, probably better than legislation. The adjudicatory adversarial process fares well because it invites disagreements on questions of facts, opinion, and law. It thereby creates a forum where the judges' normative and empirical horizons are constantly challenged by the conflicting perspectives of the participating

---

91. Even if one insists that such an axiom is justified in the discussion of democracy-based legitimacy, it is out of place in the discussion of legitimacy in a democracy. As the text implies, the latter, broader type of legitimacy that concerns me here accommodates differing types of citizens' participation and of decision-makers' accountability.

92. Another reason relates to comparative costs: voters "often face a far less expensive road [than litigants] to registering their needs ... in the political process." NEIL K. KOMESAR, IMPERFECT ALTERNATIVES: CHOOSING INSTITUTIONS IN LAW, ECONOMICS, AND PUBLIC POLICY 127 (1991).

93. To preempt a possible objection, I may add that the notion that judicial passivity can upset the marginality of these topics within our public discourse does not seem particularly plausible.

94. *See generally* JESSICA LITMAN, DIGITAL COPYRIGHT (2001).

parties, which present a microcosm of the social dilemma at hand.[95] Moreover, as Neil Komesar shows regarding tort law, adjudication sometimes seems to provide a qualitatively better forum for the participation of affected parties. One instance are cases showing sharp "distinction between *ex ante* and *ex post* stakes," so that the low *ex ante* probability of harm may obscure an important perspective rendered vivid in the *ex post* litigation triggered by the unfortunate realization of such harm.[96] Certain important developments of property institutions, such as marital property, cohabitation, and leaseholds, by the judiciary may also fit well into this category.

But legitimacy should perhaps require only decision-makers' accountability rather than citizens' participation. Accountability is a more modest standard: it does not require active participation or deliberation but merely insists that decision makers be responsive to citizens' values and preferences. As with participation, the accountability requirement may in the abstract appear as a trump in favor of elected legislators vis-à-vis unelected judges, given that reelection is a rather potent guarantee of responsiveness. But my previous observations regarding skewed participation in private law matters immediately and detrimentally affect legislators' responsiveness as well. If most or many private law matters are either politically marginal or dominated by interest groups, the legislators' expected responsiveness is likely to be rather limited. Likewise, an outright dismissal of judges' responsiveness seems exaggerated. As Llewellyn insisted, in their opinions judges need to "account to the public, to the general law-consumer" on a regular basis and in detail. They must persuade not only their brethren but also the legal community, including losing counsel, "that outcome, underpinning, and workmanship are worthy" and that their judgment was formed "in terms of the Whole, *seen whole*."[97] Although real-life adjudication surely falls short of these ideals, having these standards in place is nonetheless significant because it affects judges' utility function and thus informs judicial behavior, as even the tough-minded portrayals of judges as maximizers of their utility function admit.[98]

* * *

Even if judges can legitimately affect our private law, is granting judges the power to apply a rather diverse set of collective values not tantamount to inviting them to apply subjective and thus illegitimate unbounded discretion?

---

95. *See supra* section III.B.1 of Chapter 2; Matthew Steilen, *The Democratic Common Law*, 2011 J. JURIS. 437.

96. *See* KOMESAR, *supra* note 92, at 135–36.

97. LLEWELLYN, THE COMMON LAW TRADITION, *supra* note 17, at 48, 132; LLEWELLYN, *American Common Law Tradition and American Democracy*, in JURISPRUDENCE, *supra* note 7, at 282, 309–10.

98. *See* RICHARD A. POSNER, HOW JUDGES THINK 11–12, 60–61, 371 (2008); *see also* LAWRENCE BAUM, JUDGES AND THEIR AUDIENCES: A PERSPECTIVE ON JUDICIAL BEHAVIOR 16–21, 90, 106 (2006); Frederick Schauer, *Incentives, Reputation, and the*

I do not think so. Different types of human interactions and, consequently, different categories of private law doctrines, call for different balances of the (indeed limited number of) values relevant to any given private law institution. Here, as elsewhere, the requirement to explicitly apply judgment, which needs to be normatively and contextually justified, is a real constraint.[99] In some categories of cases, this contextual normative inquiry might indeed lead to a standoff, with reason unable to adjudicate between two or more competing accounts. The relevant question, however, is not whether such cases are possible. The sheer existence of hard cases scarcely undermines the determinacy or the integrity of our private law, especially given that purely doctrinal reasoning, the main alternative to openly normative legal reasoning, is hopelessly malleable and thus indeterminate.[100] Rather, the question is whether cases of contextual-normative deadlock are prevalent enough so that they threaten a conception of private law premised on these guidelines, that is, whether we are indeed unable to use reason as the arbiter for identifying the most normatively desirable regulative principle of the private law institution at hand. As I attempted to demonstrate in my books on property and on restitution,[101] a sufficiently robust contextual normative account can often have quite sharp doctrinal teeth. Although some of my analyses may be controversial, they can hardly be challenged by the sheer difficulty of measuring or balancing the private law values I employ or by the possibility that there are other pertinent values. To challenge my approach, a detailed demonstration of the superiority of a competing account is needed, and a blanket claim that a better account will always be available will not suffice.[102] (Furthermore, recall that private law pluralism is committed to providing a rich variety of institutions both between and within social contexts, so that people who want, for example, to become homeowners, engage in business, or enter into intimate relationships have more than one option. Thus, private law pluralism allows individuals to navigate their course so that they bypass certain legal prescriptions, which means that judicial errors are less worrisome than they are in a monist private law regime.)

Let me again take an example, then, from the law of common-interest communities. My example this time deals with another constitutive characteristic of this important property institution, which is improperly marginalized in the exclusionary conception of property: inclusion. Since the landmark case

Inglorious Determinants of Judicial Behavior, 68 U. CIN. L. REV. 615, 615–17, 619–21 (2000).

99. *See, e.g.*, MICHAEL MARTIN, LEGAL REALISM: AMERICAN AND SCANDINAVIAN 39–40, 76 (1997); Joseph William Singer, *Normative Methods for Lawyers*, 56 UCLA L. REV. 899 (2009).

100. *See supra* text accompanying note 61.

101. *See* DAGAN, *supra* note 5; DAGAN, *supra* note 30.

102. *Cf.* RONALD DWORKIN, LAW'S EMPIRE 76–86 (1986).

of *Shelley v. Kraemer* held that judicial enforcement of racially restrictive covenants is an exercise of state action that violates the Fourteenth Amendment,[103]
some rights to entry in defiance of the property owners' will have become
inherent in a significant segment of housing law in America. With the enact-
ment of the Fair Housing Act,[104] discrimination in the sale or rental of residential dwellings on the basis of race, color, religion, sex, familial status, national
origin, or handicap is indeed currently prohibited.

Given its constitutional origin, the right to fair housing is usually analyzed as an external qualification of the owner's exclusionary prerogative,[105]
rather than as an internal entailment of the meaning of the right to property in common-interest communities (or of landlords' property right). But
this seems to be wrong or at least incomplete because, as Carol Rose insisted,
Shelley poses "a state action enigma": both prior and later decisions show that
the bare potential for judicial enforcement of private arrangements and preferences does not transform them into state action. Although Rose's specific
solution to this puzzle seems to me unsatisfactory,[106] her more general claim
that *Shelley* presents "some of the best instincts of property law" is precise.[107]
The nonowners' right of entry to common-interest communities is indeed
intrinsic to this property institution and should not be perceived as an external limitation or imposition.[108]

103. Shelley v. Kraemer, 344 U.S. 1 (1948).

104. Fair Housing Act, 42 U.S.C. § 3601; *see also* Civil Rights Act of 1866, 42 U.S.C.
§ 1982, which prescribes that "all citizens of the United States shall have the same
right, in every state and territory, as is enjoyed by white citizens thereof to inherit,
purchase, lease, sell, hold, and convey real and personal property." *Jones v. Alfred Mayer
Co.*, 392 U.S. 409 (1968), held that this prescription applies not only to public discrimination, but also to private discrimination.

105. *Cf.* Richard A. Epstein, *Covenants and Constitutions*, 73 CORNELL L. REV. 906,
918–19 (1988); Stewart E. Sterk, *Minority Protection in Residential Private Governments*,
77 B.U. L. REV. 273, 281 (1997).

106. Rose suggested that this puzzle can be solved by reference to the welfarist commitment of property law to minimize negative externalities on third parties who may
not share the preferences of the existing transactors. But, as Rose herself admits, making the protection of third parties from the idiosyncratic preferences of current transactors the core of property raises difficult questions for cases such as *Shelley*, where
third parties are likely to share these current preferences.

107. Carol Rose, *Shelley v. Kraemer*, *in* PROPERTY STORIES 169 (Gerald Korngold &
Andrew P. Morriss eds., 2004).

108. *Cf.* Noble v. Alley [1951] S.C.R. 64 (Can.), invalidating racially based restrictive
covenants because they referred to the identity of users/owners rather than to any
actual use of the pertinent land. Not only is this reasoning from within property, but it
also (implicitly) relies on the raison d'être of the property institution of covenants as a
means to facilitate landowners' ability to commonly enjoy the benefits of private land
use controls along the lines discussed above (*supra* text accompanying notes 50–51).
Understanding covenants in these terms does, on its face, make references to the identity of users and owners suspicious.

To see why, and to appreciate the constraining power of contextual normative reasoning regarding private law institutions, consider the way the right to entry to common-interest communities is grounded in the very reasons—the very same property values—that justify the support of our legal system for this property institution.[109] Consider, in other words, why *Shelley* is correct notwithstanding the state action enigma, and why the basic entry rule set by the Fair Housing Act should likewise be treated as a statutory specification of the regulative principle of common-interest communities (refined in *Neponsit*) rather than as a public law intervention.

Consider first the justification common to all property institutions as means for securing people's ability to be the authors of their lives. Limiting the opportunities of certain people to buy or lease houses or apartments in a certain geographical area undermines this role of property in facilitating people's self-determination. For this reason, exclusionary practices that unreasonably limit the mobility of the excluded persons (a mobility crucial to them in forming, revising, and pursuing their own ends) must be invalidated. In some settings, the concern for the autonomy of entrants is defeated by the autonomy and personhood concerns of property owners: the Fair Housing Act vigorously protects the right to exclude in intimate settings, where the personhood value of the owner (potential landlord) trumps any possible interest of potential tenants.[110] The Act, however, reverses this rule and recognizes a rather capacious right to entry where the lessor is a commercial entity. Because negative liberty is not an ultimate value but rather a means for self-determination, a claim by one who wishes to establish her life in a certain locus must override that of someone who perceives that property as a fungible asset.

Thinking about common-interest communities as a property institution aimed at fostering the community value of property, thus conceptualizing covenants along the lines of the regulative principle identified in *Neponsit*, leads to similar conclusions. This perspective sanctions exclusionary practices of residential communities only in limited circumstances. In particular, it implies that law should not authorize such practices insofar as they are used against, rather than by, cultural minority groups.[111] It also requires that the law should make sure that the limits on entry applied by "thin" common-interest communities are indeed necessary in order to ensure that "bad cooperators" likely to jeopardize the success of the commons property are excluded. This means

---

109. The following paragraphs draw on DAGAN, *supra* note 5, at ch.2; *see also* Sophia Moreau, *What Is Discrimination*, 38 PHIL. & PUB. AFF. 143 (2010).

110. See the Act's exceptions for intimate associations: single families (§3603(b)(1)) and small owner-occupied multiple unit dwellings (§ 3603(b)(2)).

111. Or, for that matter, by other types of groups, such as where a common-interest community is organized around a commitment to, say, vegetarianism. *Contra* Austin, *supra* note 60, at 27–29.

that courts need to supervise both the admissions criteria of such communities and the way they are practiced on the ground. One implication of this prescription is that rejections of applicants for admissions must be reasoned, and that the reasons must be sufficiently detailed so that both their evaluative and factual components can be properly scrutinized.[112]

CONCLUDING REMARKS

The most charitable reading of private law theorists' resistance to embrace the structural pluralism typical of private law is the concern that, by endorsing this feature of our law, they could end up exacerbating its deficiencies concerning both the conception of the rule of law as guidance and its understanding as constraint. As I tried to show in the preceding pages, however, these concerns are exaggerated if not simply wrong.

Properly interpreted, private law pluralism does not endorse ad hoc decision making, which is indeed detrimental to guidance, and is often supportive of rule-based decision making. As any (sensible) understanding of the rule of law as guidance acknowledges, however, private law pluralism does need to resort to standards in certain cases. Rather than undermining guidance, however, its standards are frequently conducive to guidance because they build on the character of the private law institution at hand, which is typically the basis of most people's expectations.

Private law pluralism need not raise serious concerns of unconstrained judicial power either. To be sure, legislatures in a democracy can legitimately play a role in the development of private law, which shapes and reshapes our social order, adjusting it to new circumstances, challenges, and opportunities. In some contexts, judges should possibly refrain from taking part in this drama,[113] but in many others, courts enjoy no less legitimacy—from a participation or accountability perspective—in the shaping of our private law institutions. Likewise, although the plurality of values involved in the molding of these institutions' regulative principles makes the enterprise challenging, we have no grounds for assuming that a normative contextual inquiry cannot lead to just and principled results.

112. And there is no way to avoid the hard questions of distinguishing appropriate goals of common-interest communities from illegitimate ones. *Contra* Austin, *supra* note 60, at 27–29, who implies that common-interest communities can never relate to the identity of their members.

113. Typical types of cases calling for significant deference are those of newly enacted private law legislation, as well as of private law innovations that require a regulatory structure, depend on specialized knowledge available elsewhere, or involve excessive widespread redistribution. *See* Dagan, *supra* note 89.

Demonstrating the alliance of private law pluralism with the rule of law is not only intrinsically significant; it is also instrumental for the goal of this book as a whole. My account of private law pluralism, like the other specific topics addressed in Chapters 3–7 of this book, is informed by the reconstructed account of the realist conception of law (offered in Chapter 2) as a set of ongoing institutions that embodies three constitutive and irresolvable tensions: between power and reason, science and craft, and tradition and progress. Throughout this book I argued that this subtle understanding of law is valuable and worth revitalizing. This legacy, I claimed, captures a deep truth about the law, which is obscured both by legal formalists and legal monists as well as by the purported heirs of legal realism who discarded it in favor of a refinement of one feature of this complex conception of law. I further contended that this realist legacy deserves renewal because it provides important lessons, which can both improve our understanding of specific legal topics (such as the relationships between rights and remedies), and guide our endeavors in promoting law reforms and developing legal theories. This last chapter is aimed at completing my effort of revival, demonstrating that contrary to some of its caricatures, legal realism should not be equated with nominalism—the archenemy of the rule of law—as, in fact, it offers a viable, indeed attractive, understanding of the rule of law and thus of law's promise of freedom and autonomy.

I hope that these accounts demonstrate the importance of legal realism in any exercise of legal discourse and thus justify its renewal as a mainstay in American legal discourse. But I have no pretense for closure. There are probably many additional insights that are worth mining from the heritage of legal realism, just as there are likely to be further refinements that may be needed for the realist contributions I have explored in these pages. I welcome these additions and possible debates, hoping they will further contribute to the long-overdue resurrection of legal realism in America.

INDEX

The table in Chapter 7 is indicated by t following page numbers. Footnotes are indicated by n following page numbers.

Formalism. *See also headings starting with*
  "Doctrinal"
  alternative conceptions of, 16*n*
  autonomy and closure of legal world,
    17
  as cover-up, 23–24
  critique of, 15–28. *See also* Critique of
    formalism
  defined, 16–17
  lawyers' authority and, 24
  normative nature of criticism of,
    18
  predominance of formal logic within,
    17
  private–public distinction as residue
    of, 113–114
  reconstruction after formalism,
    25–28. *See also* Reconstruction after
    formalism
  as state of art legal theory paradigm,
    104
Forum of reason, law as, 39, 95
Foundational pluralism, 172–174
Frank, Jerome, 3, 76
"Frankified" subjectivism, 25–26
Freedom of contract. *See* Contract law
Freedom of speech, 175*n*
Functions of law, 93*n*, 177. *See also*
  Expressive function of law
Fungible land, 159

Gender inequality and marital property,
  117–119
Global coherence, rejection of, 66. *See
  also* Structural pluralism of private
  law
Globalization of private law
  promoting competition and trading,
    104
  substantive irrelevance of, 128*n*
Gordon, Robert, 32
"Grand Style" of the common law, 61
"Groupness of the group," 40

Hale, Robert, 42*n*
Harris, J. W., 196*n*
Hart, Herbert Lionel Adolphus (H. L. A.)
  on Holmes's "bad man" analysis,
    71–72
  predictive theory of law and, 29–30

response to realist claim of doctrinal
  indeterminacy, 4
rule indeterminacy and, 18–19
on tension between coerciveness and
  normativity, 34
Hayek, F. A., 202*n*
Heller, Michael, 81
Hohfeld, Wesley Newcomb
  on legal rights, 23, 145–147, 150
  on property, 185–186
Holmes, Oliver Wendell
  "bad man" analysis of, 30, 32,
    71–72
  on coercive power of law, 29–32,
    35
  on lack of self-evident propositions,
    39
  on legal tradition, 60–61
  on mathematical conception of law,
    38
  realism and, 3
  on rule indeterminacy, 22
  on social ends of law, 85–86
Human heterogeneity. *See* Rationality,
  ambivalence of law and legal theory
  toward
Hunch theory of law, 25

Idiosyncrasy wing of legal realism,
  25
Incommensurability
  pluralism claim to, 172*n*
  repressiveness of monism due to,
    174*n*
Individual cases vs. narrow categories,
  54–56
Inequalities, law as cause of, 42*n*
Injunctions, 156*n*
In rem rights, 146
Institutional virtues, 51–53,
  90–91
Institutions
  configurations of entitlements and,
    186, 198
  diversity within structural pluralism,
    174–175
  grounding in social reality of, 181
  ideals of, 200
  internal coherence of,
    209–210